KARL KORSCH

Also by Patrick Goode

AUSTRO–MARXISM (*editor and translator, with T. B. Bottomore*)

KARL KORSCH

A Study in Western Marxism

Patrick Goode

© Patrick Goode 1979

Softcover reprint of the hardcover 1st edition 1979

All rights reserved. No part of this publication may be reproduced or transmitted, in any form or by any means, without permission

First published 1979 by
THE MACMILLAN PRESS LTD
London and Basingstoke
Associated companies in Delhi
Dublin Hong Kong Johannesburg Lagos
Melbourne New York Singapore Tokyo

British Library Cataloguing in Publication Data

Goode, Patrick
   Karl Korsch
   1. Korsch, Karl
   335.4'092'4   HX273.K74

ISBN 978-1-349-03658-5   ISBN 978-1-349-03656-1 (eBook)
DOI 10.1007/978-1-349-03656-1

This book is sold subject
to the standard conditions
of the Net Book Agreement

TO MY PARENTS

Contents

	Acknowledgements	ix
	Introduction	1
1	Korsch's Early Years	5
2	*What is Socialisation?*	17
3	*Labour Law for Factory Councils*	37
4	*Marxism and Philosophy*	62
5	Political Debates, 1923–8	97
6	*The Materialist Conception of History*	114
7	*Karl Marx*	136
8	Beyond Marxism?	170
	Notes	188
	Bibliography	217
	Index	235

Acknowledgements

I would like to thank the supervisor of my D.Phil. thesis at the University of Sussex, Professor T. B. Bottomore, for his invaluable advice and assistance; Mr F. Halliday, who generously made available a copy of his interview with Frau Korsch; Miss Julia Brittain of The Macmillan Press for checking the text so carefully; and Dr G. Langkau, Head of the Central European Department of the International Institute of Social History, Amsterdam, who made accessible the Institute's collection of manuscripts by Korsch.

The publishers and I also wish to thank the following who have kindly given permission for the use of copyright material:
Associated Book Publishers for extracts from *Karl Marx* by Karl Korsch, published by Chapman & Hall Ltd, 1938.
Europäische Verlagsanstalt for extracts from *Arbeitsrecht für Betriebsräte* by Karl Korsch.
New Left Books for extracts from *Marxism and Philosophy* by Karl Korsch translated by F. Halliday.

London *Patrick Goode*
March 1978

Introduction

Karl Korsch is best known to students of Marxism for two works: *Marxism and Philosophy* (1923) and *Karl Marx* (1938). Both these books reflect the changing fortunes of the revolutionary working-class movement in Europe. In the early 1920s, until the defeat of the German Communist Party (KPD) in October 1923, which was followed by a series of reverses in other countries, this movement was in the ascendant. During the period there was a fruitful examination of the foundations of Marxism by revolutionary Marxists, in which all the basic questions of Marxism were re-examined: namely, the relation of Marxism to its predecessors, the validity of its economic analyses, and the connection between Marxist science and political action. The best-known part of this debate concerns the first question – the Hegelian dimension of Marx's thought. The revival of interest in this problem was initially stimulated by various remarks of Lenin, which were acted on by a number of writers.[1] The most significant contributors to this debate sympathetic to such a philosophical examination of Marxism were Korsch and Lukács. The discussion was soon cut short as Stalin's faction in the Comintern began to gain control. Thus at the Fifth Congress of the Comintern, the first after Lenin's death, both Korsch and Lukács were subjected to a crude, demagogic denunciation by Zinoviev.[2]

The subsequent fate of Korsch's ideas among the 'orthodox Marxists' of the KPD and their successors is typical. Almost from the time of his expulsion from the party (May-June 1926), he has either become a non-person, or the references to him are quite meaningless. For example, even as late as 1951, when he was no longer politically active, he was being referred to as 'an agent of US imperialism'.[3] Despite the brief thaw which followed the revelations of the Twentieth Party Congress in the USSR (1956), numerous oppositional or dissident communists remain unknown to the movement of which they once formed part. If their names are known, their ideas have been distorted beyond recognition. In one of the most recent histories of the German working-class movement, there is no mention of Korsch or other 'ultra-lefts', such as Ruth Fischer, who at one time had important posts in the leadership of the party, and commanded the sympathy of substantial sections of the membership.[4]

For different reasons, this neglect and distortion of the ideas Korsch put forward in *Marxism and Philosophy* was to apply to his later work also. By the time he wrote *Karl Marx*, the balance of class forces had completely changed. The working class was very much on the defensive: fascism had been victorious in a number of European countries, and threatened to exterminate the working-class movement in the remaining 'democracies'. The Marxist movement lay almost entirely under the dead hand of Stalinism. Outside this, it survived in small groups which had little contact with the working-class movement and within which the level of theoretical debate was extremely low compared with the previous period. Although *Karl Marx* was not written with the polemical intention of *Marxism and Philosophy*, it does represent an interesting interpretation of Marxism which, because of the prevailing situation, was hardly discussed at the time.

But the aim of this work is not simply to rescue Korsch's own ideas from oblivion. It also aims to examine Korsch's theory and practice as part of the interpretation of the Marxist system by the communist movement in Western Europe. The distinctive feature of Korsch's Marxism is his stress on practice: an active effort of the will is needed in order to transform society in a socialist direction. Marxism is not a passive scientific evaluation of history, it is an active factor in the struggle to change society. For Korsch, political practice is always the supreme criterion of the validity of ideas. This applies even to his most abstract ideas on philosophy; as he said of *Marxism and Philosophy*: 'It had a rigorously scientific character but did not deny that the problem was practically related to the struggles of our age which were then raging at their fiercest.'[5]

Introduction 3

In his concern for an active involvement in working-class politics, and the economic and political problems this required him to confront, Korsch differs from the usual run of 'Western Marxists' whose position has (in my view, correctly) been characterised as follows:

> The progressive relinquishment of economic and political structures as the central concerns of theory was accompanied by a basic shift in the whole centre of gravity of European Marxism towards *philosophy*. The most striking single fact about the whole tradition from Lukács to Althusser, Korsch to Colletti, is the overwhelming predominance of professional philosophers within it.[6]

In fact neither Korsch nor Lukács (in the 1920s at any rate) form part of this tradition, in that they were only concerned with the problem of Marxism and philosophy in so far as it enabled them to rediscover the revolutionary method of Marxism in order to apply it to current problems of the class struggle.

Another aspect of Korsch's basic difference from this tradition is his orientation to Lenin's ideas. In the two major works written during his membership of the KPD, *Labour Law for Factory Councils* and *Marxism and Philosophy*, he was concerned to apply Lenin's conceptions of the state and imperialism to the problems of law and philosophy respectively. Even after his expulsion from the KPD, his main point of reference was Leninism: his arguments on the state, philosophy and the problems of working-class revolution were negatively determined by his attempts to refute Lenin. In this respect his work has quite a different orientation from other 'Western Marxists'—it is not concerned with analysing 'superstructures' or criticising contemporary bourgeois culture;[7] nor does it accept the customary superficial rejection of Lenin's theories as being quite inapplicable to Western Europe, the starting point of 'Western Marxism' and its current political expression 'Eurocommunism'.[8] It will be argued that both his attempted application and his rejection of Leninism were based on a failure to grasp the essentials of Lenin's thought—the analysis of imperialism, the class nature of the state, and the nature and necessity of ideological struggle. In certain respects, when their political and philosophical concerns coincided, during the early 1920s, Lukács showed a superior understanding of Lenin's method. Yet because Korsch was attempting to work out a revolutionary programme for the working class in Western Europe (as was Lukács during the 1920s, before his retreat to aesthetic questions) Korsch's work is of enduring theoretical and practical interest for those concerned with the application of Marxism in a practical political context.

1 Korsch's Early Years

Karl Korsch was born on 15 August 1886 in Tostedt on the Lüneberg Heath.[1] Like many other Marxist intellectuals, he came from a family upwardly mobile from the lower middle class. Originally his father was from a farming background, but by hard work he rose to be the vice-president of a bank in Meiningen, where Korsch went to grammar school (*Gymnasium*).[2] After taking his *Abitur*, he began to make the rounds of the universities in the normal fashion of German students of that period. He spent most of his time at Jena, but visited Geneva and Berlin, and also had one term in Munich.[3]

Philosophy would have been his own chosen area of study, but his father insisted on law. Korsch compromised by specialising in jurisprudence and the more philosophical aspects of law. Eventually he submitted a thesis on a technical aspect of jurisprudence, the application of the rules of proof in civil proceedings and admissible depositions, which was published in Bonn in 1911. As an early statement of his general views on the relations between abstract ideas and practice, it does contain some illuminating passages. For example, in the introduction to the thesis, he states that its guiding idea is that

> previously, in dogmatic jurisprudence [*Rechtswissenschaft*], the question of the abstract content of the valid legal norms [*Rechtssätze*] has taken up far too much space. By contrast, the question of how and in what way the valid legal norms are to be applied in practice has been given too little attention, has

scarcely even been recognised as an independent task of dogmatic jurisprudence.[4]

Apart from this, however, the remainder of his thesis is too specialised to be of general interest.

He passed his law exams with high marks, and after taking the state board exam in law, he went on to do *Vorbereitungsdienst*, the equivalent of being 'in chambers'.[5] He did not, however, take up legal practice: he had never intended to do so, since he had always been more interested in the philosophical aspects of law. He never returned to the study of law—even as a professor of civil law in the 1920s he concentrated on jurisprudence.[6] This being so, it is his interest in social and political thought in this period which will now be examined.

I shall argue that throughout this pre-war period, Korsch's ideas were neither individual nor Marxist, being instead typical of the ideas common to young middle-class Germans of the period. This was a time of great upheaval in German economic and social life, when the whole of German society was experiencing a profound structural change. The rapid industrialisation of the period 1890–1914 meant, on the one hand, the rise of the giant industrial corporations, and, on the other, the ruin of many of the smaller producers and the steady drift from the land into the industrial *Grosstädte*. This was the time of the sensational growth of the Social Democratic Party (SPD), the main—often the only—democratic party in Wilhelmine Germany; the traditionally dominant Junkers and the Prussian state bureaucracy felt the firm ground of traditional moral values slipping from beneath their feet. The resultant crisis in cultural and political life affected the educated *Mittelstand* in general, but was reflected at its most extreme in the youth and student movements. It is with the latter that Korsch was mainly concerned.

In the nineteenth century student organisations had formerly been dominated by the *Burschenschaften*. Originally founded in Jena in 1815, these were, like the *Studentenkorps*, anti-Semitic, militaristic and reactionary, their principal activities being mainly duelling and drinking. Membership was used mainly as a means of gaining influential positions in later life.[7] In opposition to these conservative organisations there arose two reform movements among the students: the student sections of the youth movement[8] and the free student movement. The latter has been described as follows:

> The Free Student movement began as an emancipation movement of the non-incorporated students, who since the beginning of the social upheaval in the student body in the last third of the 19th century, increased in numbers, and particularly in the universities in the great cities came to make up by far the greater part of the student body.[9]

What was Korsch's relation to the Free Student movement? Organisationally, he took a leading role in it, and travelled all over Germany as a speaker on its behalf.[10] He also became the editor of the *Jenaer Hochschulzeitung*, the organ of the 'Free Students', to which he also made numerous contributions.[11] But the mere fact of his membership does not in itself tell us very much. It was a movement united only in its opposition to the traditional student bodies: outside this negative orientation, its positive solutions were rather diverse and often unclear. The vagueness of its aspirations can be seen from the first number of the *Jenaer Hochschulzeitung*:

> New life is springing up everywhere: the long germinating seed thrusts towards the light. In the social era, the struggle gets hotter and hotter; new life seethes and grows . . .[12]

Korsch's position within the 'Free Students' can be defined by referring to another movement of this period—the movement for 'social policy' (*Sozialpolitik*).

The expression 'social policy' first became popular in 1872 when Adolph Wagner and Gustav Schmoller founded the 'League for Social Policy' (*Verein für Sozialpolitik*). At first the League concerned itself with protective legislation for the working class, but later extended its activities to all economically weak strata of the population. It was not a socialist movement: it was concerned with measures to redistribute wealth, rather than with the transformation of the relations of production within which such wealth was created. In fact, it tried to pre-empt the appeal of socialism by proving to the working class that its interests could be protected under capitalism.[13] The movement grew, and in the period under consideration many leading intellectuals (such as Max Weber) contributed to its journal.[14]

In so far as there is a discernible tendency informing the articles Korsch wrote for the *Jenaer Hochschulzeitung* at this period, it is toward such a reformist 'social policy'. This tendency appears in the articles he wrote on the reform of law and legal studies, on land reform, on secondary schools, and on women's emancipation.[15] He also seemed to support the general aim of the 'Free Students' of bridging the gap between the intellectuals and the working class. The idea that the working class has its own interests irreconcilable with those of other classes is, not surprisingly, absent.[16] At Jena, there were plenty of opportunities for contact with members of the working class politically conscious enough to be interested in such questions. Through a friend in the SPD, he arranged a meeting between a group of 'Free Students' and SPD workers and socialists.[17] As far as can be ascertained, this was the limit of his involvement with the SPD, while a student. There is nothing in any of his published articles of this period which indicates a definite socialist orientation, even though Hedda Korsch suggests that he was a convinced socialist much earlier—by the time of his last year in school.[18] Although his liberal 'social policy' position was quite consistent with the ideas of the more moderate 'revisionist' members of the SPD, it cannot be said that as yet he had adopted a definitely social-democratic, let alone Marxist, position.

Leaving behind the early formative years, we find that in the next period his ideas begin to assume a more definite shape. He began to contribute to *Die Tat* after the end of his student years. The periodical had originally been founded by the Horneffer brothers in 1909, and three years later was taken over by the publisher E. Diederichs as a kind of house journal for his publishing company. Diederichs was convinced that religion and religious-ethical education must be made the foundations of German society. Politically, he favoured a German people's state, and wished to see aristocratic ideas supplemented by democratic action. His periodical was originally subtitled *Ways to Free Humanity*: later (August 1916) this was changed to *Monthly for the Future of German Culture*. Diederichs himself cannot have assigned great importance to it, since he gives it only a passing mention in his autobiography.[19] Like the *Jenaer Hochschulzeitung*, the publication with which Korsch was now connected was 'radical' in the most general sense of the word—its ideology belonged to neither the established left nor the right. None of Korsch's articles fit in with the more mystical tendencies of *Die Tat*, since he certainly did not share Diederichs' philosophical or political positions. He wrote on a variety of topics, usually concerning questions of 'social policy', e.g. on the agrarian question; on the reform of law; the women's movement; and in particular a number of articles on eugenics, to which he seemed favourably disposed.[20]

Although most of the articles he wrote during this period appeared in *Die Tat*, it was only the vehicle for ideas he was developing in quite a different direction. The most important influence on him now was the Fabian Society. After finishing his studies, he went to England to work with Sir Ernest Schuster on the translation of a book on English civil law and procedure. That work itself was not important—in fact it was never published.[21] What was important was that Korsch joined the Fabian Nursery, the branch of the Fabian Society for younger members.

The Fabian Society was then experiencing a period of great success. Between 1900 and 1913 its London membership quadrupled.[22] It was a peculiarly English institution, being very different, for instance, from the German SPD. The Society had never had a Marxist wing and from the time of its foundation was separate from the various Marxist groupings. It could be openly anti-Marxist in a way that the 'revisionists' could not yet afford to be. Engels himself had remarked on the anti-Marxist character of the society, describing it as

> a clique of bourgeois 'socialists' of diverse calibres from careerists to sentimental socialists and philanthropists, united only by their fear of the threatening rule of the workers and doing all in their power to spike this danger by making *their own* leadership secure, the leadership exercised by the 'eddicated'.[23]

Ideologically, it was more of a liberal reform movement, similar in its aims to the right wing of the SPD. It has been claimed that there was a close connection between Fabianism and Bernstein's revisionism:

> For the most part ... Bernstein's revisionism was only Fabianism, oriented to a German social-democratic audience

and attuned to German conditions.[24]

But unlike the SPD, which was overwhelmingly working class, the Fabian Society had very little connection with the working-class movement.[25] Sociologically, its membership was mainly middle-class; more exactly, as Korsch himself put it:

> Their [the Fabian Society's] most numerous and active members belong to the daily growing class of 'clerks', the 'new middle class', as we would say in Germany; the technical workers in commerce and industry and those working in municipal and state offices, who are on the same level; in addition, some students, young authors, members of all theoretical and practical professions.[26]

I have shown that previously Korsch did not support even the moderate kind of socialism represented by the Fabian Society. Did his membership of the Society therefore mark a significant change in his opinions? There can be no doubt that at that time he did support its aims. Although much later he was to say that during his membership of the Fabian Society he was an oppositionist, there is no sign of such opposition in anything he wrote during this period.[27] What the Society meant to him is shown by his article, 'Die Fabian Society', written for *Die Tat* soon after he joined. He argued that the programme of the Society

> has an entirely democratic-socialist content. In addition to a fully democratic form of government, it demands the socialisation of all the means of production, land and capital. The Fabians aren't 'well-meaning friends' of socialism, they are democratic socialists.[28]

He even goes so far as to say that

> The Fabian Society shares with German Marxism the conviction that economic and political socialism (the socialisation of the means of production) comes by itself, however much we as individuals desire or oppose it.[29]

But, in his view, the Fabian Society differed from the SPD in two respects. One is that

It adds to this theoretical insight a very important orientation of the will [*Willensorientierung*]. The practical will: to ensure that, in this inevitable transformation of human economy, human culture, the ideal of humanity is also advanced.[30]

This is explained more concretely in connection with his views on the socialisation of industry, outlined in his article of 1912.[31] This stress on the 'practical will' being necessary to achieve socialism was to be constantly repeated throughout the rest of his life. Here it is allied to an idealist aim, 'the ideal of humanity', but it persisted even in his more materialist days.

The other difference, apparently unconnected with the first is that

> the Fabian Society is not a political party and does not aim to be. A political party must concern itself with increasing its membership, in order to eventually attain the majority, and carry out its political ideals ... The Fabian Society knows that the transition to socialist state forms may not, even if it could, be compelled by an individual party, however strong. The majority is not the whole [*Gesamtheit*].[32]

Despite the important change marked by his joining the Fabian Society and his apparent acceptance of its programme, Korsch had not yet abandoned his earlier ideas in favour of a total commitment to socialism. His ideas still retained a rationalist 'social policy' tendency, rather than a narrowly or dogmatically socialist one. He could even describe the nationalisation of the railways as a measure of 'social policy'.[33] In order to make his characterisation of the Fabian Society more comprehensible to his German readers, he argued:

> In the university towns, the Fabian Societies satisfy the same needs as the 'Free Students' do in German universities ... But the Fabian Societies also do this outside academic circles. This need is, for the most part, not satisfied in Germany.[34]

A more fundamental political reason why he saw the Fabian Society as corresponding more closely to a liberal reform movement like the 'Free Students' than to the orthodox Marxist wing of the German SPD, was his estimation of the democratic character of English life. Other Fabians noted that the existence of democracy in England fundamentally affected the struggle for socialism:

> The Socialism advocated by the Fabian Society is State Socialism exclusively ... England now possesses an elaborate democratic State machinery ... the opposition which exists in Continental monarchies between the State and the people does not hamper English Socialists. For example, the distinction made between State Socialism and Social Democracy in Germany ... has no meaning in England.[35]

Korsch commented favourably on the democratic aspects of English life as compared to that in the Prussian state. Although he pointed out how in practice freedom in England was limited, he also thought that once the working class had decided on broad demands on the state, such demands could soon be fulfilled via the democratic process.[36] In England, there was much more freedom of speech than in Germany.[37] The judicial system in England also has a much more democratic character because the judge comes under public scrutiny.[38] The open nature of English society is further exemplified by the role of the press in bringing the results of all kinds of cases, not merely sensational ones, to the attention of the public. The newspapers also assist the democratic process by the way in which they edit their correspondence pages, an important feature of the English press. As these do not have to follow the 'party line' of the newspapers concerned, they allow minority opinions to be expressed.[39]

Thus, given the existence in England of a vigorous democracy, the politics of the Fabian Society were preferable to those of the German SPD. He summed up their respective merits thus:

> They [the Fabians] have not shied away from theory—as Englishmen usually do. But they have not raised it to an end in itself as Germans do.[40]

He still remained wary of the orthodox Marxism then represented by the SPD. There are two examples of this. The first concerns a rather curious view of examinations:

neither the liberal nor the social democracy has yet displayed an adequate understanding of the fact, that the problem of the 'exam' is the core problem of democracy, rightly understood.⁴¹

The second occurs in an approving comment on a eugenics programme:

> the social programme advanced here means . . . the attempt to replace the previous politico-economic foundation of socialism (Marxism) by a biological one, and by this means to give a new and more urgent emphasis to the most essential demands of social reform.⁴²

It is not possible to determine precisely what he knew of Marxism at this period, since he does not refer to any of Marx's works, nor to contemporary writers such as Kautsky or Bernstein. To such an outsider to the debates in the SPD, Bernstein would no doubt seem as much a representative of Marxism as Kautsky would. The more radical critics of Bernstein, such as Luxemburg (let alone Lenin), would probably be quite unknown to him.

The fact remains that Korsch's membership of the Fabian Society does mark an important step in the direction of socialist ideas. What he valued in the Society was that it was eminently practical in its attitude to socialism, in that it had actually drawn up plans for the future socialist society. He was particularly impressed by the *Committee of Inquiry on the Control of Industry*, which aimed at giving a detailed account of how socialism was to be achieved. The object of the inquiry was to work out

> the main lines on which in the control and management of . . . industry and commerce . . . we can combine the widest measure of personal freedom and initiative with the maximum of democratic control; the largest national product with an equalised distribution of services and commodities among the whole people.⁴³

It noted that 'socialisation' was an ambiguous concept. More important was a passage which Korsch himself quoted:

> The existing chaos and disorder among socialists, whenever we are asked for constructive proposals, together with our ap-

parent inability to state, with any degree of unanimity or precision, what we are asking for with regard to the future organisation of industry and commerce will lose us our hold on the younger intellectuals.[44]

The practical character of this committee is attested to by the introduction to its report, in which Mrs Webb seems to show most enthusiasm when it comes to explaining the methods of inquiry to be followed, and the sub-committees between which the work is to be divided.[45] Korsch might have added that the society had also drawn up detailed plans for the nationalisation of the railways. Shortly after his article was written, it was also to demand the nationalisation of the mines.[46]

These ideas were discussed in his most significant pre-war article, 'Die sozialistische Formel für die Organisation der Volkswirtschaft'.[47] Even after the war, he still referred to this article as being relevant to any discussion of the socialisation movement.[48] Its main thesis is that the formula 'socialisation of the means of production' which serves state socialists, syndicalists, trade unions and 'many other tendencies' is a negative one: it only means the 'annihilation of private property in the means of production'. It has no content as a positive formula, so that

> If a socialist is asked what he means by 'socialism', the best answer one will get will be a description of 'capitalism' and the observation that 'socialism' will replace capitalism by the socialisation of the means of production.[49]

Provided the practical realisation of socialism is not an immediate question, this lack of content does not matter, but

> It becomes harmful, the moment that socialism anywhere comes into power and is required to carry out the socialist organisation of the economy.[50]

Only six years later these words proved to be prophetic, when the Majority SPD government showed itself incapable of utilising a very favourable situation to carry out any positive plans for the transition to socialism. But in this article Korsch was criticising the negative character of the socialist formula not so much because it would pose such difficulties when the socialists gained power, but because it failed to distinguish them from the syndicalists. He makes this point clear in the following passage:

> For Germany too the socialists must become clearer on this question. Not because it is to be expected that they will shortly be summoned to establish the socialist state of the future, but because even with us the ruling dogmas of Marxism are considerably shaken by the demands of syndicalism, which are so much more simple, and closer to the factory worker. Given that this disintegration has begun, it will be worth finding a new way, of integrating the German socialist movement internally, and distinguishing it from other movements.[51]

It should be noted that this criticism was not made from a Marxist or even a socialist standpoint: it is a criticism which would occur to anyone who rationally examined the programme of the SPD. This passage is sometimes taken as evidence that Korsch was at this period strongly inclined to syndicalism.[52] But there is very little direct evidence for this. Earlier in this article, he refers to the pressure put on the socialist movement by the growth of syndicalist tendencies: the invasion of syndicalism from France is beginning to shake the complacency of the 'old socialism'.[53] This development had not gone unnoticed by the Fabians. In Mrs Webb's report it is suggested that it is necessary to work out practical proposals for socialism so as to avoid seeming too passive in comparison with the 'anarchists'.[54] As I have said, Korsch's own views on anarcho-syndicalism are not discernible in this article. Although he later claimed that he was attracted to syndicalism during this period,[55] the article as a whole neither supports nor refutes this claim, since it is quite neutral as to the merits of syndicalism, merely drawing attention to its impact on the orthodox conception of socialism. Indirectly syndicalism may have attracted his sympathy by virtue of its stress on activism and direct action: it did seem to offer more possibilities for the immediately active will than the apparently more cautious and contemplative scientific socialism.

To sum up. In the first period of Korsch's creative work, distinctive positions have not yet emerged. Certainly his writings for the 'Free Student' movement do not express a clear or coherent world view, such was the vague character of his ideas on 'social policy'. Unfortunately, he did not describe in any detail his philosophical positions. This is regrettable in as much as he appears to have been interested in philosophy from the beginning of this period. Nor was this omission remedied during his membership of the Fabian Society—in fact it was not until 1923 that he wrote directly on philosophical problems. But his connection with the Society does signal a change in his political views, a more definite turning away from the reformist liberalism of his earlier views toward a more socialist orientation. As yet, however, this is not as radical as even the rather diluted nominal Marxism of the reformist wing of the SPD. The trait which does begin to emerge most clearly from the period of both the Free Student movement, and the Fabian Society is his emphasis on the active practical will as a crucial factor in any scheme for the improvement of society. It is precisely this *Willensorientierung* which he found to be lacking when only six years later the SPD found itself in the position considered in 'Die sozialistische Formel' as a purely hypothetical case: i.e. of being a socialist government in power. This crucial experience, and the position Korsch took towards it, will be examined in the next chapter.

2 *What is Socialisation?*

By the time Korsch had finished his legal work with Schuster, it was the summer of 1914. He was summoned by his regiment in Meiningen to report for extraordinary manoeuvres. His return to Germany was apparently not from patriotic motives, but because he did not wish to be imprisoned somewhere as an alien without any contact with the mass of socialist workers, even when they were misguided enough to support a patriotic war. This meant being in the army, so he was in uniform training recruits before the war actually started. Because of his complaints against the violation of international law by the march through Belgium, he was demoted to the ranks. His form of protest against the war was never to carry a rifle or sabre, because he personally did not intend to kill people. Instead he considered it his mission to bring home alive as many soldiers as possible. However he carried out his military duties with enough ability to be eventually awarded the Iron Cross (first class) and to be recommissioned. Towards the end of the war, his company was all for revolution and for ending the war by not fighting any longer. His company was not demobbed until January 1919 because the government did not want to let the soldiers loose in a volatile political situation.[1]

In January 1919 Germany was facing a severe political crisis. At the end of the war, the old order of the monarchy had collapsed. Before it was possible to effect a gradual change to a parliamentary democracy, the whole of Germany was covered with a network of workers' and soldiers' councils (*Arbeiter– und Soldatenräte*)[2] which threatened to provide an alternative to parliamentary democracy even before it had become established.

The councils' movement (*Rätebewegung*) made a great impression on Korsch. He argued that the revolutionary movement of 1918 in Germany was part of an international movement in Italy, France, Great Britain and the USA, comparable in significance to the French revolution of 1789.³ However, he was not directly involved in the councils' movement. The major formative experience for Korsch during this period was the Commission on the Socialisation of Industry. This was the one apparently positive step taken by the Social Democratic government, its only measure of a definitely socialist and not merely democratic character. The Commission was brought into being on 18 November, only nine days after the outbreak of the revolution. It consisted of eleven members: Ballod, Cunow, Francke, Hilferding, Bochum, Kautsky, Lederer, Schumpeter, Umbreit, Vogelstein and Wilbrandt.⁴ It had its first session on 5 December, and issued a statement on its plan of work on 11 December. Not surprisingly in view of its composition, it did not emerge with any very radical proposals.⁵

Korsch took part in the meetings of the Commission as scientific assistant to Robert Wilbrandt. Wilbrandt was a professor at Jena University who before the war had already written on 'social questions'. There was a certain identity of views between Korsch and Wilbrandt on the question of 'practical socialism'.⁶ At no time was Korsch a member of the Commission. Nor does the official *Protokoll* contain any reference to the nature of his work with the Commission itself.⁷

The Commission had a short and uneventful life. Its ponderous legality was largely by-passed by more direct attempts at enforcing socialisation. From the beginning of December, there were isolated seizures of factories in Berlin. In January, there was a powerful movement in the Ruhr, signalised by the decision of the Essen workers' and soldiers' councils to proclaim the socialisation of the mines, on 13 January 1919. A similar movement took place in Merseburg–Halle.⁸ Rather than attempting to assert their national authority over such movements, the Social-Democratic government sent three SPD Majority members to participate in the 'Commission of Nine' set up by this meeting of workers' and soldiers' councils, to ensure the socialisation of the mining industry in Essen. Meanwhile, the Commission on the Socialisation of Industry had followed up its initial publication of a work plan with a report on its activity. This essentially repeated the idea of the initial plan that socialisation must be carried out according to the state of maturity of the various industries concerned. The mines were judged to be already in this state of 'maturity' (7 January 1919).[9]

The activity of the Commission was completely ineffective in another respect. While it did not have any connection with the more elemental movement for socialisation, its recommendations were also ignored by the higher-level authorities.[10] The socialisation law of 3 March 1919 effectively made the Commission redundant. The decisive paragraph 2 of the law ran:

> The nation is empowered, by means of legislation, given suitable compensation ... to take over into the community economic enterprises fit for socialisation, in particular those which profit from the land and exploit the forces of nature; in cases of urgent need, it may regulate the production and distribution of economic goods.[11]

The only significant piece of work it had carried out was its report on the state of the mining industry, and the desirability of its socialisation. At the time Korsch thought that this report did propose useful measures on the way to a fully socialised economy. He later added that this report was the most important application of the 'guild principle' to one particular section of the economy.[12]

The major statement of Korsch's position on socialisation in early 1919 appears in *Was ist Sozialiserung?* (*What is Socialisation?*) (March 1919).[13] This was the first in a series of 'socio-political writings' which he edited for the newspaper *Freies Deutschland*, which stood on the left wing of the SPD.[14] His connection with the newspaper is the most definite indication of his political affiliations at this period which I have been able to find. It had an ethical, rather than a Marxist, tendency—it regarded its task as 'convincing the widest possible circles of our German people of the high value and the moral seriousness of the socialist demands'.[15] He was still very sympathetic to Fabianism and was certainly not yet a member of the Independent Social Democratic Party (USPD).[16]

Let us now examine his political positions of this period. First, we shall see how his position had changed in comparison to his writings of the pre-war period. In *What is Socialisation?* he makes a decisive break with the *'Sozialpolitik'* which had been the dominant feature of his earlier ideas. According to this view:

> By means of a gradual socio-political limitation of the authority of the private proprietor, private property is to be changed into public property by means of a continuous development.[17]

Korsch now thinks that this is incorrect because

> In reality *social policy* which by definition assumes the private property of the capitalist and only intends to conciliate the conflict between the capitalist's own rights and the claims of the whole society, can never be transformed into a true socialisation ... without *'a leap and a radical change'*.[18]

This meant that there can be

> no socialisation of the means of production without the total exclusion of the private property owner from the social process of production, at once or gradually.[19]

Later in 1919, he came to oppose *Sozialpolitik* not only in the sphere of the socialisation of industry, but also in its more general application. The scientific discoveries of Marx had shown that it was impossible to change the relations of distribution without changing the underlying relations of production. By confining itself to the former, *Sozialpolitik* was bound to fail.[20] But at this stage his criticism was confined to *Sozialpolitik* as it applied to socialisation, although this is of course a criticism of one of the basic positions of *Sozialpolitik*.

That Korsch is moving away from *Sozialpolitik* towards a much more openly socialist position is shown by his statement in the opening paragraph of *What is Socialisation?*

> The socialisation demanded by socialism means a new regulation of production with the aim of replacing the capitalist private economy by the socialist community.[21]

The first step towards this was the socialisation of the means of production. Genuine socialisation meant the elimination of private property in the means of production, and not merely sharing this property out among new owners. On this basis he rejected some socialisation schemes as being merely 'half-measures', e.g. Kautsky's proposals for 'stateisation' (*Verstaatlichung*); the projects of well-meaning capitalists for 'profit-sharing' schemes; and plans for 'industrial democracy', in which the workers participate in the running of the factory while the proprietor still manages the enterprise.[22]

In explaining his own views, Korsch used two terms, '*Sozialisierung*' and '*Vergesellschaftung*' more or less interchangeably.[23] In his article 'Grundsätzliches über Sozialisierung' (1920), he notes that

> The word socialisation (Sozialisierung) was first adopted in general use only after the November revolution. There are isolated instances of it previously. As far as I can establish, it was used for the first time in 1875 by . . . Eugen Dühring.[24]

The article goes on to discuss three groups of contemporary ideas about socialisation—as represented by the Wissell–Mollendorff plan, Rathenau's idea of the 'autonomous economy' and the revolutionary councils' movement—but space forbids a detailed discussion of this grouping.[25] Korsch claims that the word 'socialisation' is to be found in the early writings of the English Fabian Society.[26] He was most concerned to distinguish 'socialisation' from 'stateisation' (*Verstaatlichung*) or any of its forms, such as 'municipalisation' (*Kommunalisierung*).[27] This distinction is of more than terminological significance: it is in fact essential to differentiating his position from the state-socialist conceptions of the Majority SPD, which confounded the two terms.[28]

In Korsch's view, the state-socialist position is open to the two following objections. After the capitalist class has been excluded from the sphere of production, any socialisation plan has to take into account the fact that two antagonistic interests are present, those of the consumers and those of the producers. If the interest of either is preferred, then all that will result will be a new type of capitalism. In the case of stateisation (*Verstaatlichung*), either through municipalisation (*Kommunalisierung*) or through the units of production joining consumers' co-operatives, the consumers' interest will be preferred. Such 'consumers' capitalism' is in no way a means to introducing new social conditions for those directly involved in production—in fact, it is only 'state capitalism'.[29] By contrast, Korsch constantly stressed that the demands for the socialisation of the means of production and the freeing of productive labour, required the transformation of a historically specific form of production relations.[30]

A common objection to state socialism is that it leads to bureaucratisation, schematisation and thereby to the deadening of individual initiative.[31] Korsch does not comment on this directly. What he is more concerned to show is that even if 'stateisation' did lead to an increase in the productivity of labour, this would not mean an emancipation of the labourer:

> Even if 'stateisation' were possible without paralysing the forces of production, under the present conditions it would never bring us the socialism which the working people demand ... the class of economically active workers will as such not be freer, or have a more human way of life and work, if an official employed by the state government or the municipal administration replaces the manager employed by private capital.[32]

This is an important aspect of his ideas at this period—his concern with the possibilities of socialisation leading (to some extent) to the immediate emancipation of the worker. While recognising that all large-scale machine industry is organised labour, and thus requires uniform direction, perhaps by one man, he hoped that since that manager would be chosen by the workers, the effect would be that 'the machine and the whole mechanism of work and its organisation, necessary for life, shall cease to enslave man'.[33] Thus in his two-phase model of socialisation, the first phase would involve an emancipation of labour: 'Its first phase consists of the socialisation of the means of production and the emancipation of labour which this produces.'[34] While state socialism did not lead to the emancipation of labour, it had also failed to consider the possibility of an antagonism between producers and consumers continuing to exist even if their plans for the socialisation of industry were realised, because their notion of socialisation was basically a negative one. Thus:

> It can be maintained that, right up to the moment when they

gained power, the German Social-Democracy concerned itself very little with finding a positive formula for the socialist organisation of the economy, therefore with the practical solution of the socialisation question.[35]

Thus the Majority SPD's proposals were of a purely negative character, guided by the idea that 'socialisation is the abolition, removal, overcoming of the "private property" or of "capitalism", and concerned themselves very little with 'what other relation should replace the abolished private property'.[36] In fact, the party of 'scientific socialism' prided itself on its rejection of any clarification of the question of how the socialist world of the future would look, on the grounds that this was quite 'utopian'.

Korsch therefore rejected the state-socialist conception of socialisation because it did not lead to the emancipation of labour, and, because it did not do away with the antagonism between producers and consumers. But this antagonism may persist in other socialisation plans, more specifically, 'in any attempt at socialisation which tends to the productive-cooperative movement and modern syndicalism ("the mines to the miners", "the railways to the railwaymen")'.[37] Syndicalism was not a very strong tradition in the German working-class movement. After the initial conflict between localised and centralised trade unions in the 1890s,[38] the politically conscious sections of the German working class adhered overwhelmingly to large, organised, state-socialist bodies (i.e. the SPD and the trade unions associated with it).

Thus, because syndicalism was of less importance in German conditions, Korsch did not criticise it quite so thoroughly as he did state socialism. His main objection to the syndicalists' conception of socialism was that it would lead to the danger of producers' capitalism,[39] and thus the old antagonism between producers and consumers would be perpetuated. Later in the year, however, writing for the USPD paper *Der Sozialist*, he argued that syndicalism did embody the important insight that

> the centre of gravity of the revolutionary struggle for socialisation is not in the area of state politics, but in that of economics. A monopoly of trade, stateisation of production, municipal socialism, and the other 'political means' are in themselves insufficient to 'improve the fate of the working class, to increase

their mental powers, and to raise their enjoyment of work'; these will only be achieved, an adequate ... 'socialisation' will only be created, when the workers have become full ... participants in production on the road of direct socialisation.[40]

Thus no socialisation plan can be considered a satisfactory fulfilment of the socialisation idea unless it takes into account the notion of the direct control and 'co-ordination' (*Mitbestimmung*) of every branch of industry, if not of every individual factory, by the community of the workers employed in that industry, and the institutions they have set up.

But in rejecting both the state-socialist and the syndicalist conceptions of socialisation, Korsch did not revert to reformist or gradualist solutions. He rejected as insufficient all those measures which

> amount to a distribution of power and profit between the non-working proprietor on the one side, and the non-possessing worker on the other.[41]

On this basis, he criticised three kinds of 'socialisation' plans: Kautsky's proposal that certain enterprises be leased out by the state, but should carry on as private concerns; all 'profit-sharing' schemes, an idea which well-meaning employers had been attempting to use for 100 years; the idea (which went under the false name of 'industrial democracy') that those working in a particular factory should choose representative assemblies of workers and employees (workers' committees, factory committees, employees' committees), while the direction and administration of the factory is fundamentally still in the hands of the capitalist owner.[42]

Thus from *What is Socialisation?* onwards, Korsch rejected reformist *Sozialpolitik*, state socialism and syndicalism. What was his own solution at this stage? It consisted in the introduction of 'industrial autonomy', which means the following:

> in every factory, the participating workers ... exercise their rule over the production process in place of the previous private property owner ... while at the same time, the

limitations placed by state 'social policy' on the private capitalist property in the means of production ... are further developed into an effective .... property of the totality.[43]

The autonomy of the socialised industry would have three aspects: the syndicate controlling all the branches of the socialised industry would be autonomous with respect to the central state government; the individual factory would possess a limited autonomy with respect to the centrally determining syndicate; various groups of workers and employers would possess a limited autonomy with respect to both the central state and the central syndicate.[44]

How were these ideas for socialisation to be put into effect? The final section of *What is Socialisation?* 'What Should We Do?—Education for Socialism', in answering this question, reveals Korsch's notion of socialism at this period. After stating that he has attempted to give a sketch of the goals of 'practical socialism', he describes three means for achieving these goals: political action for socialising individual branches of industry, by 'state legislation', or 'municipal decree'; work in the co-operatives; and political and economic action by the working class to compel the employers to recognise the rights of collective bargaining and co-determination.[45] However, the 'heroic' period of direct action for socialisation could only be expected to be effective as long as revolutionary times persisted. Thereafter what was needed was tireless educational activity directed to the rising generation entrusted with the building of socialism.[46]

In this the first and most lengthy of his writings on socialisation the Fabian influence is very noticeable. A significant part of it is concerned with the problem that even after the capitalist property owner has been eliminated from production, there may be two opposed interests in the economic life of a human community.[47] However, at this point I do not intend to assess this in any detail, as I wish to look at his other writings of this period on socialisation.

During 1919–20, Korsch wrote a number of articles on the socialisation question. They show a tendency to accept Marxism to a greater extent, and to stress the role of the councils more fully. In *What is Socialisation?* there are two quotations from Marx—from *Wage-Labour and Capital* and the *Communist Manifesto*;[48] a reference to the production of surplus-value;[49] and, in Sections 2–6, a basic exposition of Marx's ideas on production, the means of production, capital, the capitalist social order and economic and social power:[50] yet he does not avow himself to be a Marxist. Nor does he make any reference, direct or indirect, to the councils' system (*Rätesystem*), contrary to what later commentators have claimed.[51]

The article 'Grundsätzliches über Sozialisierung', which appeared in February 1920, less than a year after *What is Socialisation?*, marks an important change (by this time of course he had joined the USPD). He now claims to belong to those who 'today claim for ourselves the legacy of Marx and Engels'.[52] He feels able to criticise other Marxists for not grasping the point that 'scientific socialism' is not only a special theory of historical knowledge, but carries with it practical obligations;[53] and to refer to certain ideas as being so much part of the ABC of Marxism that they are not worth discussing.[54] Equally striking is the importance he ascribes to the 'councils', which he had not mentioned at all in *What is Socialisation?* Although his ideas do change, I would claim that there are enough similarities in his writings on socialisation in this period for them to be validly grouped together for analysis. I will concentrate on the two main features of these ideas: his conception of 'practical socialism', and his criticism of state socialism.

His criticism of other socialists' plans for socialisation was essentially a practical one:

> Only a few theorists and practitioners of socialism endeavoured, in opposition to the accepted dogma, to have a *positive* idea of the socialist form of society they aspired to.[55]

In the earlier part of this period, when he was still inclined to Fabianism, he claimed that it was wrong to say that the Fabians were 'mere revisionists', 'social reformers'—they, too, were 'practical socialists'.[56] By this he meant that

> Differing from the majority of present-day 'Marxists' and in conformity with a deeper understanding of Marx, 'practical socialism' stresses the insight that the only means to the real completion of the transition to the socialist organisation of society and the construction of socialism is conscious human activity (Marx's 'revolutionary praxis').[57]

'What is Socialisation?' 27

Likewise, when assessing Marxism itself, he stresses its practical character:

> For Marx, the 'materialist' knowledge of social development is ... from the very beginning not merely a theoretical grasp of an essence under the form of the object or of contemplation, but always at the same time subjective, human-sensuous, practical-critical, therefore 'revolutionary activity'.[58]

This emphasis is important, not only in relation to his writings on socialisation, but also as a manifestation of a tendency which was to be very prominent in the whole of his intellectual life, i.e. the concern with practice. Right from the start, his Marxism was as much, if not more, a question of practical as well as intellectual conviction. In his assessment of the socialisation question, we see that concern with practice which had been present in his pre-war writings. It was the practical failure of the Social-Democrats when faced with their greatest test, and not so much the disparity between a theory he already accepted and a practice contradictory to that theory, which convinced him of the need for a more intransigent Maxism. It was precisely this 'activist' strain which, as we shall see, was to lead him (from 1926 onwards) into conflict with the other Marxist orthodoxy, that of the Communist Party. The experience of the socialisation movement was decisive in giving a further impulse to the practical orientation of his thought.

It is also important to see this experience as part of the raw material out of which he fashioned *Marxism and Philosophy*. In the latter work, he treats these questions in a very rarefied and abstract way. This is of course entirely justified. But it is important to see that this philosophical abstraction drew on the experience of a particular situation, with all the limitations that that imposes. In Germany at this period, the majority of the population was both suffering from the extremes of material deprivation, and was actively dissatisfied with the old regime—an explosive combination. This seemed to be the ideal situation for a Marxist revolution: a trained proletariat with a long tradition of struggle, the ruling class in great difficulties. What happened? After a period of great difficulties the old ruling classes hoisted themselves back into the saddle with the help of the great Marxist party of the Second International, the SPD. It was quite clear that the determinist formulae of the 'orthodox' Marxists of the Second International were seriously at fault. In the heat of battle, they had, as Korsch saw it, not only been passive in leading their own supporters into the struggle for practical socialist measures, but also in many cases had proved to be in the front ranks of the defenders of the old regime.

Thus what characterises all of his positions during this period, when he moved from being on the left wing of the SPD to joining the KPD (1918–20), is a concern with the practical. Indeed a later Marxist critic was to characterise his position of this period as being purely voluntarist. In *Marxismus und Sozialisierungstheorie*, W. Greiling criticises Korsch for his tendency to see the will to socialism as basic. His conception of socialisation is thus, in its fundamentals, an organisational one. His 'deviation' from Marx thereby consists in accepting the will as a 'self-sufficient factor of development', and in neglecting the importance of objective factors.[59] It is certainly true that when he wrote *What is Socialisation?* he actually called his own standpoint, in contrast to the 'purely scientific' character of the 'orthodox Marxist' conception, and to the revisionist outlook which saw only the practical work of the immediate struggle, a programme of 'practical socialism'.[60]

What were to be the institutional means for carrying out the practice of socialisation? In *What is Socialisation?* he did not mention the councils (*Räte*), but in another article he argued that

> The way ... in which ... control from above (by the majority) and control from below (by the participants) can be safely and rapidly carried out, is the so often mentioned and so little understood 'councils' system' [*Rätesystem*].[61]

He also claimed that the operation of the councils' system in Russia showed that the most far-reaching autonomy could be combined with the incorporation of all economic bodies in a planned administration of the whole.[62]

Thus he saw the role of the councils primarily as economic, not political. It is his conception of the relation between politics and economics which grounded his criticism of state-socialist conceptions of socialisation, which we shall now consider.

In some of his more simplified statements, Korsch seems simply to equate socialisation and revolution, e.g. when he writes:

Socialisation is the social revolution, it is the socialist idea becoming flesh and reality through practical, human-sensuous activity.[63]

This messianic statement does not help one understand the difference between reformist and revolutionary conceptions of socialisation. Several years earlier Lenin had made the distinction clearly and succinctly. At the 1910 International Socialist Congress at Copenhagen, the SPD representative, Elm, argued that one should not quarrel about the expropriation of the capitalist class, but should be concerned with 'overcoming' (*Überwindung*) capitalism. Lenin replied:

> what is 'socialisation'? It can be taken to mean conversion into the property of the whole community, but it can also be taken to mean any palliatives, any reforms within the framework of capitalism, from peasant cooperatives to municipal baths and public lavatories.[64]

What we want to discuss here, however, is Korsch's position on the role of the state in the transition from capitalism to socialism. The statement above seems to ignore the state completely—is this true of Korsch's position in general?

He argued that the state socialists' plans for socialisation were incomplete in that they refused to consider the possibility of extending them to the export and import trade. The state socialists thought that this trade could be left to the initiative of the individual merchant; socialisation of this sector of the economy would be impracticable anyway until other countries had socialised their economies. As a consequence of leaving foreign trade in private hands, Korsch claimed that raw materials were being sold on the world market, much below world market prices, thus bringing about the ruin of German industry.[65] Clearly this is not a fundamental criticism of the state socialists' position, only of one of its aspects. The same holds for his implied criticism of the notion held by some Majority socialists of 'war socialism'—that socialisation should consist in extending the kind of intervention made by the state in wartime. This 'state capitalism' is not even 'state socialism'.

To understand Korsch's fundamental critique of the state socialists, let us return to *What is Socialisation?* Here we find a two-stage model of socialisation: first, the socialisation of the means of production; and second, the socialisation of work, and the gradual process of education towards socialism. Gerlach comments

> The reader will recognise here the two-phase theory of socialisation adopted by Marx (see his *Critique of the Gotha Programme*) which Korsch here takes over as a realistic prognosis of the development of socialism.[66]

In fact, Korsch and Marx have radical differences on this question. They each have quite a different conception of the relation between politics and economics, and of the 'transition period' between capitalism and socialism. The question to which Marx primarily addressed himself in his *Critique of the Gotha Programme* was that of the state. After the overthrow of capitalist society, and before the achievement of communist society, there is 'a political transition period in which the state can be nothing but the *revolutionary dictatorship of the proletariat*.'[67] Whereas Korsch argues against the state socialists that, after equating 'socialisation' with 'stateisation',[68] they add that

> 'of course' the 'state' of the socialist epoch which uniformly regulates production and consumption as a whole would be quite a different state from the previous 'class state'.[69]

Thus Korsch views even a different kind of state as not much of an improvement.

Elsewhere, he claims that in the minds of many workers, the idea of 'socialisation' is replacing the earlier socialist teaching that, first, political power in the state is to be gained by the vote (*Stimmzettel*), and then the means of production shall be transferred to the majority by legal means[70]—i.e. his criticism is not merely an ideological one, it represents an idea that is already taking root in the working class.

It is clear that by 'state socialists' he meant the Majority SPD. The events of 1918–19 had shown that what they meant by a class state was the political system of Imperial Germany: the three-class electoral system and the predominance of the Junkers. What they wanted to replace this by was the 'classless' system of 'parliamentary democracy'. This was made particularly clear by their attitude to the councils. They held that the councils were 'caretaker' organisations, to be dissolved as soon as the National Assembly could be convened. Ebert represented this view with great clarity at the December 1918 Congress of Workers' and Soldiers' Councils.[71]

Apart from the passing reference to the vote[72] Korsch said very little of any consequence in this period about parliamentary democracy and its relation to the councils or the soviet system. He seems to have thought that the councils were primarily economic organisations. Thus in one passage he argues that the system of workers' democracy in socialist society is based on 'industrial workers' councils', built on the factory assemblies of every individual factory.[73]

It is instructive to compare Korsch's ideas on this question with those of Lenin and the Bolsheviks. In a certain sense they, too, considered themselves state socialists. As early as 1899 Lenin had specified the task of the Russian Social-Democrats as being the leadership of the revolutionary movement of the working-class towards the seizure of state power.[74] In *State and Revolution*, he made it clear that the crucial question concerning the transition to socialism was not whether or not a state would be necessary, but what kind of state.[75] His view was borne out by the practice of the Bolsheviks.

In the chaotic period of workers' control in the Russian Revolution, which lasted from April 1917 to well after the Bolshevik seizure of power in October, isolated factories were seized, and others were run under the direction of factory committees. But the Bolsheviks did not welcome the spontaneous elements of such movements as uncritically as Korsch did. They saw the direct action of the workers in taking over their factories as a means of breaking the power of the capitalists, but the anarchic elements in this kind of action could equally well jeopardise the operation of a centralised socialist plan. Therefore they had to be replaced by the centralised direction of the economy by the workers' state. This was to direct the economy for the benefit of all, and to avoid the 'anarchy' which would result from local autonomy. Lenin in particular had a much more realistic view of the possibilities of the continuing involvement of the whole of the working class in the direction of the economy, once the initial revolutionary *élan* had resulted in victory. The predominance of the Bolshevik workers would be inevitable given the generally low levels of education and training that the majority of the small

Russian working class had received. Until this could be corrected by a drastically reshaped education system, the mass activity of the Soviets which had characterised the period February to October 1917 would almost certainly subside. Of necessity, the central organs of the new state power would then play the leading role.[76]

Thus Korsch's critique of state socialism at this period distanced him from both the Bolsheviks and the Majority SPD. At a later period, as a member of the KPD, he was of course an orthodox 'Marxist–Leninist' on this question, insisting on the class nature of the German state, and of the need for a new kind of state power.[77]

Thus in conformity with the USPD[78] he held a 'centrist' view on the councils and their relation to the state. His ideas are very much like those of the Austro-Marxists, Adler and Bauer, in seeing the councils as economic institutions, although he does not seem to agree that parliament should continue to exist as a political institution. Thus Adler proposed that

> the system of workers' councils ... will become a real organ of socialisation ... the Assembly [i.e. parliament] ... would be the essential instrument in the transitional period, which safeguards the proletariat and assures a continuous and peaceful development, far from the storms of civil war. To maintain the National Assembly as well as the central council of the workers' councils is much less dangerous for the social revolution inasmuch as its importance is bound to decrease as the propaganda for socialism asserts itself, which is much more powerful by speeches and writing than by the machine gun and the special court.[79]

Likewise, in *Der Weg zum Sozialismus*, Bauer had proposed plans for socialisation rather like those of Korsch[80] and he criticised state socialism in remarkably similar terms:

> Who is going to administrate the socialised industry? The government? Certainly not! If the government administrated all the industries without exception, it would render itself too powerful with respect to the people and national representation. Such an increase in the power of the government would administer the socialised industry badly, because no one ad-

ministers industry worse than the state. Also we socialists have never demanded stateisation, but the socialisation of industry.[81]

The evasive character of such formulae is particularly clear with respect to the question of the state. While the reformists were content to use the old machinery of the Junker state, and while Lenin was proposing what he considered to be a radically new form of state, the centrist proposals, in virtually ignoring the problem, are a utopian ambiguity. This is all the more surprising as the traditional role of the state in liberal-democratic theory, the ideology of *laissez-faire* capitalism, which was that its intervention would be kept to a minimum, had been seriously challenged by the extensive interference of the state in the German war economy. This posed a difficult problem for Marxists, since it seemed difficult to reconcile with traditional conceptions of socialism and capitalism.[82] Where the state is not just a repressive power apparatus, as it was in Russia, coercing by naked force, this poses a difficult ideological problem anyway for Marxists.[83]

However, one must remember the differences between Korsch and the Austro–Marxists. The comparison just made with Bauer and Adler is only partly justified in that they did recognise the importance of the problem of the state: a more apt comparison would be with two other movements—the anarcho-syndicalists and the English Guild Socialists.

In *What is Socialisation?* Korsch implies that syndicalism would lead to 'producers' socialism'.[84] The most extended discussion of this question is to be found in the article 'Das sozialistische und das syndikalistische Sozialisierungsprogramm', in which he is quite sympathetic to syndicalism. He praises it for realising that the important focus of the struggle for socialisation is economic not political; and that it does not fall into anarchist simplicities such as 'socialism without rulers': in both cases it is in line with modern socialist and communist thought.[85] Much later (in 1951) he wrote that syndicalism had attracted him before 1914, and that it was his interest in it which led him into the councils' movement 'during and after World War I',[86] but in his published writings of the immediate post-war period he was no more than mildly sympathetic.

The other non state-socialist tendency to which his ideas at this period bear a remarkable similarity was the Guild Socialist group of G.D.H. Cole. There is only explicit reference to the 'guild principle' in Korsch's writings,[87] but it is not unlikely that he was acquainted with their ideas given his continuing interest (at the beginning of this period, at any rate) in the Fabians.[88]

The Guild Socialist movement is worth examining briefly, not only for its theoretical similarities to Korsch's ideas, but also for its attempt to put these ideas into practice. The Guild system won substantial support in the engineering shop-stewards movement in England during the war, and also among the miners, railwaymen and postal workers. The end of the war, and the disbandment of the munition workers, weakened its hold among the engineering workers in particular. But, despite this, in 1920 S. G. Hobson actually launched a National Building Guild. This met with some success, until the government contracts on which it had been based were withdrawn. This was effectively the end of the Guild movement, although it was not formally wound up until 1923.[89] Like Korsch, the Guild Socialists rejected both the syndicalist and the state-socialist conceptions of socialisation. Similarly, they required not merely a rejection of these dangers, but a positive plan:

> for the constructive task of social reorganisation more is needed than a plan for the assumption of power by a social class however equipped. There is also needed a positive plan of action for that class to pursue both in the course of and after its assumption of power.[90]

For this end, they proposed a system of National Guilds. Cole defined these as:

> A Nation Guild would be an association of all the workers by hand and brain concerned in the carrying on of a particular industry or service, and its function would be actually to carry on that industry or service on behalf of the whole community.[91]

The system of National Guilds aimed to ensure the greatest possible amount of autonomy to the local group. The general structure would be a national commune into which would enter representatives of the Guilds' National Councils and Regional Communes.[92] The Guild System is interesting not only for its practical demonstration of the inadequacy of these ideas in practice, and for its similarities to Korsch's proposals, but for the way in which the logic of the ideas is brought out. This is how the elements of politics and economics involved in such proposals exist side by side in an eclectic compromise. On the one hand, the primacy of politics is denied:

> the transformation required is fundamentally not political but economic ... It is the economic, rather than the political power of the workers that will avail to overthrow capitalism.[93]

This was, on the other hand, linked with the claim that Guild Socialism is not a purely industrial theory. It rested upon a different conception of democracy from that of the nineteenth century. Democracy is to be extended into all parts of society: the theory was worked out mainly in relation to the industrial sphere, because that is basic.[94] Looking back, Cole reassessed his earlier doctrine thus:

> Guild Socialism was fundamentally an ethical and not a materialist doctrine. It set out, as against both State Socialism and what was soon to be called Communism, to assert the vital importance of individual and group liberty.[95]

Summing up Korsch's writings of this period, we can see the gradual emergence of explicitly Marxist ideas, in comparison to the commitment to a more Fabian approach—still dominant when he wrote *What is Socialisation?*. The notion of 'practical socialism' reveals a voluntarist tendency in his ideas, more marked than in the pre-war days, which was to continue throughout his political life. This tendency was reinforced by his view of the reasons for the failure of the socialists after November 1918:

> when the political power organisation of the bourgeois class had collapsed, and there was nothing externally standing in the way of the transition from capitalism to socialism, the great opportunity was however to lapse without being exploited because the *social-psychological* conditions for making use of it were to a large extent lacking.[96]

Arguably, the experience of the socialisation movement thus

provided him with the raw material of which he was to make a more exact analysis in *Marxism and Philosophy*: i.e. a specific instance where the objective conditions for revolution were present but the ideological preparation (in the terms of *Marxism and Philosophy*), or the 'social-psychological' conditions, (in the terms of 'Grundsätzliches über Sozialisierung'), were lacking. Indeed on one occasion he speaks of the Second International's failure in terms quite reminiscent of the later work.[97]

But he was not yet concerned with such philosophical questions. His immediate concern was with the political problems facing the socialisation movement. In a somewhat different form, these were the subject of his next major work, *Arbeitsrecht für Betriebsräte* (*Labour Law for Factory Councils*), which is discussed in the next chapter.

3 Labour Law for Factory Councils

The second phase of Korsch's writings on the struggle by the working class for direct control over production concerns the factory councils (*Betriebsräte*) rather than the more broadly based workers' councils (*Arbeiterräte*). This change reflects the changed focus of political life during 1920–2. In this period, the *Arbeiterräte* were non-existent, having in fact lost most of their effectiveness by the end of 1919. As Korsch pointed out:

> already in November 1919 only a tiny band of 'municipal workers' councils' was left ... of the revolutionary workers' and soldiers' councils of ... 1918 ... but since the end of 1919 we have no longer had political councils in the revolutionary sense.[1]

They were replaced by the factory councils, which were given an added importance by being granted legal status by the factory councils law of 1920. The legal recognition of the factory councils was a sign that the revolutionary movement had almost entirely disappeared, and that the normal rule of law had returned. But why had the utopian revolutionary movement of the earlier period given way to a more peaceful political philosophy of parliamentarism and the struggle for piecemeal reforms?

The answer given by the theorists of the Communist International was that it was due to a combination of the treachery of the SPD, the misleading role of the 'centrists' (the USPD) and the failure of the revolutionary elements to achieve organisational cohesiveness by forming their own independent party. During this period, the 'need for a Leninist party' was not yet as widely argued by the Comintern and its constituent parties, as it was subsequently (e.g. in the later campaign for 'Bolshevisation', of which Korsch was to be a victim). Korsch could take a somewhat different position. Recognising that the political councils, which had revolutionary implications, had been replaced by the much more conciliationist factory councils, which did not pose such a threat to the power of the state or of the employers, he argued that they had failed not for want of a revolutionary party, but because

> The most important organisational failure was that for the most part, the political councils were not chosen by the proletarians themselves, arranged according to factory and profession, which alone would have corresponded to the meaning of the councils, but were chosen by the socialist parties, usually it is true on the basis of parity.[2]

Before I discuss Korsch's writings from this period, I propose to examine the important changes taking place in political life and Korsch's position in relation to them.

Until 1914, there was only one socialist party in Germany, the SPD. The war, and the failure by the majority of the SPD leaders and their trade union counterparts to oppose it, had caused deep fissures to appear in its ranks. The first open signs of such splits were the formation of the USPD in 1917, and further to the left, but within its ranks, the Spartakus League of Rosa Luxemburg. This process was hastened by the experience of a period of the Social Democrats in office, immediately at the end of the war. Korsch's exasperation at the passivity of the socialisation commission was shared by the thousands of workers who had suffered the war patiently in the utopian expectation of radical changes in the post-war period.

None the less, at the first election to the National Assembly (in January 1919), the SPD still had a long lead over the USPD. But the USPD had made such inroads into the traditional support of the older party, the industrial working class, that in some areas including Korsch's own (Thüringia) it was in the majority. In the eighteen months after the end of the war, the USPD continued to grow rapidly, more than doubling its membership and electoral support.[3] After his disappointment with the inactivity and ineffectiveness of the socialisation commission, Korsch himself was looking for more radical solutions and so joined the USPD. But his membership of that party did not last for long, since he was shortly to be attracted to an even more radical party—the KPD.[4] This was formed as a separate party from the Spartakus League on 30 December 1918. For some time, it remained very small, even by comparison with the USPD.[5]

The situation was soon to change drastically. At their March 1919 party conference, the USPD had already come out in favour of Soviet government, and the 'dictatorship of the proletariat'. This marked a decisive break with the convinced democratic parliamentarians of the SPD. When this was confirmed at the December 1919 conference, reunification with the SPD was clearly excluded. Instead unity was to be sought with the official Comintern Party in Germany, the KPD, and an application was made to join the Comintern. Accordingly a conference was held at Halle in October 1920 to debate this momentous question. After an impressive oratorical performance from Zinoviev, it was decided to accept the twenty-one conditions for membership of the Comintern, and the fusion of the two German organisations. If he had any reservations about the decision at this time, Korsch did not express them in public (there is no record of his having spoken at the conference).[6] It is not clear exactly when he joined the KPD, but it was probably towards the end of 1920.[7] At any rate, he soon began to contribute to the communist newspaper for Thüringia, the *Neue Zeitung*.[8] Subsequently he was a prolific contributor to the communist press. Because the majority of these articles are only of occasional interest, and, though competent, are not more than that, his journalistic activity will not be discussed directly.

The main focus of his work for the first two years of his membership of the KPD was on the political problems of the day: in particular, the law on factory councils, and the establishment of legal factory councils in place of the 'extra-constitutional' political workers' councils. To understand the problem more clearly and to see how it relates to the earlier writings on socialisation, the progress of such legislation since the socialisation movement of 1918–19 must be briefly reviewed.

The socialisation commission had been content to dissolve itself after the vague legislation of 3 March 1919 concerning the socialisation of suitable economic enterprises.[9] At the same time as the socialisation commission was pondering its ineffective proposals the first steps in setting up a system of factory councils and appropriate legislation for them had been taken. On 23 December 1918, an Order was passed regulating the operation of collective agreements, and making provision for workers' committees to supervise their execution. This legislation marked a drastic improvement in the workers' legal position, in comparison with their status under the Hilfsdienstgesetz of 1916 and previous legislation.[10] It was formally codified in the Weimar Constitution (31 July 1919). Article 165, paragraph 1 stated:

> Workers and employees shall be called upon to co-operate with employers and on an equal footing in the regulation of wages and working conditions as well as in the entire field of the economic development of the forces of production. The organisations on both sides and their agreements shall be recognised. Workers and employers shall for the purpose of looking after their economic and social interests be given legal representation in factory workers' councils as well as in district workers' councils ... and in a workers' council of the Reich.[11]

The Bill was finally sanctioned on 18 January 1920. The special Betriebsrätegesetz (Factory Council Law) stated its purpose as follows:

> To safeguard the common economic interests of employees (manual and white-collar workers) with respect to the employer, and to support the employer in carrying out the aims of the factory, factory councils are to be set up in all factories employing as a rule at least twenty workers.[12]

How did the Communist Party, Korsch's new political allegiance, respond to the changed situation? It eventually adopted a sharp change of tactics. The direct insurrectionary struggle for power was not an immediate task; the new orientation was to be towards 'the struggle for the masses for the conquest of power'. This turn was not achieved without a severe internal struggle. The Spartakus League, the forerunner of the

KPD, had rejected participation in the National Assembly, and, at a different level, the factory councils were a similar kind of constitutional organisation. The left wing of the KPD was as much opposed to factory councils as it was to parliament: it stood instead for revolutionary councils. At times, during the period 1919–20, large sections of the party supported these ideas, and only the skilful manoeuvring of Levi, backed by the authority of Lenin, succeeded in steering the party away from such a position. But this was not finally achieved until the end of 1921. For example, one of the severest disagreements arose over the abortive putsch in central Germany led by sections of the KPD—the 'March Action' (1921).[13]

After this incident, the line of the Third (June 1921) and Fourth (December 1922) Comintern Congresses won the day in the KPD. This was for patient work in the mass organisations of the working class (particularly in the trade unions, which had grown enormously since the war), however 'reformist' they might be. The constituent parties of the Comintern were not to neglect any opportunity to work in such organisations and were to utilise any concession made by the employers. The factory councils presented great opportunities for this kind of work.[14]

This policy was followed for two years from the end of 1921. How successful was it? The KPD did gain significant support in the employed working class. Its co-operative attitude towards other parties, as instanced by the United Front policy, began to yield real successes in this period, especially in the factory councils. At the first congress of the factory councils (October 1920) convened by the ADGB (the German equivalent of the TUC) the left as a whole was very much in a minority.[15] In the next two years, there was a steady swing leftwards, so that by the eleventh ADGB congress in 1922, the politics of 'co-operation' (*Arbeitsgemeinschaft*) were actually condemned.[16] In September of the same year, the KPD convened its own Conference for Factory Councils, which Korsch reported on for the *Neue Zeitung*. This was attended by over 200 delegates from all over Germany. From Korsch's own district, Thüringia, there was a narrow minority against sending delegates to the conference, but elsewhere the movement even extended to traditionally less radical areas, such as Breslau/Schlesien.[17]

What was Korsch's role in this movement? Before we examine this question, we must look at the general level of development of his ideas at this period. In the first year of his KPD membership, his published work consisted of seven newspaper articles for the *Neue Zeitung*, which are not of any great significance. What he wrote in the following year, 1922, was of much greater importance. In February and March 1922 the communist publishing house Viva issued two pamphlets by Korsch: *Quintessenz des Marxismus*, and, *Kernpunkte der materialistischen Geschichtsauffassung*. As the latter discusses questions more relevant to *Marxism and Philosophy*, it will be discussed in the next chapter.[18]

Quintessenz des Marxismus resulted from the educational classes in basic Marxism which Korsch taught to KPD members. It was meant to give a popular outline of Marxism, as Korsch pointed out in his Preface, '[it] helps the beginner to make an independent study of the Marxist system'. In addition to the ABC of Marxism, 'it deals with the difficult questions of Marx's theory of economics and society, relating them to each other'.[19] The very brief first section (two and a half pages) attempts to explain 'The Marxist theory of society'. Apart from a rather curious 'diagrammatic representation of human society' displaying Marx's base-superstructure schema[20] the remainder of the pamphlet gives a simplified version of Marxist political economy.[21]

The question of political rights and their relation to the productive process had not been clearly answered in *What is Socialisation?* *Quintessenz* answers the question explicitly. The opening page states:

> The democratic-republican state guarantees its citizens political freedom only, but it does not yet do away with social unfreedom.[22]

The first clause is rather unfortunate in view of the fate of the Weimar republic. Even at the time, it was a rather curious thing to say in a country still dominated by Junkers.[23] This ambiguous view of bourgeois rights is not corrected by the fourth paragraph, the only party of *Quintessenz* which deals with this question:

> The bourgeois freedoms (e.g. free trade, free entry to education, free vote etc.) are of no use to the proletarian, because in capitalist society he is prevented from using them by his class situation.[24]

This formulation does not deal adequately with the relation between the law (rights), and, the productive system in which the law operates. There seems to be only a contingent connection between the sociological position of workers and their access to law. But in the Marxist system there is quite a different relation between law and the production process. I now wish to show this difference, first by examining Korsch's conception of the nature of law.

His early career had shown that he was not very interested in the practice of law, but, if anything, in jurisprudence. His own professional career was in the academic study of jurisprudence. From 1919 he was lecturing at the University of Jena on related topics. For example, in the winter semester of 1920/21, he held seminars on Hegel's philosophy of law, and, in the following winter, on the problems of the law and the state.[25] He was eventually appointed Professor of Civil Law at the University of Jena.[26] Even then he did not write a general treatise on the relations between law and Marxism. In the early 1930s he wrote his one article on the nature of law—a review of works by the Austro–Marxist Renner and the Soviet jurist Paschukanis.[27] In this he suggests that Lukács's argument that philosophy is a form of reified consciousness can be applied to law:

> until the present time, a clear recognition by Marxists of the fact clearly expressed by Marx was lacking, namely that even in its form so-called 'law' [Recht] was only a more fetishistically distorted form of the same social realities which make their first fetishised appearance in the form of the commodity.[28]

However, in the early 1920s, his analysis had not reached such a sophisticated level. But his general position at this period can be reconstructed. 'Law' (*Recht*) forms part of the superstructure. In his 'diagrammatic representation of human society',[29] he locates it as part of the 'superstructure' on the same level as 'morals' and 'customs':

Superstructure	(*Ideas in men's heads*
	(*Law, morals, customs*
	(*Church, school, free professions*
	(*Family, state*
Base	(*The economic order*

If the diagram represents a series of stages, then presumably the lowest level (family and state) is most closely connected with the 'base' (economy) and as one ascends, the autonomy of ideology increases till one reaches the 'ideas in men's heads'.[30] But in every case, ideology is a part of reality. There can be no question of the ideological superstructure undergoing a substantial change independently of a change of the 'base'. On this question, Marx had stated definitely that

> Right [Recht] can never be higher than the economic structure of society and its cultural development conditioned thereby.[31]

Before assessing Korsch's ideas on law, as outlined in *Labour Law for Factory Councils*, it will be useful to describe Marx's position and use that as a touchstone. Marx considered that the problem of accounting for the existence of law and the state was one of the key problems which led him to his materialist conception of history:

> legal relations [Rechtsverhaltnisse] as well as forms of state are to be grasped neither from themselves nor from the ... development ... of the mind, but rather have their roots in the material conditions of life.[32]

Unfortunately, Marx never applied to law itself the methodological outlines he had gained in this way through his studies of law.

Yet it is possible to conjecture how he would have approached this question. Marx would not have aimed at giving a sociological critique of law—i.e. how the law served the interests of certain classes—or (at a more empirical level), at investigating the class background of members of the judiciary. This is because Marx had a more fundamental aim: to show, the relations between law, and the 'material conditions of life', on which classes were themselves grounded. In the idealist system, law and rights were held to embody certain eternal human values; in Marx's system they were grounded in definite stages in the development of society. In the bourgeois revolution, the demand for certain rights, although held to be desirable in itself by those putting forward the demand, objectively had the effect of promoting bourgeois property relations.³³ In future, the demands put forward in the context of the proletarian revolution would, in the classical Marxist schema, have a different orientation. The following passage from Marx may help to clarify this point:

> The right to work is in the bourgeois sense, nonsense, a wretched, pious wish. But behind the right to work stands the power over capital, behind power over capital, the appropriation of the means of production, their subjection to the associated working class, that is, the abolition of wage labour, capital and their mutual relationship.³⁴

In short, Marxism argues that any attempt by the working class to use the law to protect and advance its interests comes into conflict with the fundamental relations of exploitation. Based on a supposed connection between law and the organisation of production, it demands a reorganisation of society in and after which law can play only a secondary role.

I now wish to assess Korsch's ideas on labour law in the light of this brief attempt to distinguish between a sociological and a Marxist explanation of law. In criticising his general approach to the question of law, I shall not look for differences with the conventional jurists. Even if relevant, this would be an enormous task, since the law elicited a great deal of legal commentary.³⁵ Further, Korsch himself did not concentrate on the interpretation of the law by conventional jurists, since he was mainly concerned with arguing against the reformist conceptions of the SPD. He attempted to demonstrate that the views of the SPD and the bourgeoisie in fact coincided. Like the conventional jurists, the SPD commentators claimed to discuss the matter objectively, giving equal weight to arguments favourable and unfavourable to the employers.³⁶

Korsch did not directly challenge the idea that the law can be analysed objectively. Instead he disputed the practical conclusions drawn by the SPD. In so doing, he had a tendency to align himself on the side of the 'class struggle':

> our *Labour Law for Factory Councils* is from its first to its last page oriented to the revolutionary class struggle.³⁷

Korsch warned that the factory councils could be used to get the majority of the workers to comply with the schemes for participation with the employers (*Arbeitsgemeinschaft*) which the moderate trade union leaders preferred. In his opinion, the councils should instead be considered as

> the most advanced outposts of the proletarian army ... as the real battlefields in an economic and social struggle, which ... at the same time necessarily means a political struggle.[38]

Their role was to promote the class struggle: precisely the opposite of the aim of the moderate leaders of the SPD and the trade unions, who preferred a policy of co-operation.

Thus in Korsch's view, the factory councils were not merely 'auxiliary organs' in the trade union struggle to maintain the workers' standard of living within the existing capitalist order, but were also to be the advanced position of the revolutionary movement: they already were a weapon of control over the running of the factory.[39] In this sense,

> the councils movement appears no longer as just a preparatory action for the coming major battle of the social revolution, but as the real and definite beginning of this decisive social battle itself.[40]

But the factory councils were only a temporary foothold. He opposed the 'reformist' notion that the factory councils and the laws relating to them could represent a permanent gain for the working class. He claimed that they were a concession given by the industrialists in their hour of danger, when it seemed that they might be engulfed by the popular wave of protest at the end of the war. Concessions were made in the hope of averting even more threatening dangers. This was so not only in this case, but in general

> undoubtedly the decisive motive for all previous social policy, however honest the intentions and motives of individual bourgeois reformers may have been, has been for the most part the pressure of the proletarian class.[41]

Reforms are conceded in order to defuse potentially dangerous movements of popular protest. For example, at the same time as the anti-socialist laws there was legislation on social insurance.[42] In reviewing the history of social policy, Korsch mentions various motives for the concession of reforms. The reform of housing conditions, for instance, was motivated by the fear that the epidemics caused by poor conditions would spread to the more affluent residential districts. Other improvements in the dietary and housing conditions of the working class were carried out to ensure an adequate supply of healthy recruits to the army.[43] Thus, like other reforms, the factory councils would not be a permanent concession to the working class. He warned that

> The German capitalist class, which tolerated 'co-operation' [Arbeitsgemeinschaft] as long as it needed it as a buffer between itself and the movement of the masses ... is today already preparing its withdrawal from co-operation and from all 'co-operative' ... institutions of the new Germany.[44]

He illustrated this point with examples from a memorandum, 'On the Economic Constitution of Germany', issued by the employers in May 1922,[45] which seemed to support his point. He claimed that the greatest danger for the working class would be *not* to use the factory councils for political ends. The greatest danger would be

> to fill ... the legal factory councils with a 'co-operative' spirit and to begin to consider them as members of a so-called 'common economy' resting on the fraternisation between capital and labour.[46]

The notion of 'anchoring' the councils into the constitution was quite utopian, and

> even this distorted caricature of a 'councils system' promised by Article 165 of the Constitution was for the reactionary forces which have re-constituted themselves more and more powerfully since 1920 still too much to tolerate.[47]

Korsch decisively rejected a reformist 'social policy' approach to the factory councils. This is hardly surprising: what is more significant is his tendency to be sympathetic towards the anarcho-syndicalists. He notes that even before the war they had at least recognised the possibilities for direct control over production by the working class. The traditional party of the working class, the reformist SPD, had entirely ignored such possibilities.[48]

So far I have reviewed Korsch's general notion of Marxism and his rejection of the reformists' views on the factory councils. I will now turn to the main ideas of Labour Law for Factory Councils itself. The detailed legal commentary on the factory councils law, which forms the second part of the book, will be referred to only in so far as it adds to or explains more clearly the argument of the first, more theoretical part.

The first part of his argument is that the antithesis between the bourgeois and proletarian classes leads to opposed notions of labour law:

> the bourgeois class considers the whole labour law essentially from the standpoint of the 'contract of labour; by contrast the proletarian class considers it essentially under that of the 'constitution of labour'.[49]

What is meant by these two notions 'contract of labour' and 'constitution of labour'? In discussing the former, Korsch does no more than repeat Marx's argument that, while the worker may be a free and equal citizen in the democratic republic, in the economic sphere he is neither free nor equal. The 'contract of labour', apparently a free contract between equals, rests on a real inequality in the sphere of production, between those who own the means of production and those who do not.[50]

The concept of 'constitution of labour' refers to certain developments in capitalism which have taken place since Marx's death. The explication of this concept forms the central thesis of *Labour Law for Factory Councils*. This central thesis depends upon a certain periodisation of capitalism, i.e. that the contemporary period is a transitional one between capitalism and socialism. Since this notion of the transitional period is crucial to Korsch's whole outlook during this period, and since it is also the basic underlying conception of *Marxism and Philosophy*, it must be examined before a detailed analysis of *Labour Law for Factory Councils* can be made.

'Labour Law for Factory Councils'

The idea that the epoch beginning around 1900 was a transitional one between capitalism and socialism formed an essential part of Comintern doctrine. It had first been put forward in Lenin's *Imperialism: The Highest Stage of Capitalism*,[51] which argued that important changes in the nature of capitalism had begun to appear around the year 1900. Previously, the driving force of capitalism was free competition; in the imperialist stage, free competition had been replaced by the operation of the giant monopolies which dominated the economy. Consequently, capitalism showed a tendency to stagnate, by comparison with its earlier stage. Lenin summarised this development as follows:

> Capitalism in its imperialist stage leads directly to the most comprehensive socialisation of production; it so to speak drags the capitalists against their will and consciousness into some sort of a new social order, a transitional one from complete free competition to complete socialisation.[52]

In this transitional epoch between capitalism and socialism, capitalism would be continually beset by economic crises leading to 'wars and revolutions'. In Lenin's analysis of imperialism, the changes in the production process are considered primary: the probability of 'wars and revolutions' is derived from this economic analysis. But Lenin did not think that there was a mechanical, rigidly determinist connection between economics and politics. The 'death agony' of capitalism may be prolonged, and capitalism might revive to enjoy periods of sustained growth, if a revolutionary party did not succeed in leading the working class to overthrow capitalism.[53] Lenin's argument is both concrete (in that it is based on a detailed economic analysis) and cautious (in its estimation that capitalism is not inevitably doomed).

The more messianic and utopian followers of Lenin in the 1920s lacked his concreteness and his caution. Lukács, for example, boldly proclaimed the actuality of the revolution;[54] Korsch simply asserted:

> At the beginning of the twentieth century, the long period of purely evolutionary development of capitalism came to an end and a new epoch of revolutionary struggle began.[55]

He does not explain the concept of imperialism in any detail, perhaps because he thought it too well-known in communist circles to require explanation. In one passage he does mention the objective basis of imperialism:

> in the beginning of the 20th century it became evident that the ... *development of imperialism* had created the objective preconditions for an ... enormous intensification of class antagonisms.[56]

But in none of his references to the imperialist epoch does he attempt to explain the particular significance of the economic changes which underlie it. Instead he concentrates on its political aspects: the 'dictatorship of the proletariat', 'increased class struggle'. To use the Marxist terminology, he only refers to the superstructural features of the epoch, an epoch in which in all areas of society two hostile classes confront each other, without either being more than temporarily dominant.[57]

Thus his conception of the transitional epoch is not explicitly stated. The few references he does make to the 'transitional period' (*Übergangsphase*) show that his conception may differ significantly from Lenin's. In *Labour Law for Factory Councils*, he compared the transitional period between capitalism and socialism to the period of the absolute monarchy, which represented a transition between capitalism and feudalism. This comparison is more clearly stated, however, in a newspaper article which, by means of a journalistic conceit, expresses the idea more sharply:

> Just as formerly the French Sun King, in the epoch of the greatest splendour of the absolute monarchy (which today seems to be a rather brief transitional period between the mediaeval state based on the estates [*Ständestaat*] and the modern bourgeois constitutional state) called out in the full glory of his rule: I am the state! so too do his powerful successors King Stinnes and Company declare the same, standing on the summit of the epoch of capitalist domination, and proclaiming ... the absolute pre-eminence of their social leadership over the democratic republic which has sunk to the level of a formal state.'[58]

This comparison is itself the conclusion of an argument about the bourgeois and proletarian revolutions. The difference between them is as follows. Bourgeois society had overthrown the tyranny of some forms of religion and state, but had not been able to achieve a comparable liberation in the economic sphere, so that

> The historical task of the struggle of the proletarian class against the bourgeoisie and all older social classes consists ... in abolishing the unfreedom of the working man in production, and thus destroying the basis of capitalist domination.[59]

He considers that the proletarian revolution is not totally different from the bourgeois revolution, only its 'deepening' (*Vertiefung*).[60]

Within this general schema, there is a great deal of complexity. The evolution of bourgeois rights was a lengthy process:

> The political freedom and equality of all state citizens in the democratic republic today was not won by the bourgeois revolution with one blow.[61]

In feudal society, decisive political power is to be found in the hands of the upper estates (*Stände*). This period is followed by that of the absolute monarchy, in which political power is held by one person alone, the absolute monarch. This represents a balance of forces between the declining estates and the rising bourgeoisie. The first step away from this towards democracy is the attainment of a written constitution limiting the rights of absolutism, i.e. a constitutional monarch, in which the monarch has control over ministers. Finally, in a parliamentary monarchy, the ruler is merely 'the dot on the i!' The most complete form of political freedom is the democratic republic.[62] Yet even in the most democratic republic, the struggles between the bourgeoisie and the proletariat 'only apparently turn around the domination of the state: in their innermost essentials, they turn on the domination of the economy, i.e. the 'constitution of labour'.[63] This schema is completed by a transitional period in which the bourgeoisie imposes its dictatorship in periods of crisis; and the proletariat attempts to replace this by its own dictatorship in the transitional period from capitalism to communism. Eventually this results in the communist society free associations in a state—and the classless society.⁶⁴

In this schema, economic and political developments do not run parallel:

> The same development which has, in the course of history, been completed in the 'superstructure' of the state community, is completed in a different tempo of development and in partly different forms in the economic base of this political community: in the 'community of labour'.⁶⁵

The individual phases of the 'community of labour' occur later than the corresponding phases of political development. For instance, despotism is the rule in the factory after it has disappeared from the political scene.⁶⁶ At the present stage, too, economics lags behind political developments:

> the present constitution of labour in such countries as Germany and Austria can be characterised as a 'constitutionalism of the professions' [*gewerbliche Konstitutionalismus*], still in its first stages. The monarchical rulers of the factories still exist even if they are for the most part no longer sovereigns totally independent of each other ... but are united in leagues and kingdoms.⁶⁷

Whereas the reformist politicians and trade union leaders had imagined that the growth of large enterprises would lead to a democratisation of the economy, precisely the opposite had occurred: the large entrepreneurs were able to exercise their despotism all the more easily.⁶⁸

The rights of co-determination attained by the workers in the sphere of the 'community of labour' fall into three groups, in the following historical sequence. First, in the sphere of social policy. The workers' gains do not affect them directly as workers, but only indirectly as 'citizens of the state'. These 'social policy' concessions were granted for the reasons discussed above.⁶⁹ The second limitation on the capitalist as 'master in his own house' is exercised by the trade union organisation of the working class. The workers gain a right of 'co-determination' of their conditions of work as owners and sellers of the commodity labour-power.⁷⁰ The third (and most recent) form of limitation on the absolute powers of the factory owners is the 'co-determination rights' gained for the workers *as such*, as members of a productive unit, the factory. The first weak indications of this were the German factory laws of the 1890s, which were strengthened in the years at the end of and after the war.[71]

Regarding the law and factory councils Korsch reaches the following conclusion:

> Despite all the concessions already made by the bourgeois mind in the present epoch of transition ... there is really no room for the concept of a 'constitution of labour' within the framework of bourgeois law.[72]

Yet at the same time, consistent with the generally transitional character of the present epoch, the present system of law also has a transitional character.[73] Thus, he argues:

> The universal character of the transition, which takes place in the present epoch, naturally must also be expressed in the legal consciousness. In ... [this] epoch, the old, purely bourgeois standpoint of private law cannot be maintained nor ... the new purely proletarian standpoint of social law.[74]

The law would govern the relations between 'collectives' rather than between individuals—for example, the law governing the relations between trade unions and the employers' federations. In his inaugural professorial lecture, Korsch makes this point even more explicitly. The greatest part of what the bourgeois jurist regards as labour law 'is on the whole on longer bourgeois law and cannot be ... subsumed under the so-called public law of present-day bourgeois society'.[75] What is it being replaced by?

> In labour law the old ... law of declining bourgeois society and the declining bourgeois state is opposed within this state and society by the new proletarian law of the working class; just as in classical Natural Law from Grotius to Hegel the ... rigid law of declining feudal society was opposed by the new bourgeois law of the third estate.[76]

The 'constitutional' or rather 'pseudo-constitutional' character of the present organisation of the economy is most clearly revealed by the constitution of the individual factory, as laid down in the factory councils' laws and other related laws.[77]

What strategy follows from this analysis? The faltering steps taken in the direction of 'industrial democracy' by the concession of a written constitution and the right to consultation, must be made more decisive. That the relation between workers and factory-owners is written down in the factory councils law is an achievement analogous to that of a written constitution.[78] But there are limits to this process of democratisation:

> Today it is not yet possible to speak of the full achievement of 'industrial democracy'; the development of freedom in the community of labour has not even reached 'parliamentarism'.[79]

The argument is concluded as follows. Just as in the political 'community of labour' a phase of constitutionalism was only a transitional period between absolute monarchy and complete bourgeois democracy, so, too, in the development of the constitution of the 'community of labour' there must follow a phase of complete 'industrial democracy'. He warns that anyone who believes that, through a planned development of all these various forms of the co-determination of the workers in production and conditions of work,

> the desired 'industrial democracy' in the community of labour can be fully realised without a violent overthrow of the existing bourgeois-democratic state institutions, is overlooking the immense difference between the bourgeois-capitalist state as the 'ideal capitalist as a whole' ... and the state of the proletarian dictatorship, as the 'collective proletarian ideal'.[80]

Capitalism places certain insuperable limits on the development of such co-determination rights. They may only develop in so far as they do not clash with the profit-making interest of the capitalist class. If these rights ever become more than bridgeheads for the attack on capitalism, then they will be withdrawn by the capitalist class.[81]

The main immediate practical consequence of this strategy was that the factory councils are not to be considered mainly as auxiliary organs (*Hilfsorgane*) of the economic struggle—they are of decisive importance in the struggles for the control of production. This does not mean that trade union organisation according to profession (*Berufsverband*) is quite unsuitable. But to serve revolutionary ends, the normal form of trade union organisations should be transformed into industrial unions (*Industrieverbände*). The argument about industrial unions is rather involved, so it will not be pursued here.[82]

I shall now evaluate Korsch's ideas in *Labour Law for Factory Councils* using the criterion of Marx's views on law. Marx's basic argument was that the evolution of law does not depend on the self-development of certain legal concepts but is conditioned by the development of the forces of production. Korsch does not accept this standpoint wholeheartedly. Formally, he does recognise the necessity of an analysis in terms of political economy. For instance, he argues that in order to understand the root cause of the lack of freedom for workers in the democratic republic 'we must, following Marx's teaching, descend into the most fundamental stratum of human life, which is denoted as the "economic" '.[83] He goes on to say that Marx's critique of political economy gave an insight into the political significance of economic facts: beneath the deceptive surface of freedom and equality, he revealed the economic unfreedom of the propertyless wage-worker. His analysis revealed the ambiguous character of the freedom gained by the modern wage-worker in the 'contract of labour': he is free in that he is no longer a slave, but he is also 'free' of the means of production, so that, if he is to survive, he must subject himself to someone else economically.[84]

This argument does agree formally with the Marxist texts, if at a rather elementary level. Korsch does not go on to use this criterion of political economy to trace the connection between the productive process and law in this particular case. His analysis remains at such a level of generality that it could apply to any law. By contrast, Marx displays both the necessary abstraction and concreteness which are lacking in Korsch. This can best be seen in Marx's criticism of the English Factory Acts, 1833–64. As an extension of his earlier general critique of law and rights, Marx attempted to relate the introduction of new legislation to the continued process of the accumulation of capital. The effect of legal regulation of conditions is to introduce order, uniformity and economy into the individual factory, and in so doing to give an impetus to the introduction of technical improvements:

By maturing the material conditions and the combination on a social scale of the processes of production, it matures the contradictions and antagonisms of the capitalist form of production and thereby provides, along with the elements for the formation of a new society, the forces for exploding the old one.[85]

When Korsch has a formally correct position, he is not able to apply his analysis. On other occasions, when he does attempt to trace a connection between the economy and law, he does not use the same criterion as Marx. Despite his formal criticisms, he essentially accepts the 'bourgeois' conception of rights and law, and simply wishes to extend it to all spheres of social life. As he himself admitted, he saw the proletarian revolution as merely the 'deepening' (*Vertiefung*) of the bourgeois revolution. This is clearly evident when he writes:

> for this demand [i.e. industrial democracy] the working class can bring into the field all those arguments which the bourgeois class itself developed in its struggle against the despotism of princes and the privileges of estates, for a liberal state constitution and for 'political democracy'.[86]

That is, the same kind of rights workers enjoy as citizens must be extended to the sphere of work, because 'the capitalist, who may outside his factory be enthusiastic about freedom and human rights, still wants to remain very much 'master in his own house'.[87] Marx, on the other hand, when discussing the right to work, saw a qualitative distinction between the bourgeois conception of rights and his own. The socialist demand for rights should not concentrate therefore on 'more of the same', nor on extending legislation, etc.[88]

Korsch's comparison of the modern factory owner with the absolute despot reveals a failure to understand the position of the individual capitalist within the production process according to the Marxist system. Korsch holds an ambiguous position on this matter. On two occasions, he does recognise that capitalists are subject to some external laws independent of their will.[89] The partial truth in Korsch's argument is that the individual entrepreneur does hold unlimited sway within the factory. But, as the passage quoted clearly indicates, Marx is concerned with the laws governing production as a whole, to which the entrepreneur is himself subject. The absolute monarch, on the other hand, is not subject to such pressures at all. Whatever agitational value the comparison between the power or wealth of the absolute monarchy and that of the German capitalists may have, it is not soundly based on a Marxist analysis of the personal role of capitalists in the production process.

This confusion about the nature of this law—was it to be entirely ignored, while the factory councils were used to further the revolutionary struggle? Or could it be utilised?—was not peculiar to Korsch, but was shared by the KPD. In a resolution submitted to the eleventh congress of the German trade unions, the KPD proposed:

> the congress requests the national executive to work out a new factory councils law within two months ... the draft law shall establish ... thorough-going control of production, trade and commerce.[90]

Korsch's notion of 'industrial democracy' is in fact surprisingly similar to that held by two writers not otherwise sympathetic to his political aims—namely, Sidney Webb and Otto Bauer. In the case of the former, the similarity extends even down to the terms used:

> The captains of industry like the kings of yore, are honestly unable to understand why their personal power should be interfered with, and kings and captains alike have never found any difficulty in demonstrating that its maintenance was indispensable to society. Against this autocracy in industry, the manual workers have, during this century, increasingly made good their protest. The agitation for freedom of combination and factory legislation has been in reality a demand for a 'constitution' in the industrial realm.[91]

There is also a very remarkable similarity to Bauer's *Der Weg zum Sozialismus*. This contains a schema of rights for factory workers which is almost identical to Korsch's, as can be seen in for instance the following passage:

By the establishment of factory committees, we arrive in the factory at a constitutional monarchy: legal sovereignty is shared between the boss, who governs the enterprise like an hereditary monarch, and the factory committee, which plays the role of Parliament. Beyond this stage, one goes on to the republican constitution of industry. The boss disappears; the economic and technical direction of each branch of industry is entrusted to an administrative council.[92]

But to understand why Korsch draws such similar political conclusions, we must examine his analysis more closely. *Labour Law for Factory Councils* is not simply a continuation of *What is Socialisation?*, which stood even closer to Bauer and Webb. It does contain one new idea which is formally much more in line with his new political affiliation, i.e. the notion of the transitional epoch.

Korsch's understanding of this idea is open to two objections. The first concerns the central notion of 'social law' (*Sozialrecht*). If Korsch was merely arguing that the pressure of the working-class movement in the post-war period had enabled it to gain considerable legal concessions, e.g. the legal recognition of workers' organisations—a concession which seemed to break with the traditional concept that law applied to private individuals only and not collectives—then this would be partly untrue and rather uninteresting. But Korsch's argument is more ambitious: it is that a new *principle* of law has already begun to replace the old— 'social law' instead of 'private law'.

In my opinion, this reveals a mistaken understanding of Lenin's concept of the transitional epoch—it attempts to extend the application of this concept from economic to cultural problems, i.e. legal and political rights. To use the Marxist terminology, his argument rests on an analogy between base and superstructure: just as the monopoly organisation of production means the replacement of the individualistic production of the *laissez-faire* era by socialised production, so, too, in the realm of ideas individualism is replaced by more collective conceptions.[93] Large-scale socialist production has an embryonic existence in the organisation of large monopolies; likewise socialist ideology exists embryonically in such principles as 'social law'. Although Korsch formally acknowledges that such possibilities can only be fully realised under the 'dictatorship of the proletariat', he still claims that the new principle already exists. He takes this argument to its practical conclusion: the essential task for the working class is

> to maintain those positions, at which today a conflict between the bourgeois-legal and the social-legal conception of the labour relation has already broken out or at least is about to break out. In the second place, in all these particular positions, the attempt must be made to draw the consequences of the social-legal conception with a sharpness corresponding to the present historical situation.[94]

This conclusion does follow from his argument: it is this basic argument which is mistaken. The mistake lies in the assumption that whatever may be said about the 'base' may also be said about the 'superstructure'. This criticism of Korsch's position is of course independent of the validity of the arguments of Lenin's *Imperialism*. Korsch's notion goes against the more dialectical relation of base to superstructure, of ideology to reality, which he was to argue for in *Marxism and Philosophy*. Whereas Marx would argue that ideas can persist long after their material base has disappeared, Korsch appears to argue the converse: that in fact ideas can anticipate changes in the material base.

This erroneous argument may explain why Korsch's understanding of how the transition to socialism is to be achieved is unclear. In one passage he suggests that

> In the epoch politically characterised as the transitional period of the 'proletarian dictatorship', a proletarian *constitution of labour*, resting on the firm foundation of 'industrial democracy', and with it a real *councils' system* will, after long, difficult and ruthless struggles in the *whole economy*, and in all individual *branches of the economy* and in every individual factory, be gradually realised by the state power placed at the service of the proletarian class.[95]

This is a curiously 'gradualist' statement for a 'revolutionary Marxist' to make, but at least it does indicate some sort of strategy for the transition to socialism. On other occasions, he merely draws an idealised contrast between the present situation and an imagined future. The fulfilment of the economic and political demands requires the construction of a system of economic councils, controlled by the proletarian state. He then quotes from the 'Labour Code' of the Soviet Union, and presents an ideal schema describing how a system of economic councils would work. This is the ideal. He then compares this to the less acceptable reality of the current German situation, in which the councils were being anchored into the constitution.[96] He does not mention any strategy by which the present factory councils could play a role in the concrete transition from unacceptable reality to the utopian ideal: he simply proposes that they play a 'class struggle' role, instead of a 'co-operative' one.

In some respects, *Labour Law for Factory Councils* does not deal with any of the concrete problems that the factory councils were facing. It deals with the question of workers' rights, the relation of the factory councils to the political councils, and the need for industrial unions. But because it does not deal satisfactorily with the abstract problem of the relation of law to production, it is unable to produce a concrete programme dealing with the problems facing the German proletariat at that time, such as inflation, and the maintenance of working class living standards. Korsch can say in general terms that what is needed is an orientation to 'class struggle'. But in only one instance does he say what the content of the class struggle was at that period: it concerned 'resistance to longer hours of work, unbearable tax burdens, and the struggle for bread'.[97] He only makes a brief mention of the fact that at that period there were important struggles by the working class for the control of prices and production. Korsch was perfectly well aware of these struggles, for he wrote about them for the KPD's newspapers.[98] It is strange then that he does not indicate how, in a concrete manner, the factory councils might be used to assist the prices' committees in the struggle for control over production.

In this chapter, we have seen that Korsch attempted to apply the Leninist conception of imperialism as a transitional epoch to the nature and development of labour law (especially as applied to the relations between worker and employer). I have shown that Korsch was not entirely successful in this attempt. By the criterion of consistency with Marxism, his *Quintessenz* does not show an adequate understanding of the relation between law and the economic system. Thus, when he comes to apply his notion of Marxism to current problems, he adopts quite erroneous positions. More generally, he has an idiosyncratic view of the relationship between (in the Marxist terminology) 'base' and 'superstructure'. This has not been fully examined here, for it is more relevant to the next chapter, in which we shall see how Korsch thought that, just as Lenin had rediscovered the orthodox version of Marx's theory of the state, he himself had succeeded in a similar restoration of Marx's concept of philosophy.

4 Marxism and Philosophy

The immediate post-war years had seen Korsch closely involved with the concrete political problems of the day—first the socialisation movement, then the factory councils. But at the same time he was writing on the basic aspects of Marxism, as they related to such problems, for example in the *Quintessenz* and the *Introduction to the Critique of the Gotha Programme*. His next work, *Marxism and Philosophy*,[1] seems to mark a departure. At first sight, the relation indicated in the title seems to be only a 'history of ideas', and of the most arid variety, tracing the influence of A upon B, and, in the case of Marxism, requiring the painstaking exegesis of fragmentary texts. This might give interesting information about the genesis of Marx's ideas, and the logic of their development, but it does not seem to have that relevance to practice with which Korsch was always concerned. Yet at the time it was thought that this apparently scholastic question did have a bearing on practical problems of the highest importance; so much so that in 1924, the year after Korsch's *Marxism and Philosophy* and Lukács' *History and Class Consciousness* were published, it became the centre of heated debates in the Communist International. To understand why this was so, the debate has to be seen in its political context. Since this is only partly made explicit in *Marxism and Philosophy*, a brief sketch will be offered here.

Despite the tremendous convulsions of 1918–19, the old order in Germany had largely survived intact. Even in a situation as apparently favourable to communist ideology as that of 1918, with the openly 'bourgeois' parties discredited by their presumed responsibility for the war, and the main socialist party (the SPD) losing its traditional support for the same reason, the powerful movements of protest which occurred did not effect any fundamental change in the political structure. The SPD could produce 'Marxist' explanations for its passivity and, as the communists saw it, its 'counter-revolutionary' role during this period. They argued that the *objective* conditions for a successful transition to socialism were lacking. In an economy ruined by the war, it would be utopian to undertake any 'Bolshevik experiments', which would end in disaster, as they claimed had happened in the Soviet Union. The communists, on the other hand, argued that the 'objective' conditions were completely adequate: it was the *subjective* factor, the will of the conscious political organisation aiming to seize power, which was lacking.

Translated into philosophical terms, the Communist criticism of the Social-Democrats emphasised the factors of will and consciousness. The determinist 'scientific' formulae of the Second International seemed to be seriously at fault in ignoring the necessity for conscious action, if capitalism was to be overthrown. But at the same time, how could Marxism's claim to be a science, with the 'determinism' that such a claim involves, be justified? It was considered necessary to return to the *locus classicus* of the discussion of such questions: the philosophical debates about freedom and causality, determinism and voluntarism—i.e. back to Kant and Hegel.

To understand their ideas on these questions, it would be necessary to see them in their social context. Korsch drew the following parallel between philosophy and social movements:

> Since the Marxist system is the theoretical expression of the revolutionary movement of the proletariat, and German idealist philosophy is the theoretical expression of the revolutionary movement of the bourgeoisie, they must stand intelligently and historically (i.e. ideologically) in the same relation to each other as the revolutionary movement of the proletariat as a class stands to the revolutionary movement of the bourgeoisie in the realm of social and political practice.[2]

Conventional historians of ideas are quite prepared to admit that Kant and Hegel did make an intellectual revolution; but they conceive of it as 'a nice quiet process that takes place in the pure realm of the study and far away from the crude realm of real struggles'.[3] The two great German philosophers of the bourgeois revolution were quite aware of the connections between their intellectual revolution and the real revolution in France. Their ideas cannot be appreciated unless this connection is taken into account.[4] Only by rediscovering the practical element in their philosophy can the distinctive point of view of Marxism be understood. Korsch aimed to go back to the roots of Marxism in order to re-establish an authentic version, which, being quite distinct from the vulgar Marxism of the SPD, would offer a satisfactory practical alternative.

Before I review the results of this inquiry, the limits of this chapter must be defined. It will take us to the point at which Korsch had evolved a coherent system of philosophical ideas, which were for a time more or less compatible with membership of the KPD. Some references will be made to the *Present State of the Problem of Marxism and Philosophy*, in which he answered criticisms of the original work made by Social-Democrats and Communists. These replies to criticism will be introduced only in so far as they are made from the same standpoint as *Marxism and Philosophy*. A later chapter[5] will examine the new positions to be found in the *Anti–Critique*, in particular his revised views on Lenin's philosophy, which are connected to a much broader change of opinion about the nature of the Soviet State, and to an even more fundamental change in his estimation of Marxism itself.

Let us now turn to his ideas on Marxism and philosophy during this earlier period. *Marxism and Philosophy* begins by showing that after 1850 there was very little interest in Hegel or the young Hegelians, and that Marx's philosophy attracted even less attention. In the opinion of the professors of philosophy, 'Marxism was at best a rather minor sub-section within the history of nineteenth-century philosophy, dismissed as "The Decay of Hegelianism"'.[6] But even the Marxists placed very little value on Marx as a philosopher. The problems of Marxist philosophy had not played a major part in the theoretical discussions of the Second International. Korsch stated this point very forcefully:

> The prominent Marxist theoreticians of the period regarded concern with questions that were not even essentially

philosophical in the narrower sense but were only related to the general epistemological and methodological bases of Marxist theory as at most an utter waste of time and effort.[7]

In more detail the argument is as follows. There are three limits to the bourgeois history of philosophy, which have meant that bourgeois philosophers and historians have progressively abandoned the *dialectical* conception of the history of philosophy. First, a 'purely philosophical' limit: they did not see that the ideas contained in a philosophy can live on not only in philosophies, but also in the positive sciences and social practice. Secondly, a 'local' limit: German professors in philosophy failed to see that, although the Hegelian system no longer flourished in Germany, it continued to do so in other countries. Thirdly, a 'class' limit: bourgeois philosophers could not transcend the bourgeois class standpoint.[8] Thus, given that Marx's materialist philosophy emerged from 'the most advanced systems of revolutionary bourgeois idealism' and that bourgeois historians of philosophy were prevented by the limits mentioned from understanding Hegelian idealism, it is clear that they would completely ignore Marxist philosophy.[9] To grasp this connection between German idealism and Marxism, Korsch claims that it is necessary to adopt an approach that need not be specifically Marxist but is just *'straightforwardly dialectical'* in the Hegelian *and* Marxist sense.[10]

The argument so far is only an introduction to the main theme: Is Marxism itself a philosophy? Korsch answers that a necessary result of the new dialectical-materialist standpoint was the supersession not only of bourgeois idealist philosophy, but *simultaneously* of all philosophy as such.[11] Without developing the argument at this point he draws a parallel between the abolition of philosophy and the abolition of the state and asks what is the significance of the fact that both these problems were neglected by the Marxists of the Second International.[12] He now states the central, extremely ambitious aim of his work:

> we must try to understand every change, development and revision of Marxist theory, since its original emergence from the philosophy of German Idealism, as a necessary product of its epoch ... More precisely, we should seek to understand their determination by the totality of the historico-social process of which they are a general expression.[13]

Applying Marx's principle of dialectical materialism to the whole history of Marxism, he finds that three major stages of development through which Marxism has passed since its birth can be distinguished. In the first period, from 1843 (*Critique of Hegel's Philosophy of Right*) to the revolution of 1848 (*Communist Manifesto*), Marxist theory is still permeated through and through with philosophical thought. The second period extends from 1848 to the end of the century. In this later phase, the various components of the theory of Marxism are further separated out into economic, political and ideological elements. Yet the unbreakable connection between theory and practice was in no way abolished in the later form of his system. In the third phase, which extends '... from the start of this century to the present and into an indefinite future' (*Marxism and Philosophy*, p. 51), Marxists came to regard scientific socialism as a set of purely scientific observations, without any *immediate* connection to the political struggle. Marxism then tended to become either a kind of heuristic principle of specialised theoretical investigation or a general systematic sociology.[14] This applied to both the 'revisionists', such as Bernstein, and the defenders of 'orthodoxy', as represented by Hilferding, who argued that the Marxist conception of socialism as a necessity did not lead to any particular practical orientation.

Why had these changes taken place in Marxism? Korsch's answer is that

> the decline of the original Marxist theory of social revolution into a theoretical critique of society without any revolutionary consequences is for dialectical materialism a necessary expression of parallel changes in the social practice of the proletarian struggle.[15]

There was a long period in the second half of the nineteenth century when it had no practical revolutionary task to accomplish. This was the basis for revisionism in the Marxist movement. But the twentieth century has placed revolutionary tasks before the working class, and the apparent revival of original Marxist theory in the Third International is a result of the revival of the revolutionary workers' movement. In this revival of Marxism Lenin re-established the connection between theory and practice in relation to the problem of the state; Korsch aims to do

'Marxism and Philosophy'

the same for the problem of philosophy.[16] What does this entail?

At this point, Korsch mentions philosophy only briefly before passing on to another argument. He repeats the point that scientific socialism stands much closer to the philosophy of the Third Estate than it does to the pure sciences of bourgeois society. He now immediately passes on to the problem of ideology. To avoid the question of the mutual relations of social revolution and ideology before the seizure of state power leads to opportunism and creates a crisis within Marxism; after the revolution, it can have equally disastrous results.[17] It leads him to the question, '... how is Marxist materialism related to *ideology* in general?' (*Marxism and Philosophy*, p. 63).

Marx effected the transition to materialism in his *Critique of Hegel's Philosophy of Right*. Yet there was relatively little difference in theoretical character between the new proletarian science and previous philosophy: German idealism had constantly tended to be more than a theory—it aimed to be practical.[18] Korsch's main argument about ideology is its material reality:

> no really dialectical materialist conception of history . . . could cease to regard philosophical ideology, or ideology in general, as a material component of general socio-historical reality.[19]

By contrast, for vulgar Marxism there are three degrees of reality: the economy; law and the state; and pure ideology (p. 73). For Marx, although the critique of political economy is theoretically and practically the first priority, it includes a critique of all the forms of consciousness of bourgeois society. Thus in this critique, as in every dialectic, consciousness and reality coincide. Marx's dialectical materialism is not merely a form of thought which can be applied to any content.[20]

Here, as before (see above pp. 63 ff.), Korsch speaks of the similarities between the Marxist and the Hegelian dialectic. There are two important differences: Hegel 'inserted the world into philosophy far more than he did philosophy into the world' (p. 81); the forms of consciousness cannot be abolished through thought alone. It would be a dangerous misunderstanding of the latter point to argue that criticism in practice simply replaces criticism in theory: what is important is not only human practice but also the comprehension of this practice. Korsch's concluding argument is that

Just as political action is not rendered unnecessary by the economic action of a revolutionary class, so intellectual action is not rendered necessary by either political or economic action.[21]

Why did Korsch think that the neglect of the problem of Marxism and philosophy was so significant? The answer to this question is not easily to be found in Korsch's book—indeed, one of the problems in understanding *Marxism and Philosophy* is to determine precisely what its problematic is, because it is not set out very clearly or systematically in the work itself. Korsch's major work on philosophy, although it only runs to seventy-odd pages, is always complex and often obscure. Perhaps over-reacting to the systematisation involved in the normal presentation of German academic philosophy, Korsch presents his ideas very fluidly. The opening paragraph states rather blandly:

Until very recently neither bourgeois nor Marxist thinkers had much appreciation of the fact that the relation between Marxism and philosophy might pose a very important theoretical and practical problem.[22]

Although the problem is restated several times during the course of the work, Korsch does not give an extended systematic exposition of his own position. The problem remains of understanding *why* the neglect of philosophy and the coincidence of bourgeois (and social-democratic) views is so significant. To be properly criticised, the problematic has to be made more evident than it is in Korsch's work. I suggest that the argument can be reconstructed as follows.

The real question Korsch is moving towards via an examination of philosophical issues is that of ideology. So far in his Marxist period, he had not tackled the problem in a general, systematic fashion. Although *Labour Law for Factory Councils* had dealt with legal ideology, it contained very few statements about ideology in general: those it does make are rather crude, and approach the position criticised in *Marxism and Philosophy*, which regards ideology as immaterial. Thus in discussing the general relations between law and economy in capitalist society, he concludes:

'Marxism and Philosophy' 69

There is a glaring contradiction between the *ideology* of bourgeois society and its *reality*. The freedom and equality of the parties to the 'free contract of labour' is revealed to be merely an ideological disguise for a naked, brutal power-relationship.[23]

The 'disguise' (*Verkleidung*) could be removed at will: in fact, it is not even present in the later stages of capitalism. Capitalist ideology is itself eventually overcome as the capitalist economy develops:

> Capitalist ideology is ... eventually disproved and overcome by the development of capitalism itself ... ultimately they [the capitalists] are also compelled to throw off the ideological disguise behind which they had previously kept concealed their private class rule.[24]

This is rather a conspiratorial conception of ideology, which is much closer to the mechanical notions of ideology held by the Social-Democrats, in that it seems to suggest that ideology is merely a 'disguise' of the reality of capitalist society, which can be removed at the will of the dominant classes in that society. If this were so, then ideology could not pose an important problem for Marxists. Before the revolution, they could not do anything to combat hostile ideologies because such ideologies would only vanish at the will of the ruling powers. After the revolution, with the disappearance of these ruling powers, the ideology at their disposal would vanish with them. On a less favourable reading of the second passage above, one might conclude that ideology poses *less* of a problem to Marxists than it did previously. This would be quite consistent with the notion of *Sozialrecht* developed in *Labour Law for Factory Councils*.[25]

Yet in *Marxism and Philosophy* Korsch holds that the question of ideology is of the highest importance:

> To avoid these questions in the period before the proletarian revolution leads to opportunism and creates a crisis within Marxism just as avoidance of the problem of State and revolution in the Second International led to opportunism and indeed provoked a crisis in the camp of Marxism.[26]

He makes an even stronger claim, that a neglect of this problem has very serious consequences not only before, but also after, the revolution. If the lack of a clear theoretical understanding is not remedied, the construction of socialism could be seriously hampered.[27]

The reference to the 'problem of the state' in the passage quoted above is significant. Korsch saw the main aim of his work as doing for the question of ideology what Lenin had done for the question of the state. This was part of the 'renewal' of Marxism:

> A fresh examination of the problem of Marxism and philosophy, would also seem to be an important part of this restoration.[28]

He adds that the attempt to 'restore' the Marxist method in connection with the problems of ideology poses great problems. What is meant here by 'restoration'? Korsch explains this by using the example of Lenin's work. Its significance was that it had rediscovered the method of Marxism; but this was not simply a textual 'restoration', a 'correct reading', but a further development of Marxist thought using his method:

> the preface and first page of *State and Revolution* prove that he was also just as far from considering the main purpose of this theoretical work to be the ideological 're-establishment' of true Marxist doctrine.[29]

Korsch was heavily influenced by Lenin's recent pronouncements on philosophy, in favour of studying Hegel. Indeed, this may be said to be one of the immediate motives for Korsch's writing *Marxism and Philosophy*—namely, to fulfil Lenin's injunction 'We must organise a systematic study of the Hegelian dialectic from a materialist standpoint'[30] which appears at the beginning of the book. The full extent of Lenin's 'Hegelianism' was not known at the time. He had read Hegel's *Logic* for the first time during the war, and kept a series of notebooks (not published until 1929) in which he recorded his impressions.[31] These private notes on 'Hegelianism' were very forceful:

> It is impossible completely to understand Marx's *Capital* and

especially its first chapter, without having thoroughly studied and understood the *whole* of Hegel's *Logic*. Consequently half a century later, none of the Marxists understood Marx.[32]

His study of the Hegelian dialectic and its influence on Marxism revealed itself in a number of articles; for example, those on the trade union question, and the article on 'militant materialism' from which Korsch's quotation is taken.[33] The published pronouncements from such an authority in the Communist movement as Lenin gave an added impetus to the Hegel renaissance in Marxist circles.

Despite the importance of Korsch's work, the leading figure in this renaissance was Lukács. His major published contribution to the debate was the immensely influential *History and Class Consciousness*, a collection of essays published in 1925 and written in the preceding four years.[34] In addition to this work there were at the time extensive discussions of these problems, which unfortunately went unrecorded. In the summer of 1922, for example, Felix Weil sponsored a 'Marxist work week' which met in Ilmenau, Thüringia, and in which Lukács, Korsch, Wittfogel and other leading Marxist intellectuals took part. Korsch had published Weil's monograph on socialisation in 1921 and was one of the first people to interest him in Marxism.[35] Much of the time was apparently devoted to a discussion of Korsch's manuscript for *Marxism and Philosophy*. Expectations of a second work week came to nothing when it was replaced by a much more ambitious venture—the Frankfurt Institut, which was officially set up on 3 February 1923.[36] Thus there was a close personal and ideological link between Korsch and Lukács, and it is a central aim of this chapter to examine their similarities and differences.

Apart from continuing Lenin's work of 'restoring' the Marxist method and applying it to new problems, is there any connection between the two questions (that of the state, and philosophy) which the 'revisionists' had overlooked? Rather formally, Korsch claims that they had neglected the two problems because 'the problems of the revolution in general hardly concerned them [the Marxists of the Second International]'.[37] This criticism is itself too general, and offers an instructive contrast between the methods of Lenin and Korsch. Lenin did not have a theory of revolution in general, nor for that matter a theory of ideology in general, nor of any particular ideologies—of the state, philosophy, economics, or anything else. He always criticised particular ideologies as they presented themselves as concrete questions in the course of the class struggle. Thus, chronologically, Lenin analysed the development of capitalism in Russia, the agrarian question, philosophy (empirio-criticism), imperialism, the state, and so on. He was never concerned with 'the problems of the revolution in general', only with the *specific* problems facing the revolutionary movement.

Perhaps what underlay Korsch's argument was a notion that was to become dominant later in 'Western Marxism': that the problem of ideology was much more important for the revolution in Western Europe than it had been for Lenin and the Bolsheviks. In this conception, the main function of the state itself was, in Western Europe, ideological, not repressive. The model statement of this 'Western Marxist' perspective was made by Gramsci:

> In Russia, the State was everything, civil society was primordial and gelatinous; in the West, there was a proper relation between State and civil society, and when the State trembled a sturdy structure of civil society was at once revealed. The State was only an outer ditch behind which there stood a powerful system of fortresses and earthworks.[38]

It was the conventional wisdom of the Comintern itself that it would be much more difficult in the countries of Western Europe for the proletariat to seize power, but that, thereafter, it would be much easier for them to retain and expand their power.[39] While the Comintern held this view, it did not expand on these difficulties, particularly in the arena of ideological struggle. Korsch seems to have thought, without making it as explicit as this, that *Marxism and Philosophy* would supplement Lenin's work in precisely this way. This is the reason behind his statement that

> Therefore we must solve in a dialectically materialist fashion not only 'the question of the relationship of the State and of social revolution to the State' (Lenin) but also the 'question of the relationship of ideology to social revolution and of social revolution to ideology'.[40]

Let us now examine Korsch's argument more directly. Since Korsch did not define ideology very precisely at any point, a formal comparison of the definitions he gave is not very revealing. He says that in the 'vulgar Marxist's' conception, there are three stages of reality:

> (1) the economy, which in the last instance is the only objective and totally non-ideological reality; (2) Law and the State, which are already somewhat less real because clad in ideology and (3) pure ideology which is objectless and totally unreal ('pure rubbish').[41]

The definition he suggests is:

> In their [Marx and Engels's] terminology only the legal, political, religious, aesthetic or philosophical forms of consciousness are ideological. Even these need not be so in all conditions, but become so only under specific conditions.[42]

He even suggests that at one time Marx himself had a philosophical standpoint—which he would, according to the later use of the word, have characterised as thoroughly ideological. Marx only freed himself from this youthful error by a long and difficult process of reasoning.[43]

The problems of defining Korsch's concept of ideology is not made any easier by the fact that he never explains what he means by 'science'. He constantly criticises the positivist notion of science which was implicit in the 'scientific socialism' of the Second International, but mainly on the grounds that it does not lead to revolutionary practice: science remains a passive instrument of analysis, not a guide to action. Because he does not give an adequate exposition of his concept of science, his concept of ideology remains unclear. Thus we cannot learn from the formal definitions alone. To get round this problem, I shall look more closely at the problems in connection with which he uses the concept; namely, the category of totality, the reality of ideology and the relationship of theory and practice.

The 'strong' thesis is sometimes stated in respect to Korsch's view of totality; i.e. that 'Like Lukács, Korsch's key concept is that of totality'.[44] That this is an exaggeration can be shown by examining Lukács' statement of the 'strong' thesis. Totality is central to Lukács' problematic, which he states as follows:

> It is not the primacy of economic motives in historical explanation that constitutes the decisive difference between Marxism and bourgeois thought, but the point of view of totality. The category of totality ... is the essence of the method which Marx took over from Hegel and brilliantly transformed into the foundations of a wholly new science ... *The primacy of the category of totality is the bearer of the principle of revolution in science.*[45]

Korsch does not accept or give the category of totality such a central place in the Marxist system. But he does share the 'weak' thesis with Lukács. In their search for science, the Social-Democrats had effectively disintegrated Marxism into a number of separate sciences—economics, history, the theory of law and the state. In opposition to the atomising tendencies of such a scientific approach, Korsch argues that Marxism stands for totality. For example, the critique of political economy and, the critique of ideology are in no way to be mechanically separated, since both form 'a unified whole, whose parts cannot be simply separated and set apart from each other'.[46]

Instead of this tendency to separation, the opposite is to be found because

> In Marx and Engels however this [separation] never produces a multiplicity of independent elements instead of the whole. It is merely that another combination of the components of the system emerges developed with greater scientific precision and built on the infrastructure of the critique of political economy.[47]

But for Korsch this is merely part of his case against the version of science accepted by the 'revisionists'. This category of totality has a much more negative character, it is in no sense elevated to a central organising principle, as it is by Lukács. For Korsch, the tendency of bourgeois science to fragmentation could not be countered simply by postulating that in Marxist science the individual sciences of economics, history, etc., are not self-sufficient, but are components of a totality. This would still leave those sciences devoid of content, which is in fact a result of

Lukács' position. Lukács' concept of totality is therefore quite formalistic.

In order to give a distinctive content to the Marxist critique of ideology, we must turn to the second aspect of Korsch's concept of ideology. Korsch emphasised that, no less than economics, ideology was a material reality. This is perhaps the most distinctive feature of Korsch's position. The 'orthodox Marxists' had known how to state this truth abstractly in opposing the anarchist denial of certain 'superstructural elements' such as the state and politics. Whereas in the critique of anarchism, it was conceded that these were realities, yet

> In spite of this, many vulgar-marxists to this day have never, even in theory, admitted that intellectual life and forms of social consciousness are comparable realities. Quoting certain statements by Marx and especially Engels they simply explain away the *intellectual (ideological) structures of society* as a mere pseudo-reality which only exists in the minds of ideologues—as error, imagination and illusion, devoid of a genuine object.[48]

Political and legal concepts are at least related to something real, namely, the state and politics: they thus derive a kind of secondhand reality. Other varieties of ideology remain simply 'ideas in men's heads'. This view of ideology is, in philosophical terms, a variety of idealism, in that ideas are not thought to reflect anything objective in the real world. This idealist standpoint had been explicitly criticised by Marx in his Preface to *A Contribution to the Critique of Political Economy*, in which he stated that he had taken a major methodological step forward in understanding that ideas are rooted in material reality, and themselves form part of this reality.[49]

Korsch had already made this point about the relation of ideas to reality in a commentary on Engels' *Socialism: Utopian and Scientific*. He quoted a well-known passage from Engels' book ('Scientific socialism . . . is the expression of the proletarian movement') and commented:

> This means: a). It is not a thing for itself . . . but a *component* of real events, a 'movement', more precisely; of 'action', the action of the 'oppressed class', the proletariat. b). it is a special

component of this movement, something special within the whole.[50]

The view of the 'immateriality' of ideologies has important political consequences. It renders the ideological struggle unnecessary both before and after the revolution. It implies a certain conception of the relation of ideas to reality, in philosophical terms naïve realism:

> [which] considers thought independent of being and defines truth as the correspondence of thought to an object that is external to it. It is only this outlook that can sustain the view that all forms of economic consciousness ... have an objective meaning because they correspond to a reality.[51]

When ideas are conceived in this way as mere 'images' (*Bilder*) of the external world, they will naturally vanish with a transformation of the external world. This philosophical correlate of the SPD's view is not extensively criticised at this point.[52] Here, too, bourgeois views on philosophy and on the state coincide:

> Bourgeois consciousness necessarily sees itself as apart from the world and independent of it as pure critical philosophy and impartial science, just as the bourgeois State and bourgeois Law appear to be above society.[53]

But there is a problem with this notion of the materiality of ideology. It seems quite appropriate to apply the thesis that socialism as an ideology is a material part of the movement of the 'oppressed class' to the period in Marx's lifetime when he was involved with such movements—e.g. the period of the *Communist Manifesto*.[54] But is it appropriate to other periods—e.g. when the 'mature' Marx was writing more detached works such as *Capital*? Korsch claimed that in fact the stimulus for writing even *Capital* came from the movement of the 'oppressed classes':

> the new autonomous science of the working class attained its developed theoretical form in literature at the same time as the new autonomous movement of the proletariat achieved its practical form in history.[55]

What he was referring to was the London building workers' strike and the founding of the First International.⁵⁶ Despite Korsch's answer the concept of ideology does undergo numerous changes in Marx's works. This warrants closer examination of the relation of the earlier writings to the 'more mature' works such as *Capital*.

In fact, a key point in Kautsky's criticism of Korsch concerned the two parts of Marx's work. In general terms, he includes Korsch in a criticism of all communists who

> prefer to rely on primitive Marxism, on the apprentice works which Marx and Engels [wrote] from before their thirtieth year up to the 1848 Revolution and its after-effects. Apart from individual phrases, they don't know what to do with their later works, i.e. 'Capital'.⁵⁷

Marx himself, continues Kautsky, had admitted that many of the analyses and demands made in their early period of involvement in a revolutionary movement had become out-of-date. It is precisely these obsolescent features of Marxism which were adopted by Marxists. They had taken over a programme which Marx had prepared for absolutist conditions in Germany in the 1840s, and applied it to similarly absolutist conditions in Russia. Yet when faced with the very different situation of a democratic England, Marx and Engels had been scientific enough to change their views.⁵⁸

This problem of the relation of the 'philosophical' young Marx to the 'scientific' author of *Capital* has come to the fore again recently, in the work of Althusser, who takes a similar position to Kautsky's.⁵⁹ By contrast, Korsch insisted that even in the later works 'this revolutionary will is latent, yet present, in every sentence of Marx's work and erupts again and again in every decisive passage, especially in the first volume of Capital'.⁶⁰ However, he admits that in their later work, Marx and Engels had transcended philosophy. In the form in which it appeared at the time of the *Theses on Feuerbach*, dialectical materialism was in essence still a philosophy, even though they thought that its main task was to change the conditions of social existence which produced philosophy.⁶¹ Marx's opinion of this was shown by the fact that:

he would ... no longer allow this work to be printed, and in the real mature period of his life did not place a great value on the 'critique of ideology'.[62]

Thus the historical relation of philosophy to the rest of Marx's work is clear. But what of the logical status of philosophy in his later work? I will conclude my analysis of his concept of ideology before dealing with this problem.

The last element on Korsch's concept of ideology follows from the preceding argument. If ideas have no materiality, then there is no sense in which the unity of theory and practice can be achieved. This was one of the major points of his critique of the 'orthodox Marxists' conception of science. They held that the impartiality and objectivity of science are guaranteed by the fact that it is not biassed by any preconceptions. In Korsch's view, Marxists should not contest the results of 'bourgeois science', but should oppose this whole way of thinking about science:

> While, therefore, bourgeois philosophy and science chase after the delusive phantom of 'being without assumptions', Marxism rejects this illusion in all its parts. It does not aim to be a 'pure' science or philosophy, but instead aims to criticise the 'impurity' of all previous bourgeois science and philosophy by a ruthless exposure of its tacit 'assumptions'.[63]

Here he was on good authority as far as Marx's own writings were concerned. In *The Poverty of Philosophy*, Marx had claimed that the conventional economists had been able to explain how production takes place given certain presuppositions which remained tacit: it was those very presuppositions which needed explanation.[64] In the 'revisionists' view, Marxism was a pure science quite unrelated to any particular class or class struggle:

> Later Marxists came to regard scientific socialism more and more as a set of purely scientific observations without any *immediate* connection to the political or other practices of class struggle.[65]

This conception of Marxism as a science would turn Marxism into a science which accepted 'bourgeois' methodology, but simply achieved different results. Not only conventional Social-

'Marxism and Philosophy' 79

Democrats, but also some theoreticians of the Comintern (chiefly Bukharin) had a tendency to accept a positivist methodology of this kind. All such thinkers

> believe that the question of 'scientific' method is solved once and for all in the empirical method of the natural sciences and the corresponding positive-historical method.[66]

However, a thorough critique of positivism would go farther. It would examine the adequacy of the positivist conception of natural science itself—and not merely its notion that the methods of natural science should be applied to the social sciences. Korsch did not carry his criticisms thus far, being mainly interested in criticising the attempt to class Marxism as a science under the heading of sociology. At this stage his rejection of sociology is quite emphatic: he dismisses it as one of the 'special sciences' of bourgeois society, merely distinguished by its newness as compared to older sciences such as the science of law (*Rechtswissenschaft*). But he warns against the tendency infiltrating the Third International:

> There are some modern Marxist theoreticians who belong in practice to revolutionary communism but who come near to equating the Marxist conception of history with a 'general sociology'.[67]

The two works he claims belong to this tendency are Wittfogel's *Die Wissenschaft der bürgerlichen Gesellschaft* and Bukharin's *Theory of Historical Materialism*.[68] In the present context, the latter is more significant, since it does show a marked tendency to turn Marxism into a 'systematic general sociology'. The work itself is actually subtitled: *A System of Sociology*. Bukharin states that 'the theory of historical materialism ... is not political economy nor is it history; it is the general theory of society and the laws of its evolution, i.e. sociology'.[69] He was not to undertake a more detailed analysis of Marxism and sociology until he wrote *Karl Marx*.[70] At this period, he held a very definite view of the place of sociology in the Marxist system; namely, that it is political economy which is the basis of Marxist science. He explains what he means by this in *Labour Law for Factory Councils*:

We must consider not only the state and the law, but also that deeper layer, the economy, *in political terms*. We must not pursue, as the bourgeois does, 'economics' on the one side, 'politics' on the other, but 'political economy'.[71]

The fundamental characteristic of Marxism is not that it deals with classes rather than individuals in its explanation of history, but that such classes are economically determined: 'the conditions of material production ultimately determine all other conditions of human society'.[72] In his system, Bukharin sees matters quite differently: it is technology which is given the decisive place:

> the combinations of the instruments of labour (the social technology) are the deciding factor in the combinations and relations of men, i.e. in social economy'.[73]

Korsch criticises this view sharply, showing how much it diverges from Marxism, while not however ascribing it to Bukharin: ' "Political economy" is therefore not "technology", but is always the science of a "social subject" '.[74] We may note at this point that Lukács' objections to these works were quite different from Korsch's. His central objection to Wittfogel, for example, was that he adopted a sociologically uncritical attitude towards the method of the natural sciences, and that Wittfogel had not dealt with the connection between the rationalising method of the natural sciences and the economic development of capitalism.[75]

The significance of this difference is that Lukács adopted a definite position on one question which Korsch did not examine at all in *Marxism and Philosophy*; namely, the dialectics of nature. In fact, the main attacks on *History and Class Consciousness* centred on this very question. Lukács had made the following criticism of Engels:

> The misunderstandings that arise from Engels' account of dialectics can in the main be put down to the fact that Engels—following Hegel's mistaken lead—extended the method to apply also to nature. However, the crucial determinants of dialectics—the interaction of subject and object, the unity of theory and practice, the historical changes in the reality underlying the categories as the root cause of changes in

thought, etc.—are absent from our knowledge of nature.[76]

It is not necessary to discuss this question here, for *Marxism and Philosophy* did not say anything about the dialectics of nature. Yet the critics of Lukács and Korsch who bracketed them together quite failed to mention that this question was not discussed in *Marxism and Philosophy*.[77] Nor did Korsch make his position on this specific problem clear in any of his other published writings of this period. In an 'Afterword instead of a Foreword', Korsch said that he agreed with the general outlines of Lukács' approach, while reserving a more detailed opinion on particular points for a future time.[78] Looking beyond this period, a statement of 1925 repudiated the idea that there was a very close connection between them: 'I have never stated that I was a disciple of Lukács' theory'.[79] In his *Anti-Critique* in 1930, he was to argue that his statement that he would reserve a detailed exposition of his differences with Lukács had been taken by his critics in the KPD to mean complete agreement. At that time he had not been clear about their disagreements, but

> Nevertheless I still believe to this day that Lukács and I are objectively on the same side in our critical attitude towards the old Social Democratic Marxist orthodoxy and the new Communist orthodoxy.[80]

To return to Korsch's main argument, his chief concern in criticising Bukharin and Wittfogel was to stress the practical aims of Marxism. In doing so, he did not mean to argue for pragmatism, but rather for a dialectical relation between theory and practice which would avoid two theoretical mistakes, criticised by Marx himself, present in the history of the German socialist movement at an early date. Lassalle, of the 'practical' party, thought that practice would abolish ideology. On the other side of the debate, the 'philosophical' party believed that there could be a purely philosophical transcendence (*Aufhebung*) of ideology. These opposite mistakes could be summarised thus:

> If therefore the theoretical party believes that philosophy can be (practically) realised, without (theoretically) transcending it, so, equally incorrectly, the practical party aims to transcend philosophy (practically), without realising it (theoretically), i.e.

without grasping it as reality.[81]

The solution was to be found practically, not pragmatically, since the comprehension of this practice was equally necessary:

> It is not in 'human practice' alone but only 'in human practice and in the comprehension of this practice' that Marx as a dialectical materialist locates the rational solution of all mysteries that lure theory into mysticism'.[82]

But is the unity of theory and practice postulated here possible without changes taking place in society? This is surely problematical. It forms one of the central points of Kautsky's critique of Korsch:

> For Korsch, Marxism is nothing but a theory of social revolution. In reality, one of the most outstanding characteristics of Marxism is the conviction that the social revolution is only possible under certain circumstances, and thus only in certain times and countries. The communist sect to which Korsch belongs has quite forgotten this. For them, the social revolution is always possible, everywhere, under all circumstances.[83]

Kautsky's criticisms, published one year later, do raise a problem about Korsch's conception of the relationship between theory and practice. This criticism could also be applied to Lukács, who opened his book on Lenin with the statement that: 'Historical materialism is the theory of the proletarian revolution'.[84] Kautsky asks: Isn't the materialist conception of history the result of a scientific investigation of history, which took place *before* the revolution? Looking forward, will the Marxist theory not be still valid after the proletarian revolution when the proletariat no longer exists?[85]

These criticisms do reveal certain weaknesses in Korsch's position. From an activist point of view, his position appears more promising in that it attempts to tie Marxist theory more closely to the class struggle and the problems of the transition to socialism. But, by stressing this practical side, it ignores the other side: the question of science. Where does the objective and necessary character of the activity of the proletariat come from? In what objective conditions is it possible to stress the active factor, the will, without falling into an empty voluntarism? Korsch's criticisms of Kautsky's passivity may be correct, but without a much more all-embracing conception of the scientific nature of Marxism and its particular view of 'science' (*Wissenschaft*), it will not be possible to arrive at a more adequate understanding of the unity of theory and practice. In fact, at one point Korsch goes so far as to suggest that

> the sharp differentiation between theory and practice (characteristic of precisely this bourgeois epoch), which was unknown to philosophy even in the classical and mediaeval periods, is superseded for the first time in recent history, after Hegel had prepared its supersession by the formation of his 'dialectical' method.[86]

This is surely an overstatement of the case for the practical bias of Marxism. It is difficult to understand how a theory could *by itself* overcome this dualism. The dualism between the kind of revolutionary 'activism' which Korsch espouses and the scientific 'passivity' of the Marxism of the Second International cannot be resolved within the bounds of Marxist theory itself: it would be idealist to consider the possibility of such a merely intellectual transcendence.

I will now summarise what has been said so far about Korsch's concept of ideology. In his view the critique of ideology was important because ideology formed a material part of the society Marx aimed to change. The difference between Marxist and bourgeois science did not simply lie in the different analyses they put forward. It lay in a different relation between theory and practice: Marxism aimed to understand the world in order to change it. The conflict with ideologies was of practical and not merely theoretical significance.

The reasons Korsch gives for the necessity of Marxists undertaking a systematic study of the problem of ideology are to some extent valid and consistent. But the next step in the argument is not so clear. What is the link between the problem of ideology, and philosophy? After all, Korsch himself said of philosophy that

> The theoretical and practical criticism of philosophy is henceforward [after their early writings] relegated to the se-

cond, third, fourth or even last but one place in their critique of society.[87]

One indirect link might be through the study of philosophy—one might thereby grasp the method of Marxism, which could then be applied to ideology. While he was writing this first critique of political economy, Marx himself had said:

> In the method of treatment the fact that by mere accident I have again glanced through Hegel's Logic has been of great service to me ... If there should ever be time for such work again, I should greatly like to make accessible to the ordinary human intelligence ... what is rational in the method which Hegel discovered but at the same time enveloped in mysticism.[88]

How much emphasis Korsch placed on the understanding of method can be seen by comparing his position with that of Lukács, who showed the most extreme kind of preoccupation with method when he wrote at the beginning of the chapter entitled 'What is Orthodox Marxism?':

> Let us assume for the sake of argument that recent research had disproved once and for all every one of Marx's individual theses. Even if this were to be proved, every serious 'orthodox' Marxist would still be able to accept all such modern findings without reservation and hence dismiss all of Marx's theses in toto—without having to renounce his orthodoxy for a single moment. Orthodox Marxism, therefore, does not imply the uncritical acceptance of the results of Marx's investigations. It is not the 'belief' in this or that thesis, nor the exegesis of a 'sacred' book. On the contrary, orthodoxy refers exclusively to method.[89]

This is surely a remarkable statement of extreme 'methodologism'. It is also the foundation for the claim that in effect what Lukács was doing was to found a new idealist philosophy:

> Lukács' youthful extremism is ... so to speak a methodological extremism, which, transcending the empirical con-

tent of the problematic of the proletarian revolution ... assigns to theory an eminently philosophical role, proposes to theoretical Marxism the elaboration of a dialectical philosophy, which is historicist and humanist, and substantially modelled after the great Hegelian example.[90]

As Vacca rightly points out, Lukács' concept of method is quite formalistic in its indifference to the content to which the method is to be applied. It appears to imply that such crucial empirical findings as the falling rate of profit, or indeed any of the propositions of Marxist economics, could be rejected without the validity of Marxism being questioned. Yet Lukács as well as Korsch felt that only if Marxism could be understood as a living method and not as a series of received truths would it be possible to escape from the dogmatic straitjacket placed on it by the Marxists of the Second International.

How is this dilemma to be resolved? There is a very important point about method here which Korsch correctly makes in opposing the tendency to place the dialectic as a formal principle above and beyond any particular content—a tendency to be found in Lukács. The method of dialectical materialism cannot be separated from the material to which it is to be applied, and displayed as a set of formal principles. This is his solution to the problems involved in the two following conceptions of dialectics. The classic statement of the formalist position Lukács adopts was made earlier by Engels. In the *Dialectics of Nature*, Engels tends to isolate the dialectic and formalise it—as in the famous three laws: negation of the negation; the transformation of quantity into quality; and the unity of opposites.[91] This approach stresses the formal necessity of the dialectic. On the other hand, the social-democratic critique of Lukács went to the opposite extreme. For example, in a general critique of neo-Hegelian conceptions of the Marxist dialectic, Marck wrote: '[the dialectic] ... becomes for [Lukács] a philosophical world view, it is no longer a heuristic principle of research'.[92]

Marck thus proposes that, as a useful heuristic principle, the dialectic can merely contingently grasp empirical content. Thus form and content are separated, which results in the familiar philosophical dualisms of necessity—contingency, universality—particularity, and so on. But the dualisms involved in both these viewpoints had already been resolved in philosophical terms by Hegel. His advance over Kant was to show that 'pure reason' is in fact historicisable, because it could not in any of its forms be abstracted from the content in which it appeared. The merely formal universal laws of thought, which Kant proposed in opposition to the concrete particularity of the empiricists, were to be transcended by the 'concretely universal' operation of the dialectic. Korsch grasps this point when he writes:

> Hegel has already taught that a philosophico-scientific method was not a mere form of thought which could be applied indiscriminately to any content ... Marx made the same point in an early writing. 'Form has no value if it is not the form of its content'.[93]

This is a crucial point in Marx's methodology. Unfortunately, Korsch does not show in detail how this relationship is exemplified in the major concepts of Marx. This relation between form and content is itself grasped formally by Korsch. Thus there is only a passing allusion to this method, in his introduction to Marx's *Critique of the Gotha Programme*:

> Marx did not proceed to criticise the Gotha Programme by revealing the false and superficial general principle that clearly underlies all its particular sentences and demands, and then simply counterpose the truer and deeper principle of his materialism to it in an equally general form. He proceeds inversely, by criticising in the greatest detail each individual passage in the Programme.[94]

The greatest danger which could arise from a tendency to separate the materialist method from its content would be the setting up of a new philosophy of 'dialectical materialism'.[95]

So far, we have seen that Korsch did not propose to work out a new philosophy. The crucial significance of philosophy lies in the fact that the task of a dialectical-materialist restoration of the Marxist position on the problem of ideology

> can only be resolved by first investigating the problem which led Marx and Engels to the question of ideology: how is *philosophy* related to the social revolution of the proletariat and how is the social revolution of the proletariat related to

philosophy?⁹⁶

As has already been seen, Korsch was interested not in a chronological but in a logical understanding of the Marxist system. This was because it arose out of real conditions, and expressed the real relations of production which brought forth a progressive historical class. Marxism was not an ideology: its content was given by the historical conditions which gave birth to the proletariat. But how was it structured formally? Korsch answers:

> According to Engels, socialism in its *content* is the product of new conceptions that necessarily arise at a definite stage of social development within the proletariat as a result of its material situation. But it created its own specific scientific *form* (which distinguishes it from utopian socialism) by its link with German idealism, especially the philosophical system of Hegel. Socialism which developed from utopia to science formally *emerged* from German idealist philosophy.⁹⁷

In reconstructing Marxism it was important to demonstrate the crucial role philosophy had played in Marx's own intellectual history. Philosophy was a *logical* moment in the construction of Marxism, and a necessary element in Marx's working out a scientific form for the new historical content—the working-class struggle for socialism. On the one hand, philosophy is a moment in the scientific critique of capitalism. On the other, it cannot, simply as a matter of merely intellectual supersession, be replaced by this critique. Korsch attempts to resolve this antithesis by referring to the problem to which he was attempting an analogous solution; namely, that of the state. The 'economic theories of Marxism',

> as a refutation and supersession of bourgeois science and philosophy remain, on one side of their being, inevitably philosophy and science. On the other side, they step beyond the horizon of bourgeois science and philosophy.⁹⁸

In the same passage, he draws the analogy with the state which the proletariat will set up immediately after its expropriation of the capitalist class. On the one hand, it will still have the character of the state as we know it today. On the other,

> in its capacity as transitional stage to the classless (and thereby stateless) communist society of the future, it will no longer be just a 'state', but already something higher than a state.[99]

It is necessary to carry out this reconstruction because, as with the question of the state, it cannot be assumed that later Marxists were as clear as Marx was on this question. Thus since Marx's death we have seen the degeneration of Marx's teaching into the vulgar materialism of the Second International.[100] Marxism itself has to be seen as something variable and part of the historical process. If this is done, it is not possible to regard the crisis of Marxism as arising from the cowardice or deficient revolutionary spirit of those who adopted a vulgar Marxist position. Nor must this 'restoration' of Marxism be merely a re-reading of the basic texts. What is necessary is to use the Marxist method which has previously been applied to the philosophy of German idealism, and the Marxist theory which emerged from it, to develop Marxism further. Namely:

> we must try to understand every change, development and revision of Marxist theory since its original emergence from the philosophy of German Idealism as a necessary product of its epoch (Hegel). More precisely we should seek to understand their determination by the totality of the historico-social process of which they are a general expression (Marx).[101]

It is clear from this passage that Korsch had a specific intention—the examination of the further development not of Marxism in general, but of the relation between Marxism and philosophy in subsequent periods. It was in missing this point that his 'orthodox' critics made their major mistake. For example, Kautsky's criticism was that Korsch's periodisation referred to the general level of development of Marxism.

The deterioration which Korsch saw in the period after 1848, the 'impoverishment' of Marxism which:
> occurred during the lifetime of Marx and Engels, at a time when the First International was founded and *Capital* was published. Marx and Engels were supposedly to blame for this

'impoverishment' themselves.[102]

Korsch replied to such critics in his *Anti-Critique*, and in doing so summarised his own position:

> They have not tried to show that this periodisation was useless even for the specific purposes of my investigation. They prefer to accuse me of tending to present the whole history of Marxism after 1850 in a negative light, as a single, linear and univocal process of *decay suffered by the original revolutionary theory of Marx and Engels*—not only in the domain of the relation of Marxism to philosophy but in every domain.[103]

One of the strengths of *Marxism and Philosophy* is its avoidance of the pitfalls of a crude sociology of knowledge approach, often equated with Marxism. This approach argues that ideas serve the interests of particular classes *tout court*: that is, an unmediated application of Marx's notion that in any society the ruling ideas are those of the ruling class. Korsch ascribes this idea to the 'vulgar Marxists', as their explanation of the persistence of philosophy:

> The fact that there are still so many men who are preocuppied by such philosophical 'fantasies', appeared to them [the vulgar Marxists] to rest only on the circumstance that ... the present ruling capitalist class has an equal interest in maintaining these philosophical 'superstitions', as it does in maintaining 'religious' and all kinds of other specters.[104]

He might have added that this crude position is also to be found in Bukharin's *Historical Materialism*, which argues that 'bourgeois ideology' is just what members of the bourgeoisie think:

> The bourgeoisie also has created its own social sciences, based on its own practical requirements ... the first bourgeois economists were great practical merchants and government leaders, while the greatest theoretician of the bourgeoisie, Ricardo, was a very able banker.[105]

Korsch rightly calls the claim that the bourgeois philosophers placed their philosophy or their history of philosophy consciously in the service of one class a 'coarse notion'.[106] Further, the relations between the individual thinker and social classes are more complex than would be indicated simply from fitting the thinker into a sociological slot, and then 'explaining' ideas on this basis. Marx's position in the *Eighteenth Brumaire* is that

> Just as little must one imagine that the democratic representatives are indeed all shopkeepers or enthusiastic champions of shopkeepers. According to their education and their individual position they may be as far apart as heaven from earth. What makes them representatives of the petty bourgeoisie is the fact that in their minds they do not get beyond the limits which the latter do not get beyond in life.[107]

While certain problems have been avoided, it is evident from the foregoing that the important question still remains: is philosophy particularly important in the reconstruction of Marxism? Korsch himself point out that one of the intellectual limits on the bourgeois history of philosophy is that the ideas of philosophy can live on outside philosophy:

> the ideas contained in a philosophy can live on not only in philosophies but equally well in positive sciences and social practice ... this process precisely began on a large scale with Hegel's philosophy.[108]

If this is so, what is the point of studying philosophy as a particular discipline? Although *Marxism and Philosophy* convincingly demonstrates the need for Marxists to have a firm grasp of philosophy, in itself it does little to satisfy that need by providing a substantive exposition of philosophy. In fact, there is very little explicit philosophical content in Korsch's work. This may seem rather paradoxical, so to explain this point it is necessary to see what conception of philosophy remains implicit in the book, and then to indicate what lines of actual philosophical inquiry might have been followed.

Consider Hegel's conception of the relation of philosophy to the empirical sciences, and his definition of the object of philosophy (I have chosen Hegel as an example, because Korsch himself regarded him as the last and most important of bourgeois philosophers):

> The method of empirical science exhibits two defects. The first is that the universal or general principle contained in it ... is ... not on its own account connected with the particulars of the details ... The second defect is that the beginnings are in every case data and postulates, being neither accounted for nor deduced. In both these points the form of necessity fails to get its due.[109]

As we have seen, Korsch does not actually discuss whether philosophy shall be 'queen of the sciences', nor does he discuss 'empirical science' as such, but only the positivist conception of philosophy. A Marxist analysis of philosophy would surely have to concentrate on a demonstration of the nature of dialectical logic, and an explanation of how it differs from formal logic—in their opposition as logics of proof and discovery.[110] At the very least it would have to demonstrate Hegel's refutation of Kant's warning against 'dialectic':

> it may be noted as a sure and useful warning that general logic if viewed as an organon is always a logic of illusion, that is, dialectical. For logic teaches us nothing whatsoever regarding the content of knowledge but lays down only the formal conditions of agreement with the understanding ... [that] any attempt to use this logic as an ... [organon] ... can end in nothing but mere talk.[111]

This is a much more fundamental approach. It would deal with the key question of the formal side of Marxism, as its most general, in terms of the problem of the necessity of the dialectic, while at the same time showing what was meant by its contingency. Korsch does not approach the question at such a level of philosophical complexity. However, it does seem to have been his original intention to deal with these questions. When *Marxism and Philosophy* first appeared as an essay in the *Grünberg–Archiv*, he said that it was the first part of a longer work of historicological investigation into the question of the Marxist dialectic.[112]

I feel that he was in fact concerned with a much narrower philosophical problematic than the one outlined above; namely, the antinomy between freedom and causality, which was stated by

Kant in the *Critique of Pure Reason* as follows:

> Causality in accordance with laws of nature is not the only causality from which the appearances of the world can one and all be derived. To explain these appearances it is necessary to assume that there is another causality, that of freedom.[113]

The 'determinist' antithesis is that 'There is no freedom: everything in the world takes place solely in accordance with the laws of nature'.[114] In my opinion, Korsch is mainly concerned with *one* of the dualisms first stated by Kant. Unlike his contemporary Lukács (who devoted a long essay in *History and Class Consciousness* to this question), he does not examine dualism as a basic feature of all modern philosophical thought. In his brilliant essay 'Reification and the Consciousness of the Proletariat', Lukács set himself the task of analysing the 'antinomies of bourgeois thought'.[115] Basing himself on Marx's economic analyses, and going on to discuss the problems growing out of the fetish character of commodities, Lukács' philosophical analysis was much more sophisticated and wide-ranging than Korsch's:

> Modern critical philosophy springs from the reified structure of consciousness. The specific problems of this philosophy are distinguishable from the problematics of previous philosophies by the fact that they are rooted in this structure ... But as the problems and solutions of the philosophy of the Ancients were embedded in a wholly different society it is only natural that they should be qualitatively different from those of modern philosophy.[116]

Korsch's philosophical critique is by comparison rather superficial and not so clearly or explicitly linked to the fundamentals of the Marxist system. His purely philosophical critique is therefore not fundamental enough.

Thus for the reconstruction of Marxism, his analysis of the logical position of philosophy—the relation of Marx to Hegel and Kant—is inadequate. This might not matter so much if the proposals for the part to be played by the critique of philosophy in the development of Marxism were at all satisfactory. But in terms of Korsch's own criterion—that is, practice—they are equally inadequate. The practical proposals are stated at the end

'Marxism and Philosophy'   93

of *Marxism and Philosophy*, as follows. The economic action of the proletariat needs to be supplemented not only by political, but also by 'intellectual' (*geistige*) action. Before the seizure of power, this applies to a 'revolutionary-scientific' critique of existing society, and, at a less rarefied level, to agitational work. When the proletariat is in power, it must exercise an 'ideological dictatorship'. What is valid for the intellectual action against the forms of consciousness of existing society, is especially valid for philosophical action:

> Bourgeois consciousness ... must be philosophically fought by the revolutionary materialistic dialectic, which is the philosophy of the working class. This struggle will only end when the whole of existing society and its economic basis have been totally overthrown in practice and this consciousness has been totally surpassed and abolished in theory.[117]

Such proposals for 'intellectual action' are, it has to be said, rather vacuous: it would be difficult to draw any specific directives from them. This is a serious failing in a work whose central aim is to analyse philosophy primarily from a practical and not simply a theoretical point of view. Given this emphasis on practice, what is most surprising is that there is no mention of the role of the party. By the time Korsch wrote *Marxism and Philosophy* the question of the party had already been extensively discussed at the Third (1921) and Fourth (1922) Congresses of the Comintern. Given that during this period Korsch did follow the orthodox line about Leninism and the party, his failure to discuss this question here is rather surprising. In this respect, Lukács succeeded in drawing political conclusions from his philosophical analysis of Marxism: for example, in the essay 'Towards a Methodology of the problem of organisation' and the study on Lenin, published only one year after *History and Class Consciousness*.[118]

In this chapter, I have criticised some misconceptions about *Marxism and Philosophy*, mainly concerning the differences between Korsch and Lukács on this question, as well as examining the work itself. I now want to briefly summarise my findings on these two questions.

Ever since Zinoviev bracketed Korsch and Lukács together at the Fifth Congress of the Comintern, this amalgam technique has been uncritically repeated by most subsequent writers, friendly or hostile. Unfortunately the revival of interest in their philosophical work initiated by Merleau-Ponty's *Les aventures de la dialectique* (1955) repeated this mistake.[119] In the earlier criticisms (in the 1920s) this also meant ascribing to Korsch positions he did not in fact hold (on the dialectics of nature), as well as failing to distinguish more carefully between his and Lukács' ideas on other questions. Following Zinoviev's lead, other Comintern critics hurried to the attack:

> a disfigured, falsified Marxism is beginning to take shape in their [the European Communist Parties'] ranks. As an example of such deformations and morbid growths, the philosophical performances of Lukács, Korsch, Fogarasi and others are outstanding.[120]

As I have shown, there are in fact important differences between Korsch and Lukács. Korsch shows a superior understanding of Marxism, and, by any criterion, has a more justifiable position in relation to two questions. Firstly, he realises that it is incorrect to make such a rigid separation between form (method) and content as Lukács does. In some sense, a method has to be justified by the content it is able to establish. Lukács over-reacts against empiricist conceptions of verification to fall into the formalist trap of elevating method into a self-sufficient principle. Korsch recognises that, in Marxism, form and content are intimately linked. Secondly, he argues (correctly in my view) that the concept of totality does not have such a pre-eminent place in Marx's system as Lukács suggested. Korsch does agree that, unlike 'bourgeois' social science, Marxism attempts to integrate the separate 'disciplines' of sociology, economics, politics, history, etc., into a unified whole, and that 'totality' is an important feature of the Marxist system—but not the dominant one.

On the other hand, *Marxism and Philosophy* has two important faults: one in relation to Lukács' arguments, the other in relation to the problem of philosophy. In his critique of 'Second International Marxism', Korsch tends to ignore the variety of forms it could adopt. Thus he concentrates on its determinist-positivist aspect, and fails to realise that it can have the opposite aspect of voluntarism-idealism. Lukács' more philosophically sophisticated critique of the dualisms inherent in 'bourgeois' and (and hence social-democratic) thought, is able to show how these opposites can co-exist in an unresolved dualism. This point can be strikingly illustrated by referring to two positions held by Hilferding. In *Marxism and Philosophy* Korsch rightly draws attention to the determinism implicit in the position taken by Hilferding in his Preface to *Finanzkapital*. Yet only four years after *Marxism and Philosophy*, Hilferding could write:

> We have always thought that the fall of the capitalist system is not to be expected in a fatalistic manner—it will not be a result of the inner laws of the system, but the fall of the capitalist system must be the conscious deed of the working class ... Marxism has never been fatalism, but on the contrary the most extreme activism.[121]

The point is that Korsch's outlook could not allow for such a swing from one polar opposite to the other.

More fundamentally, Kosch's view on the relation between Marxism and philosophy remains unproved. He did succeed in distancing himself from the conception that it is necessary to provide a philosophy for Marxism as, for example, Max Adler had suggested:

> Kant's ethic is the philosophical expression of the human goals of socialism ... the categorical imperative is the idea of a universal lawgiving by the will, in which there can no longer be any *oppression* by any willing subject; the demand that no man is to be used only as a means, but is also to be regarded as an end, is an idea which totally excludes exploitation.[122]

Korsch also succeeded in showing the importance of philosophy as a historical component in the development of the Marxist system; but the logical status of philosophy is not clear. His argument stops at the very point at which it should have begun. He seems to accept a position similar to that put forward by Engels in *Ludwig Feuerbach and the End of Classical German Philosophy*:

> with Hegel philosophy comes to an end: on the one hand, because in his system he summed up its whole development in the most splendid fashion; and on the other hand, because, even though unconsciously, he showed us the way out of the labyrinth of systems to real positive knowledge of the world.[123]

But he does not explain what is meant by 'positive knowledge', nor does he provide any instance of such knowledge about ideologies. Thus his work is only a part of the prolegomenon to the study of *Marxism and Philosophy*, but an indispensable part none the less.

It is perhaps ironic that *Marxism and Philosophy* attracted such bitter and unjustified criticisms from the defenders of orthodoxy, since it is much more faithful to the letter of Marx and Lenin's writings than is *Labour Law for Factory Councils*. But, unfortunately, in the year following its publication, the 'Bolshevisation' campaign began in all the European Communist parties. In the next chapter we shall see how Korsch, who initially was a fervent supporter of the campaign, soon became a victim of it.

5 Political Debates, 1923-8

For the next five years after the appearance of *Marxism and Philosophy*, Korsch was intensively involved in party political activity. In bewildering succession he found himself a Communist Minister in a regional government (1923); in a leading position in the left turn made by the KPD (1924) after the defeat of the German revolution; attacked as an 'ultra-left' as the party turned rightwards (1925); finally, expelled from the KPD, and the leader of a small splinter group around the periodical *Kommunistische Politik*.

During this whole period, he did not write any major theoretical work of the stature of *Marxism and Philosophy* or even *Labour Law for Factory Councils*. He was confined to writing articles for the party press, editing the party journal *Die Internationale*, and, later, writing polemical articles against the party. From 1924 to 1928 he was a member of the Reichstag, and contributed to its debates on a variety of topics.[1] In the course of this political dispute, some significant differences from his earlier positions began to emerge. These were not fully expressed until he wrote *Die materialistische Geschichtsauffassung* in 1928 and his *Anti-Critique* to *Marxism and Philosophy* in 1930. In this chapter, because the emphasis is mainly on contemporary events, I shall partly abandon the earlier procedure of dealing with his writings thematically and shall adopt instead a more chronological approach.

The first political problem arose from the events of 1923, the notorious '*Inflationsjahr*', concerning in particular the role of the Communist-Social-Democratic governments in Saxony and

Thüringia (when Korsch was Minister of Justice in the latter). Let us first examine the discussion preceding the momentous events of October 1923. The most important meetings were those of the Fourth Congress of the Comintern (December 1922) and the Leipzig Conference of the KPD (January 1923). The Comintern forecast that one of the most important questions of the approaching period would be that of the 'workers' government'. This must be examined briefly, since later recriminations were mainly about this slogan. It was considered to be a continuation of the 'united front' tactic, not applicable everywhere and at all times, but

> only in those countries where bourgeois society is very unstable and when the balance of power between the workers' parties and the bourgeoisie make the decision on the question of government a practical necessity.[2]

In connection with later events, it is important to see what conditions were required for the successful operation of a 'workers' government', and what were to be its specific tasks:

> The most elementary tasks of a workers' government must consist in arming the proletariat, in disarming the bourgeois counter-revolutionary organisations, in introducing control of production, in putting the chief burden of taxation on the shoulders of the rich and in breaking down the resistance of the counter-revolutionary bourgeoisie. Such a workers' government is only possible if it arises out of the struggle of the masses and if it is based on the support of active workers' organisations involving the lowest strata of the oppressed working masses.[3]

A month later Korsch gave a leading speech at the KPD's Leipzig Conference on this very question. It is interesting to note that he attempts to conceptualise the positions taken by the various factions in a philosophical manner: i.e. as dialectical or metaphysical. The question that was posed there was whether

> certain actions, e.g. the arming of the proletariat, will be considered to be tasks of the workers' government, or conditions for participating in the workers' government.[4]

Political Debates, 1923–8

Harking back to the resolution of the Fourth Congress of the Comintern, Korsch said that everyone agreed that the 'workers' government' slogan was mainly for propaganda purposes. But there are two ways of conducting propaganda. Maslow and Fischer approach the problem undialectically, and want to use the slogan as a pseudonym for the dictatorship of the proletariat. The true dialectical position is taken by Brandler and Kleine, who regard the slogan as a means of preparing the proletariat for struggle.[5] It is interesting to note that on this question, although his own position was nearer the 'centre', Korsch sided with the 'right-winger' Brandler against the 'ultra-left' Fischer—precisely the opposite of the position he was to adopt from 1924 onwards. Eventually the conference accepted the 'Guidelines on the united front tactic and the workers' government', which were close to the Comintern resolution.[6]

In the year of this conference, the expected radicalisation which would lead to the formation of a 'workers' government' did in fact occur. On 11 January 1923, French and Belgian troops marched into the Ruhr and Rhineland in connection with claims for reparations payments. The occupation deprived Germany of the essential bases of its economy: 80 per cent of its iron and steel production; 71 per cent of the coal-mining industry. This, and the government action of printing money to cope with the situation led to a deadly combination of inflation and unemployment. At the time of the occupation, one dollar exchanged for 10,000 marks; in September, it was worth 200 million marks. The number of unemployed (and also short-time workers) rose alarmingly, the professional middle classes (*the Mittelstand*), the stable backbone of German society, were ruined; there were enormous concentrations of wealth in the hands of large industrialists such as Stinnes.[7]

Not surprisingly in such a situation, the most extreme parties began to grow rapidly. Thus, the SPD lost ground to the KPD. For example, in the only election held during this period, in the rural district of Mecklenburg-Strelitz, the KPD, appearing for the first time there in an election, got one-fifth of the votes.[8] The bourgeois government of Cunow was brought down by the general strike in August. Thereafter the situation moved at first in favour of the left, particularly in the area of Saxony and Thüringia. The first 'workers' government' was formed in Saxony. Previously, it had a government of 46 bourgeois deputies, 40 SPD and 10 KPD deputies, under the presidency of Zeigner. On 1 October, Zinoviev sent a telgram to the Communists that they were to take up ministerial posts, provided the supporters of Zeigner were really ready to defend Saxony against the fascists; they were to attempt to arm 50,000–60,000 men to do this, and to ignore General Müller.[9] At the end of his telegram giving these instructions, Zinoviev added: 'The same for Thüringia'. Accordingly, following the example of Brandler in Saxony, in Thüringia three Communists became ministers: Korsch, Minister of Justice; Neubauer, Minister for the State Police; and Tenner, Minister for Economics.[10] The following day, the government issued a statement of its intentions: to defend itself against the fascist danger from Bavaria; to secure minimal living standards for the working class; to democratise the police forces and the state.[11] At the same time, however, the KPD had entered the coalition without posing any conditions.[12]

What did the Communist Ministers do? There was no shortage of messianic appeals. A scandalised contemporary reports:

> At a funeral service in Meiningen ... the Minister for Justice (Korsch) made a speech in which he explained inter al. that he counted the Reichswehr among his sworn enemies. The workers now faced a crucial decision—they must choose between the Fascist Mussolini and the state we long for. The workers should come together in thousands and then the moment would have arrived when they could trample the Reichswehr under foot.[13]

But the three Communist Ministers made no attempt to do anything more decisive. For example, they did not try to arm the 'Hundreds' (*Hundertschaften*), a kind of proletarian militia. It has been claimed that there were as many as 250,000 men, some of them armed, in these organisations.[14] Nor did they do anything very significant about introducing any anti-capitalist measures in the factories, such as workers' control. Given the passivity of the communist ministers, the movement soon collapsed. On 29 October, using the emergency powers of the constitution, Ebert gave the order to disperse the Saxony government.[15] A week later, Reichswehr troops began to move into the area. Communists were arrested, and outdoor meetings were forbidden; Korsch and other communists left the regional government (*Landesregierung*) and fled. On 20 November, the government was reconvened; on the same day, the KPD and the Nazi Party were banned.[16] Although the KPD members of the government had only gone as far as Leipzig, they stayed underground. Korsch himself was sought by the police and his wife was arrested for a short time.[17]

The farcical proceedings in the Thüringian government, and the resounding defeat suffered by the left-wing forces, provoked severe criticism from the Comintern and sections of the KPD. At the most important meeting of the Executive Committee of the Comintern (EKKI) after October (in January 1924), a resolution was passed severely condemning the Saxony experiment, and by implication, the Thüringian one too, where 'instead of a revolutionary strategy there was a non-revolutionary parliamentary co-operation with the "left" Social-Democrats'.[18] The Executive Committee did not realise that a defeat had been suffered, and that therefore a cautious retreat was necessary—however temporary. The basic evaluation of the situation in Germany was still held to be correct. The fundamental task of the party was to remain as before—the organisation of an insurrection and the seizure of power:[19] if anything, there was a turn to the left in insisting that this was an immediate perspective.

The KPD mirrored this turn to the left, though not simply at the behest of the Comintern, for it seems to have been the genuine mood of the party, which persisted for a long time after the October defeat. In the months following the Frankfurt Conference (7–10 April 1924), at which the left was in the overwhelming majority, the lefts, led by Fischer and Maslow, became the power in the party. They were against the tactic of the 'United Front', of which the 'workers' government' was supposed to be the logical extension.[20] Thus Korsch completely changed the position he had held before the October events, and became a fervent 'leftist'. He went further than the KPD was perhaps willing to go at that time, his analysis of the defeat of 1923 anticipating the theories of social-fascism put forward by the Comintern at the end of the 1920s:

> the most disastrous mistake in our politics in 1923 was that we recognised the fascist nature of the Social-Democracy and all other bourgeois democrats in theory, and equated them completely ... with Hitler's fascism, but in our practical action we

did not draw the consequences of this view with sufficient resolution.[21]

This of course meant rejecting the 'united front' tactic which the Third and Fourth Congresses of the Comintern had taken such pains to instil in the constituent parties. Korsch wrote that, however revolutionary this tactic might be in ideal terms, in its practical application it would not serve as a clear and unambiguous guide in the struggle for the dictatorship of the proletariat.[22]

The most important question now facing the KPD was the preparation for the Fifth World Congress of the Comintern. The first point on the agenda was 'Lenin and Leninism: On the foundations and propaganda of Leninism'. What is most surprising is that in this period Korsch showed himself to be the proponent of a rigorous Leninism in its most dogmatic Stalinist form and thus naturally a fervent opponent of 'Trotskyism' and other 'deviations'.[23] This seems a far cry from the fluid methodology, the concern for ideological struggle and the critique of dogmatism which it had been the main tasks of *Marxism and Philosophy* to establish. At a different pace and with much more lasting results, Lukács, in his philosophical writings equally the opponent of dogmatism, underwent a similar evolution. This was a passing, if remarkable, episode in Korsch's life which has largely remained unaccounted for. Later commentators such as Gerlach who have admired Korsch for his anti-dogmatic positions, have largely passed over this period, or have not taken a definite position.[24] Nor did Korsch himself ever offer a satisfactory justification of his Leninist phase during this period, although he did later refer, without comment, to the articles he had written at this time.[25]

One possible explanation would be that Korsch was attempting to maintain a base for future criticism by temporarily accepting the current orthodoxy. There is very little in his published work which could be construed as any kind of criticism of the prevailing line. The one exception which has been claimed to represent an attempt at covert criticism hardly does so.[26] Of course, he may have maintained a superficial orthodoxy in his writings while attempting to spread heresy by word of mouth. But there is no evidence of this, since his opponents in the KPD would surely have brought this charge against him in the factional struggles of 1925–6, had there been any basis for it. If this was a devious way of maintaining a critical attitude while not being openly hostile to the Comintern line, it availed him little when the struggle began in earnest.

The two most significant articles by Korsch in this period are 'Lenin und die Komintern' and 'Stalin, *Lenin und der Leninismus*'.[27] The tone of these articles is perhaps as remarkable as their content: for example, the frequent references to the 'spirit of Leninism' which was to pervade the forthcoming conference, and to inspire every debate. A quote from 'Lenin und die Komintern' will illustrate this point:

> What is at issue here [referring to the agenda] is that the whole Comintern today can and must, after the shattering event of the death of its great founder and leader ... for the first time show that it is capable and willing to accept both theoretically and ideologically the legacy of Lenin.[28]

Even more remarkable is his review of Stalin's *Lenin und der Leninismus*. Describing the book as a 'study-guide for the beginner in Leninism', he asks if there are any Western European Marxists who are not 'beginners in Leninism'.[29] Quite uncritically, he quotes as valuable doctrine such statements of Stalin's as: '"Lenin is a Marxist and the foundation of his world-view is, it goes without saying, Marxism".'[30] Ironically Korsch welcomes the Congress because it will 'definitely erect bulwarks against the rising flood of Communist revisionism'.[31] He argued forcibly that it was necessary to carry out an ideological unification of all sections of the Comintern, all of which must accept one method. Those who thought of themselves only as 'practical Leninists' either accept Luxemburg's method or are indifferent to the question of method. Conveniently forgetting to mention his own earlier tendency to accept Luxemburg, he argued that such tendencies must not be allowed to flourish.[32]

Yet when the Congress came, Korsch found himself numbered among those guilty of 'Communist revisionism'. In a rather hysterical outburst, Zinoviev argued that it was necessary to struggle against 'ultra-leftism' and 'revisionism':

> When Comrade Graziadei in Italy comes out with a book ...

[in which] he turns against Marxism, this theoretical revisionism in our midst cannot go unpunished. When Comrade Lukács does the same on the philosophical and sociological level, we won't tolerate that either ... we have a similar current in the German party. Comrade Graziadei is a professor, Korsch is also a professor (Interruption: Lukács is also a professor!). We'll find that things will go badly with us, if we get a few more professors like these coming to hawk around their Marxist theories.[33]

He went on to criticise Korsch in particular for his work as editor of *Die Internationale*:

The person responsible for the periodical, Comrade Korsch, 'defends' Comrade Lenin against many deviations from Leninism. I think we should advise Comrade Korsch in a friendly manner, that he should first of all study Marxism and Leninism.[34]

The connection between Korsch's philosophy and the alleged 'deviations' was not made clear at any point. The SPD critics, Marck and Kautsky,[35] had at least made an honest attempt at criticism. Perhaps because the 'deviations' were within its own ranks, the KPD tended to be much more unreasonable and dogmatic.[36] The seriousness with which it viewed such deviations is shown by the fact that in the draft programme which emerged from this Congress there is a formal warning against 'idealism'. It is not surprising that the programme was drawn up by Bukharin, who espoused a rigid, dogmatic, mechanical materialism, in these terms:

the Communist International fights for the clarification of the class consciousness of the masses, by opposing its dialectical materialism to the theories of bourgeois ideology and thus conducts a consistent struggle against each and every kind of bourgeois influence on the proletariat—against religion, against idealist and every non-dialectical-materialist philosophy.[37]

Korsch's book also became drawn into the disputes inside the Russian party. In 1924, a Russian edition of his book appeared, with a preface and commentary by Bammel, a junior associate of Deborin.³⁸ Korsch later remarked that the latter contained the usual stereotyped arguments against him.³⁹

Pravda took up a similar refrain in an article published just after the Congress (25 July). It objected most strenuously to the claim that to regard economic ideologies as having an objective significance and all higher ideologies as 'objectless fantasies' was to subscribe to '[the] naïve metaphysical standpoint of healthy bourgeois common sense'.⁴⁰ *Pravda* remarked that the agreement of an idea with its object belonged to the ABC of Marxist philosophy: 'it is his [Korsch's] standpoint in this question which is bourgeois – an idealist mixture of identity-philosophy and Machism'.⁴¹ Despite the fierceness of these attacks, nothing happened immediately. The lefts were still in control of the party, and Korsch retained the editorship of *Die Internationale*, despite Zinoviev's recommendation that it should be placed in 'the hands of Marxists'.⁴²

The real attack was to come later. The events of this period of the 'Bolshevisation' of the Communist Party are rather involved, and Korsch's part in the more obscure aspects of this struggle is of little interest today. I shall not outline the background to this period, since this has already been done in an excellent study by H. Weber, *Die Wandlung des deutschen Kommunismus*.⁴³ The first episode was a criticism of *Die Internationale*—a delayed response to Zinoviev's suggestion. A communication from the Agitprop department of the Executive Committee of the Communist International (EKKI) which appeared in March 1925 (nine months after the Congress) argued that the journal had not followed a consistent revolutionary Marxist-Leninist line. It had published two opposed views of Trotsky's book on Lenin, and in general its editor had not exercised a sufficiently stringent ideological control. To bring it into line with Comintern policy, it was proposed that the central committee should play a larger part in directing the journal, and that the editing of all Russian questions should be entrusted to leading Russian Bolsheviks.⁴⁴ Korsch's reply effectively answered the point about the reviews of Trotsky, but concentrated mainly on the 'factionalism' of the author of the communication, Bela Kun.⁴⁵ He was, however, obliged to give up the editorship of *Die Internationale*.⁴⁶

While Korsch maintained his 'left' position, the KPD and the Comintern moved further to the right in response to the changed economic position, thus making Korsch an 'ultra-left'. The October-November 1925 KPD Congress presented a completely different picture from eighteen months previously. Before the Congress a campaign had taken place against the 'ultra-lefts', with the result that the lefts were only weakly represented.[47] A decisive factor in increasing the pressure on the lefts was the 'Open Letter' of 1 September from the EKKI. Although it did not mention Korsch by name, it contained an implicit criticism of his ideas. The main task was now said to be to draw SPD workers over to Communism by means of the 'united front', and to return to active work in the trade unions. The Fischer-Maslow leadership was severely criticised.[48]

An article in *Inprekorr* at the same period made crudely sociological innuendoes against the oppositional currents, mentioning Maslow, Scholem, Korsch and Rosenberg by name. In comparison with the healthy mainstream of progressive German workers, the oppositionists allegedly drew their support from the petite-bourgeoisie ruined by inflation.[49] This argument, of dubious relevance in any case, was not well-founded. In fact, the left and ultra-left groups were strong in proletarian areas such as Berlin-Wedding, and the Ruhr district. Admittedly, many of their members were unemployed, but the sociological composition of the opposition groups did not differ markedly from other sections of the party.[50]

The philosophical differences which had appeared at the Fifth Congress were only gradually revealed to be part of wider differences about political questions. As we have seen, the Congress had maintained that a crisis of capitalism was imminent. Events were soon to give the lie to this, for it soon became apparent in 1925 that European capitalism had achieved a measure of stabilisation. During this period, Korsch himself wrote a number of articles on the Dawes plan, which had led to a certain amount of stability in German economic life.[51]. None of these is very informative about his views, and the implicit differences with the Comintern emerge only very tangentially. More directly, it was alleged that at a party conference in Frankfurt (6 September 1925) he had spoken of the danger of the Comintern parties simply becoming agents of the Russian party. Although this was in itself unacceptable to the party leadership two of the phrases he used seemed to suggest an even more hostile view of the relationship between the Soviet Union and the

Comintern. He had spoken of 'red imperialism' and of the possibility of a repetition of the betrayal by the SPD of 4 August 1914.[52] Korsch replied that he considered the Soviet Union to be the strongest bulwark of communism. But to no avail – the signal was given for a series of articles against him.[53]

Under this pressure, the left and ultra-left groups splintered into smaller and smaller fragments. The end result of a series of splits[54] was the formation of a new group, the 'Intransigent Lefts' (*Entschiedene Linke*). The programmatic basis of the group was explained in the '*Plattform der Linken*'.[55] Although more explicit than his earlier statements, it is still quite mild in tone. His basic argument is stated in the opening paragraph—that the whole world economy presently found itself in a period of depression. This crisis extended even to the Soviet Union, which after the upswing of 1924/25 was now facing difficulties. Both Trotsky and the official leadership had made quite an incorrect assessment of the Dawes plan. They thought that it would mean the increased dominance of American capitalism over the world economy and a peaceful development of the European economies; in fact, it would lead to an increased attack on the German proletariat.[56] What were the political conclusions of these opposed perspectives? Korsch claimed that behind his opponents' talk of stabilisation

> there is in reality hidden the liquidation of the Comintern's revolutionary perspectives, the surrender of the preparation and organisation of revolutionary struggles for power, for the whole epoch.[57]

In Korsch's view, the real situation in Germany, with the continued existence of unemployment and short-time working, contained all the objective elements for revolutionary politics. The immediate day-to-day struggles must be seen in the perspective of preparing for the revolution. Beginning with the struggle for control over production, the aim must be the organisation of the dictatorship of the proletariat. In particular, the party must pay attention to the demands of the unemployed.[58] The banal parliamentary farce of the workers' government of October 1923 must not be repeated—the question of power must be clearly stated:

We must oppose to the purely bourgeois and bourgeois-reformist governmental combinations, the solution of the total power [*Alleinherrschaft*] of the revolutionary workers' councils, based on the broadest masses of the working population in town and country.[59]

In relation to the Comintern and its constituent parties, the 'Platform' implied that the Russian party played too great a role in the relations between the Soviet State and the national parties. If this development were to continue, it would eventually 'prepare the 4 August of the Comintern' (i.e. repeat the collapse of the Second International).[60] The 'Platform' was not fundamentally opposed to the Comintern as such, but to its domination by a certain group in the Russian party. Already,

> The 14th Conference of the RCP [Russian Communist Party] has shown to the world that opportunism has already gained the upper hand within our fraternal Russian party. The decisions and resolutions of the enlarged executive of March 1926 show that this opportunism is to be carried over to the whole Comintern.[61]

The 'Platform' ends with an appeal to remain within the party and the Comintern.[62]

Such attempts at conciliation notwithstanding, the political line of the document was clearly a 'deviation'. Accordingly, on 16 April, Korsch was summoned to a conference of political secretaries and editors, to defend his position. Given the general atmosphere in the party at that time,[63] it is hardly surprising that Korsch complained that what was taking place was only a token discussion which would deceive the membership, and that he expected his ideas to be falsified.[64] For example, he felt it necessary to stress:

> It is not true that this group [the Korsch-Schwarz group] starts out from the idea that the *4 August 1914* is already an accomplished fact for the Comintern and its leading party, the Russian party.[65]

Much of this speech is concerned with his attitude to various changes of position by Ruth Fischer, Urbahns and Zinoviev, and an examination of whether Otto Bauer was 'on the road to Moscow', as the KPD had suggested, or vice versa.[66] The only point which emerges much more explicitly in this speech is the following. The 'Leninism' of leaders such as Stalin represents a revision of the revolutionary theory of Lenin and Marx. The theoretical reformism of Stalin does not represent a simple return to the reformism of Bernstein. Rather,

> This new phase of development of Marxist-Leninist theory ... can be most accurately characterised as 'Bernsteinism' and 'Kautskyanism' after the seizure of power.[67]

After Korsch had defended his view in this way, the party leadership gave him an ultimatum: to give up his seat in the Reichstag. He answered that he wished first to consult his friends. Naturally, this was taken as a provocation, and an openly factional pronouncement, and he was excluded from the session. The conference then went on to vote 65:2 for struggling against the 'Intransigents'; the ultra-lefts were in general considered to stand outside the party.[68]

Just before this decisive meeting, Korsch had been instrumental in his group's issuing a periodical, *Kommunistische Politik*, the first number appearing at the end of March. The second number (mid-April) contained a justification for this step which could so easily be characterised as 'splitting', 'wishing to form a second party'. It claimed that the official party press had misquoted their platform, that dissident party branches had been dissolved or split, that party officials were selected rather than elected – these being just some of the manoeuvres used by the party leadership against the 'Intransigent Lefts'.[69]

The group gradually lost influence inside the KPD. At its Reichskonferenz in September 1926, it split into the Schwarz-Lossau group, which had a slight majority (it returned to the KPD the following year) and the Korsch group. The latter was soon reduced to a discussion group on the problems of Marxism and dissolved in 1928.[70] In November 1926, the expelled Communists of various degrees of leftism formed a Reichstag fraction of 'left communists', but their attempts to carry out common work came to nothing, because their differences were too great.[71]

Nor did Korsch's group find it possible to carry out continuous work on the international front. In the August 1926 edition of

Kommunistische Politik, there appeared an appeal for solidarity, and, still harking back to Lenin, a call to set up a new Zimmerwald left. The only group mentioned by name was the Bordiga group in Italy and France. The number of groups which could possibly have co-operated with the 'Intransigent Lefts' was quite small. On grounds of principle, it could not consider co-operation with the largest left opposition group – the 'joint opposition' around Zinoviev and Trotsky. Not only had Korsch joined in the campaign against 'Trotskyism' during his ultra-Leninist days, but now their views on the Soviet Union were quite divergent. Further, he considered that Trotsky had surrendered his position, which was shown by his giving up Mjasnikov. Trotsky was in his turn equally dismissive of Korsch.[72]

The appeal met with no response. The main opposition group to which Korsch was attracted was the Sapronow-Smirnow democratic centralist group in the Soviet Union. This opposed to the 'dictatorship of the party' the restoration of a 'councils dictatorship' which, as we shall see, was to be one of Korsch's main ideas.[73] Perhaps because Bordiga had spoken in his defence at an EKKI meeting, Korsch said in the 'Plattform der Linken' that the leftists saw in him a real co-fighter.[74] Accordingly, he wrote to Bordiga asking him to co-operate. In a cautious reply (8 October 1926) Bordiga admitted that he felt sympathetic to some of the points made by the 'Intransigent Lefts', but not to the extent of being able to collaborate politically.[75] Korsch had articles published in other groups' journals after *Kommunistische Politik* ceased publication, but this was a purely literary activity—he had no organisational ties with them.[76]

During this transitional period, his ideas focused mainly on the Soviet Union. In the 'Plattform der Linken', and the other documents published up until the time of his expulsion, he had not openly expressed the view that the policy of the Soviet Union was no longer determined by considerations of 'class politics' (the 'dictatorship of the proletariat') but by considerations of 'state necessity'. But shortly before his expulsion was confirmed by the EKKI (on 10 June 1926), Korsch, Schwarz and Schlagewerth voted against the 'friendship treaty' between the Soviet Union and Germany. Korsch made the serious charge that

> By taking this attitude towards the Russo-German treaty, the Communist Party of Germany has in fact placed itself on the

Political Debates, 1923–8

ground of 'collaboration' [Arbeitsgemeinschaft] between the proletariat and the bourgeoisie on a world scale.[77]

This charge was based on the view that Russia was a new capitalist class state, and that what now operated in Russia was a 'dictatorship of the party' (Parteidiktatur), not a 'councils' dictatorship' (Rätediktatur). He argued that the character of the Russian Revolution had changed from a radical bourgeois to a bourgeois one.[78] Perhaps the most significant change of opinion during this period was in his attitude to 'Leninism'. At the same time as the appearance of the 'Plattform der Linken', he had appealed in the 'spirit of Leninism' against the course the party was taking. While he still belonged to the party, this might be regarded simply as a tactical manoeuvre to ensure that his ideas would be heard—he could hardly expect even to get a hearing unless he made the ritual obeisance to Lenin. But that he genuinely felt it necessary to make this appeal is shown by the fact that he continued to do so even after leaving the party. For example, in his speech in the Reichstag against the Russo-German 'friendship treaty', he argued that the proposed treaty conflicted with one of the conditions for joining the Third International; at the end of his speech he appealed for a renewal of communist politics, citing Leninism as a basis on which this could be done.[79]

But by the time he came to write his last article for *Kommunistische Politik*, he had made a decisive break with 'Leninism'. He now held that it was valid for that stage of the Russian Revolution in which the task was to complete the bourgeois revolution; but during the period of the dictatorship of the proletariat, Leninist ideology was a means for suppressing the working class. The conclusion drawn was:

> For this reason, the break with this 'Leninist' ideology, which for a long time has become a chain on the proletariat's fighting energy ... is an immediate and pressing necessity for the class-movement of the Russian proletariat.[80]

It was necessary to leave behind the ghosts of 'communism' and to work for and with the real struggles of the working class, which were entering a new period.[81] The practical conclusion of this was that Leninist forms of organisation must be rejected. He now focused on quite a different form of organisation as the potential instrument for proletarian revolution: the revolutionary trade union.

He wrote a series of articles for '*Kampf-Front*, the newspaper of the Deutsche Industrieverband, the 'trade union of all class-conscious workers and employees', which was a revolutionary syndicalist union. These articles appeared as a pamphlet, *Um die Tariffähigkeit*,[82] which will now be discussed. As Korsch had already pointed out in his earlier *Labour Law for Factory Councils*, the right to 'freedom of coalition' which workers had struggled for, was showing a tendency to develop into a formal 'compulsory coalition' *Koalitionszwang*. In this later period of capitalist development, even the employers had come to stand for the principle of '*Koalitionszwang*'.[83] This does not serve as a means to strengthening the working class. On the contrary, there are concrete examples that this development leads to its greater enslavement.[84] Outside Germany,

> As in fascist Italy, so too in present-day Bolshevist Russia ... the transition from freedom of coalition to the 'ideally' higher principle of compulsory coalition is in actual praxis ultimately distorted into its very opposite.[85]

A similar situation was developing in Germany, with three trade unions—the Christian, the Hirsch-Duncker, and the 'free' trade unions—effectively being granted the legal monopoly of recognition and right to negotiation. They were given this privilege because they were economic and not political organisations.[86]

Korsch discusses three main arguments used against the revolutionary unions' having the right to make wage agreements (*Tariffähigkeit*):

1. their lack of independence from the employers;
2. their actual inability to fulfil the tasks of an economic organisation;
3. that they are predominantly political and not concerned with economic tasks.[87]

The problems he had taken up earlier in *Labour Law for Factory Councils*, such as the relations between unions, councils and factory councils, and the question of industrial unions, were not analysed at all here. The differences from his position in *Labour Law for Factory Councils* are not very obvious, perhaps because the restricted nature of these articles does not allow them to emerge. One common feature is his insistence on the dangers to the working class of accepting the leadership of the 'free trade unions'. In the concluding paragraph of *Labour Law for Factory Councils* he writes:

> Therefore the free trade unions prepare . . . their own capitulation, and at the same time a new defeat of the German proletariat . . . after all the experiences of the most recent period of historical development, there is *no doubt that they will follow this path of theirs to the end, unless before the end they are opposed by a stronger force.*[88]

Thus at the end of this period, Korsch's ideas are at a transitional stage. He still rejects the social-democratic road to socialism, but the alternative is not fully clear. During the period discussed here, he has come to see that the Leninist conception of how socialism is to be achieved is inadequate. But, as yet, 'Leninism' is only judged at a practical level—he has not criticised the basic philosophical foundations of Lenin's ideas. In the next chapter, I shall discuss how Korsch arrived at a more definite solution to these problems.

6 *The Materialist Conception of History*

In 1928 Korsch's mandate to the Reichstag expired (he did not stand again) and the *Kommunistische Politik* group dissolved itself.¹ During this period, Korsch concentrated on literary activity. Up to the time of writing *Karl Marx* (1936 onwards), the two most important works were *Die materialistische Geschichtsauffassung* (*The Materialist Conception of History*) in 1929 and the *Anti-Critique* to *Marxism and Philosophy* in 1930. The sure touch which he had shown in earlier writings had temporarily deserted him. In fact, in these years, Korsch was looking for a direction. For example, he later considered writing a long introduction to a German edition of the works of Antonio Labriola. In his opinion Labriola was 'the best interpreter of the Marxist method and in particular of its methodological ... foundations; at the same time a fundamental Hegelian'.² There were two other reasons for his interest in Labriola. First, Labriola stood at a turning point: after him came the syndicalists in France and the revisionists in Germany. Secondly, the significance of Labriola for the development of Marxism in the West is a striking parallel to the meaning of Plekhanov for the development of Marxism in the East.³ However, this remained an unrealised project and *The Materialist Conception of History* was the only book he wrote; his *Anti-Critique* to *Marxism and Philosophy* is only an extended essay.

I shall now examine the two completed works of this period. *The Materialist Conception of History* is a much slighter work than

'The Materialist Conception of History' 115

Marxism and Philosophy. The critical energy which in earlier works Korsch had concentrated to the extent that the denseness of his ideas conceals the structure (e.g. in *Marxism and Philosophy*) seems to be dissipated. On a smaller scale it is often as rambling and inconsequential as the Kautsky volume which it was criticising. He complains that there is not a strong connection between the thoughts and the chapters of Kautsky's work, but his own is hardly free of these faults.[4] For example it is overburdened with lengthy footnotes and quotations from Marx and Kautsky: in one case to the extent of a whole page of small type consisting of quotes and comments.[5] Its style is often pedestrian and indulges a rather laboured irony at Kautsky's expense. This applies particularly to the chapter on the state,[6] which discusses at great length the point that

> Not as for Marx and Engels, 'bourgeois society' ... but the 'state' forms for Kautsky the true foundation of the whole development of man in the historical period—it is the creator of all things.[7]

The work focuses too much on criticising Kautsky to be able to make any more general points and it remains very much a work of its time.

Five of the chapters of Korsch's book deal directly with Kautsky, while the sixth and last ('The historical significance of Kautskyanism') is a summary and an evaluation. He does not follow the structure of Kautsky's book very closely, nor does his book have its own integrated structure since it deals with rather loosely related themes. He claims that the 'keystone' of Kautsky's argument is his analysis of the state,[8] but as I have remarked above, he shows rather easily that Kautsky's conception of the state is different from Marx's.

Kautsky had claimed that his book was the 'quintessence' and the result of his whole life's work.[9] It is interesting to note that, in his Introduction, Kautsky reflected on the experiences of 1918–19, and drew general conclusions from them which are precisely the opposite of Korsch's guiding principle that an active effort of the will is needed in order to achieve socialism. In Kautsky's opinion, the materialist conception of history

> does not deny the power of the human will, but shows that it

only achieves a lasting and irreversible victory when it operates in the direction given by the economic conditions, and when it keeps within the limit of what is possible at the time.[10]

Perhaps the most valuable approach to such a diffuse work as Kautsky's would be to identify those elements which are important to the development of Korsch's thought at this period. We must therefore identify, then set aside those arguments which had already been discussed in *Marxism and Philosophy*.

The arguments which are repeated are as follows. Kautsky had split Marx's unified dialectical-materialist conception of history into two parts. One of these is a 'general philosophy of historical materialism' concerned with the 'laws of the materialistic conception of history as a whole'; the other contains 'only those [laws] of previous history which are discovered following research into history from the standpoint of this conception of history'.[11] Korsch argued that to regard the materialist conception of history in this way as a supra-historical principle is to commit the serious mistake of separating form from content:

> as a method and a general intellectual direction the materialist conception of history ... is the form of its content ... and this particular content, to which the 'materialist conception of history' belongs as its corresponding form, was shaped by the theory and praxis of the class action of the proletariat'.[12]

He maintains that Kautsky's ideas belong to the Kantian tradition of distinguishing universally valid laws of form and particular laws of nature (content) but does not develop this point.[13] In fact, precisely the same argument had already appeared in *Marxism and Philosophy*.[14]

The section 'Dialectics and Development' might be expected to contain a more extensive discussion of this and other points relating to abstract philosophical questions, but in it there is little that is new.[15] The section begins by stating that the central concept of the materialist conception of history is that the concept of development (*Entwicklung*) has a threefold significance in Marx and Engels, 'as Thought (dialectic), as Becoming (development in the narrower sense, in Nature and Society) and as Deed (revolutionary class struggle)'.[16] At the end of this section Korsch clearly states what he considers to be Kautsky's philosophical

'The Materialist Conception of History' 117

standpoint; namely, the naturalistic materialism of the period of the Enlightenment and the revolutionary era of the bourgeoisie—the seventeenth and eighteenth centuries— precisely that contemplative (*anschauende*) materialism which Marx had criticised in the *Theses on Feuerbach*.[17] This is an important point, which will be considered when the new aspects of Korsch's ideas are dealt with. Here I shall merely note that although he tests Kautsky's conception of development against the three aspects of the criterion which he had established (Thought, Becoming and Deed), Korsch does not attempt to justify the concept of development itself.

The second argument put forward in *The Materialist Conception of History* which merely repeats ideas to be found in the earlier work, concerns the relation of theory to practice. For Kautsky, Marxism is a ' "purely scientific theory, which as such is in no way linked with the proletariat" '.[18] This point was dealt with in my discussion of Kautsky's criticisms of *Marxism and Philosophy* in *Die Gesellschaft*.[19]

A third argument does not so much explicitly repeat as bring out a feature of the earlier work which was to become much more important later, in *Karl Marx*. This is his emphasis upon the specificity of Marxism. Whereas Marx and Engels

> grasped the laws of development of society (supposed by bourgeois idealism to be a universal law of nature) as laws linked with definite historical conditions, and appropriate only to these conditions',[20]

Kautsky 'transforms the historical laws of the development of society so far into eternally valid laws, henceforth unchangeable'.[21] It is this notion of the specificity of Marxism which underlies the schema of the different periods of Marxism, and it is the new periodisation of Marxism which is the original feature of *Die materialistische Geschichtsauffassung*.

Having dealt with these recurring points, which do however occupy a large part of the book, let us analyse the new arguments it contains. Its main aim is to re-evaluate the 'historical significance of Kautskyism' in such a way as also to illuminate the relation between it and 'Leninism'. Korsch was concerned to give quite a different answer about the nature of Kautskyism from that provided by the orthodox 'Marxist-Leninists'. It would be generally agreed that Kautskyism is not an ideology fixed for all time, but a historically variable entity.[22] The position he wishes to dispute is that of 'communist orthodoxy':

> If one determines the various phases of this historical development first of all in the usual ideological manner according to its contemporary relation to the original 'theory' of Marx and Engels, one can characterise K.'s present work, and that of recent years, as a completed transition from a concealed to an open revisionism.[23]

Let us consider the two points he makes about this method of assessing Kautskyism, and the result it usually leads to. At the beginning of the book, Korsch insists that the real significance of Kautsky's work is not its ideological content, but that it is 'a historical phenomenon, which stands in a definite relationship ... to the class struggle of the proletariat'.[24] Thus Korsch's methodological premise is that 'The following critical investigations relate ... to this real significance of K.'s theory, and the ideological expression of a definite historical movement'.[25] However, this procedure (and the accompanying caution) is not always observed by Korsch himself. He makes copious quotations from Marx, counterposing these passages to similarly lengthy excerpts from Kautsky in order to show the discrepancies between them.[26]

But when this method was followed by the 'orthodox Marxists' of the Communist Party it led to results Korsch could not accept. For them, Kautsky's materialist conception of history is quite simply the 'ideology of the Second International' which, as the representative of 'international reformism', forms a contrast to the Third International as the chosen representative of 'international revolutionary Marxism'. It is alleged by 'Leninists' that Kautsky's misfortune is that he is continually stumbling over the remnants of Marxist thought. The 'revisionist' Kautsky of today is to be compared to the Kautsky of the 'earlier, revolutionary-Marxist' period.[27] This argument implies that for the Communist Party theoretician of today there may remain much of value in Kautsky's work.[28]

By contrast, Korsch argues for an apparently more 'ideological' view than the simple one that Kautsky simply turned renegade, a view held, for example, in Lenin's 'The Proletarian

'The Materialist Conception of History'   119

Revolution and the Renegade Kautsky'[29] On the other hand, of course, Kautsky's evolution is not merely ideological:

> It is not a change in K.'s theoretical attitude towards Marxism, but only a consequence of external historical facts, that all revolutionary questions were posed more clearly and unavoidably by the heightened class struggles of the period of the war and afterwards, within Marxist theory too ... so that with increasing frequency K. now has to go over from a concealed 'orthodox' revisionism to an ... open and naked surrender of revolutionary Marxism.[30]

This is not to deny that Kautsky did play a certain progressive role: for a certain period his ideology was the only way of making Marxism useful to the masses. Korsch justifies this claim by means of a curious simile. The ideological service performed by Kautskyanism is just like that of the scholiasts (*Glossatoren*) and post-scholiasts of the Middle Ages: under the appearance of a merely orthodox interpretation of the Justinian pandects, they were able to satisfy for a time the juridical requirements of the newly rising bourgeois class.[31] Likewise, Kautsky was temporarily able to assist the working-class struggle while it had not yet developed its own theory.[32] However, the regressive side of Kautskyism will halt the development of the working class towards socialism.[33] The decisive feature of Korsch's interpretation is his location of Kautsky in a certain philosophical context. Kautsky's attacks on other non-Marxist philosophers are misplaced because

> the dominant basic tendency in both bourgeois philosophy, natural and social science of today ... does not start from a metaphysical dualistic or idealistic basis, orientation, but from precisely that 'materialistic natural-scientific' outlook for which K. too enters the lists.[34]

This is rather a difficult argument to deal with. What criterion could be employed to settle the question of whether idealism or mechanical materialism is the dominant intellectual tendency in a particular period? It is difficult to know how to evaluate such general and speculative statements. Empirical tests of any kind—however broadly conceived—would seem to be out of place. But perhaps what is more important is to establish the logical validity of these approaches. It is rather surprising that with his philosophical bent Korsch did not do this, for ultimately it would have been more rewarding, rather than making speculations (for this is all such statements can be) about which of these ideologies is dominant.

What was of value in the philosophical work of Kautsky and Lenin? They had performed a valuable service in refuting obscurantism, religious mysticism and idealism, by applying the materialist method. Lenin himself had urged that the periodical *Unter dem Banner des Marxismus* should contain refutations of religious thought, if necessary relying on eighteenth-century atheists and Enlightenment thinkers.[35] Engels had said that, if the French workers, unlike the Germans were not already atheist,

> nothing could be simpler than to ensure that the magnificent French materialist literature of the last century is widely distributed among the workers, that literature, in which the French mind has made its greatest achievements in form and content which—taking into consideration the state of science at that time—in its content today continues to be highly rated—its form has never been attained again.[36]

But Korsch's main objection is that Kautsky's 'materialist critique' is not carried through consistently. Paradoxically, this means that Kautsky is led to take up an idealist, Kantian position on philosophy.[37] The argument for this position is rather complicated. On the one hand, Kautsky supports the eighteenth-century materialists in their attack on mysticism and religion. Yet when it comes to the task he sets himself, that of bringing Marxism into line with the latest developments in science, Kautsky feels the need to supplement a materialist approach to the question with an idealist philosophy. The philosophy he chooses for this task is not that of Hegel, but Kant. Kautsky explains that the Kantian criticism ' "really could become the starting point for a higher form of materialism" '.[38] It is not easy to interpret Kautsky's position here. In his earlier period Kautsky had been one of the staunchest opponents of the neo-Kantianism which gained wide acceptance in Marxist circles, especially among the 'Austro-Marxists' Max Adler and Otto Bauer in particular. Kautsky's *Ethik und materialistische Geschichtsauffassung* had criticised their position very sharply.³⁹ Korsch claims that this tendency to neo-Kantianism was already present in a concealed form even in Kautsky's earlier critique of Kant, but his argument in support of this point is neither extended nor convincing.⁴⁰ It seems unfortunate that he does not explore this dualism between neo-Kantianism and mechanical, naturalistic materialism any further, because he would have been able to apply this criticism to some of the leading communist thinkers such as Bukharin,⁴¹ which would have given his argument a more general application.

Instead, Korsch argues at some length that Kautsky's actual knowledge of the natural sciences since Marx's time is insufficient for the task he had set himself: 'But even ... simply from the standpoint of modern bourgeois science ... his [Kautsky's] completely negative relationship to all its results and to the spirit of modern scientific investigation [reveals itself]'.⁴² He also points out that mathematics are, with the exception of some 'excessively naïve remarks', missing from Kautsky's book.⁴³ But surely the extent of Kautsky's scientific knowledge is a secondary problem: the important philosophical question is the validity of Kautsky's programme of 'revising' Marxism in the light of modern developments in natural science. Perhaps this is an early indication of Korsch's dissatisfaction with philosophy. From this period onwards he showed an increasing interest in mathematics and the natural sciences.

What is new in *The Materialist Conception of History* is the clear implication that 'Leninism' is not an adequate form of Marxism for the development of the revolutionary class struggle. If the final verdict on Kautskyanism is that it is

> the specific phenomenal form of this dialectical transformation of 'Marxist' theory accepted by the modern workers' movement as an ideology, from a form of development into a fetter on the revolutionary proletarian class struggle⁴⁴

and if Kautskyanism was ambiguous from the start, this ambiguity being shared by 'Leninism' too, then clearly 'Leninism' must also be suspect. He makes this point clear in a footnote when speaking of the 'fundamental theoretical affinity between the Leninist and the Kautskyan varieties of the so-called "Marxist centre" '.⁴⁵ Although Korsch may have shown that Lenin and Kautsky shared similar general ideological positions, formally considered, during the period of the second International, what is the relevance of this to the Marxist movement ten years after the foundation of the Third International? Whatever their previous similarities, from the outbreak of the First World War Lenin began a decisive struggle *against* Kautsky. Kautsky's ideas were of crucial danger to the Marxist movement at a specific period only, as Lukács pointed out:

> It is this diversionary strategy: *this deliberate attempt to prevent a clear and correct split* between revolutionaries and reformists in the workers' party, or—when a split has already become inevitable—the engineering of a *false split*—it is this which constitutes the historic omission of Karl Kautsky as the theoretical leader of the Centrists in the Second International.[46]

Thus although Korsch clearly showed that Kautsky had gone over from concealed to open revisionism, he failed to realise that at the same time Kautsky lost any significance for the revolutionary movement. As a concealed revisionist, Kautsky posed a danger to sections of the working class, which did not realise that, despite Kautsky's Marxist phraseology, in fundamental terms he did not differ from the open anti-Marxist reformists. In the period 1914–19, Lenin recognised this danger for the revolutionary movement and consistently polemicised against this view, on the grounds that

> the danger of Kautskyism lies in the fact that . . . it endeavours to reconcile the proletariat with the 'bourgeois labour party', to preserve the unity of the proletariat with the party and thereby enhances the latter's prestige. The masses no longer follow the avowed social-chauvinists . . . The Kautskyites' masked defence of the social-chauvinists is much more dangerous.[47]

It is because Korsch's book was directed against a thinker who no longer had any contemporary relevance for the Marxist movement that it is so unsatisfactory. Despite the correctness of many of the arguments, *The Materialist Conception of History* is a disappointment by comparison with *Marxism and Philosophy*. As we have shown above, Kautsky's work was of little political significance; nor did it require any great theoretical insight on Korsch's part to

'The Materialist Conception of History'

demolish as he did the book's theoretical pretensions. Finally, it represents a transition stage in which Korsch's repudiation of 'Leninism' is not yet completed.

To find a more extensive statement of his new ideas on 'Leninism' it will be more profitable to turn to Korsch's *Anti-Critique*, although it will be necessary to continue to refer to *The Materialist Conception of History* on some points. A substantial part of the *Anti-Critique* merely repeats arguments put forward in *Marxism and Philosophy*, and consists in refuting misconceptions of his earlier position. As such the most relevant of these counter-objections have already been examined, so that in this chapter only the new positions on 'Leninism' will be considered.

Almost from the start he states much more forcibly than he had in *The Materialist Conception of History* what is to be the new position: that Lenin in fact never renounced the Second International's version of Marxism; so that

> the real division on all major and decisive questions is between the old Marxist orthodoxy of Kautsky allied to the new Russian or 'Leninist' orthodoxy on the one side, and all critical and progressive theoretical tendencies in the proletarian movement today on the other side.[48]

He now states more explicitly than he had done in *Marxism and Philosophy* the purpose of that work: 'the ... general problem of the Marxist conception of *ideology* or of the relationship between *consciousness* and *being*'.[49] He claims that there was complete solidarity on theoretical questions between the new communist Marxist orthodoxy and that of the old social-democrats. Behind communist complaints that Korsch had presented too schematised a picture of the Second International:

> [there is] a dogmatic attempt to defend the 'Marxism of the Second International', whose spiritual legacy Lenin and his companions never abandoned, in spite of some things they said in the heat of battle.[50]

In *The Materialist Conception of History*, Korsch distinguishes between ideology and theory in the following manner. The bourgeois conception of science is ideological in that it opposes theoretical and scientific knowledge as an independent entity to historical practice; whereas the new scientific principle of the dialectical materialism of Marx and Engels is that all scientific theory is only the product of the historical movement itself. As Marx had said, the theoretical propositions of the communists 'merely express, in general terms, actual relations springing from an existing class struggle'.[51]

Lenin and Kautsky failed to make this distinction, so that in their hands Marxism became an ideology. In a famous passage discussing how the proletariat acquires a socialist consciousness, Kautsky had written:

> Socialist consciousness is therefore something that is brought into proletarian struggle from the outside and not something that grew naturally from within it.[52]

In *What is to be done?* Lenin had quoted this passage in full, and added the equally famous comment:

> The history of all countries shows that the working class, exclusively by its own effort, is able to develop only trade union consciousness.[53]

What was the philosophical character of 'Leninism'? In the first place,

> Lenin is not primarily concerned with the *theoretical problem* of whether the materialist philosophy he propounds is true or untrue. He is concerned with the *practical question* of its use for the revolutionary struggle of the proletariat.[54]

Lenin was particularly concerned that philosophical questions should not become objects of factional strife, and thus hinder the work of the Party. 'Machism' should be a private matter; the tactical differences between Bolsheviks and Mensheviks would be unnecessarily sharpened if the independent question of Marxism's epistemological compatibility with Spinoza and Holbach, or with Mach and Avenarius, were brought into the argument.[55]

Thus it seemed that Lenin was very unsympathetic to the whole problem of Marxism and philosophy—the necessity for Marxists to have a positive position on philosophy. As Korsch points out,

'The Materialist Conception of History'   125

this is the same as the Lassallean standpoint of considering that the practical political party can transcend philosophy through practice, without comprehending it theoretically—*Marxism and Philosophy* had effectively refuted this position.[56]

But there is a paradox here. Why then had Lenin, the practical politician, placed such great importance on writing *Materialism and Empirio-Criticism*? It occupied nearly a year of his time, required a special trip to London, and was regarded by him as an important task.[57] As an 'orthodox Marxist' Korsch had suggested that this paradox could be explained by referring to Lenin's skill as a tactician. In explaining Lenin's phrase about the 'historical service' performed by the Second International, he uses the same argument, but in neither case does it really explain anything.[58]

Let us continue with Korsch's analysis of Lenin's philosophy. Just as Kautsky did in his *Die materialistische Geschichtsauffassung*, Lenin thought that the dominant tendencies in bourgeois philosophy were idealism and mysticism, so that it was necessary

> to stress *materialism* against certain fashionable tendencies in bourgeois philosophy, rather than to stress *dialectics* against the vulgar, pre-dialectical and in some cases explicitly un-dialectical and anti-dialectical materialism of bourgeois science.[59]

In short, in the term 'dialectical materialism' Lenin puts the accent on materialism. While repeating his contention that the main trend in bourgeois philosophy, natural and social science is not idealism but contemplative materialism, Korsch supports Lenin's defence of bourgeois materialism against the recurrence of 'spiritualist' tendencies.[60] The problem is that Lenin gets no further than this:

> Lenin . . . goes back to the absolute polarities of 'thought' and 'being', 'Spirit' and 'matter', which had formed the basis of the philosophical and even some of the religious, disputes that had divided the two currents of the Enlightenment in the seventeenth and eighteenth centuries.[61]

Before assessing this criticism of Lenin, let us follow Korsch's argument about Lenin's philosophy to its conclusion. Apparently the Hegelian period of Lenin's philosophical writings (1914–16) which had directly inspired Korsch's own *Marxism and Philosophy*, would surely refute the idea that Lenin was always a mechanical materialist. Even after the publication of Lenin's *Philosophical Notebooks*, in which Lenin's later debt to Hegel is quite clear, Korsch clung to the view that

> A belated revival of the whole of the formerly disowned *idealistic dialectics* of Hegel served to reconcile the acceptance by the Leninists of old bourgeois materialism with the formal demands of an apparently anti-bourgeois and proletarian revolutionary tendency.[62]

What was Lenin's conception of the transition from the idealist dialectic of Hegel to the dialectical materialism of Marx and Engels? It was simply conceived of as a materialist 'transposition' (*Umstülpung*), at best consisting simply of a terminological change, in which the absolute is in the Marxist system to be named 'material' and not 'spirit'.

This concludes the strictly philosophical argument. How adequate is his evaluation of Lenin as a philosopher? There can be no doubt that until he read Hegel, Lenin's ideas did contain elements of vulgar materialism. As Korsch was to point out later, Lenin had declared in an early article (1894), 'What Marx and Engels called the dialectical method ... is nothing else than the scientific method in sociology'.[63] The positions taken in *Materialism and Empirio-Criticism* are often as philosophically sophisticated as Dr Johnson's refutation of Berkeley's solipsism. For example, Lenin glories in being a 'naïve realist':

> The 'naive realism' of any healthy person who has not been an inmate of a lunatic asylum or a pupil of the idealist philosophers consists in the view that things ... exist *independently* of our sensation ... Materialism deliberately makes the 'naive' belief of mankind the foundation of its theory of knowledge.[64]

For two of his main arguments Lenin relied on the authority of Engels, in particular the later works such as *Ludwig Feuerbach* and *Anti-Dühring*.[65] The first argument concerns the relation between ideas and reality. Engels constantly speaks in his works of things and their mental pictures or images ... and it is obvious that these mental images arise exclusively from sensations.[66]

The second concerns the refutation of the Kantian 'thing-in-itself' which in *Ludwig Feuerbach* Engels said would be the result of 'praxis, namely, experiment and industry'.[67] Thus two of Korsch's objections so far advanced would also apply to Engels, but he did not pursue this line of argument.

Further, there is a real philosophical problem here. Korsch was unwilling to accept the separation of theory from practice implied in the passive theoretical commentaries of Kautsky. But on the other hand, although he would reject the vulgar pragmatism which Lenin sometimes appears to accept, and which his disciples such as Bukharin frankly acknowledge in such statements as 'When we eat, conduct the class struggle ... none of us ever thinks of doubting the existence of the external world',[68] is Korsch's position more than a refined version of this? His tendencies to voluntarism, and the stress on 'practice', which are a constant feature of his work—do they not approach the position of Engels and even Bukharin?

In any case, the assessment of Lenin's position is not as simple as Korsch claims. Although it is undeniably true that there are elements of vulgar materialism in Lenin's views, it would be mistaken to call his philosophy 'vulgar materialism' *tout court*. For example, even in *Materialism and Empirio-Criticism*, he made formal statements about 'dialectics' which Korsch could hardly have disagreed with. In one passage dealing with Engels' critique of French eighteenth-century materialism—i.e. the very position Korsch ascribes to Lenin—two of its limitations are said to be the anti-dialectical character of that philosophical school, and its tendencies to mechanical materialism.[69] Elsewhere, Lenin explicitly states that 'Marx and Engels laid the emphasis in their works rather on *dialectical* materialism than on dialectical *materialism*, they insisted rather on *historical* materialism than on historical *materialism*'.[70] Korsch could hardly have disagreed with Lenin's emphasis. Outside this strictly philosophical work, Lenin also made impeccable statements about 'dialectics' in his polemical works; for example, at the end of *One Step Forward, Two Steps Back*.[71] If Lenin did on some occasions hold a 'vulgar materialist' position, on others he was perfectly capable of arguing for 'dialectics'.

Korsch's claim that there was a coincidence of views between Lenin and the Marxists of the Second International is much more justifiable. As has already been shown, Korsch was quite right to point out that Lenin drew on Kautsky for his criticism of Bernstein. He might also have pointed out that in Kautsky's *Bernstein und das sozialdemokratische Programm: Eine Antikritik*, Kautsky criticised Bernstein's 'mechanical' materialism and included quite a lengthy section on dialectics. Lenin seemingly agreed with this and simply gave a brief précis of it.[72] So the positions of Lenin and the Second International coincide, as it were, in their ambiguity.

Korsch also quite correctly remarked that their views on socialist consciousness coincided, as revealed by Lenin's lengthy quotation of Kautsky in *What Is To Be Done?* He could have strengthened his case by pointing out that Lenin also agreed with Kautsky over the agrarian question, which was important for Russian Marxists, and that Hilferding's *Finanzkapital* had been of great service in the writing of Lenin's classic, *Imperialism, the Highest Stage of Capitalism*.[73] Seen in this formal sense, Trotsky had even less reputable connections with the Social-Democrat and later war-profiteer, Parvus.[74]

A crucial feature of Korsch's estimate of Lenin's philosophy is his failure to understand it as a process of development. There is no doubt that Lenin's *Philosophical Notebooks* are much more philosophically sophisticated than anything he had previously written. Earlier references in Lenin's works to 'dialectics', while they refute Korsch's rather simplistic view of Lenin as a 'mechanical materialist', do show rather a formal understanding of philosophical questions. Lenin himself admitted at the time of writing *Materialism and Empirio-Criticism* that he was such a beginner in philosophical questions as to feel some hesitation in pronouncing on philosophy.[75] What perhaps complicates the issue of Lenin's 'Hegelianism' as much as anything else is Lenin's own failure to see the differences between the two philosophical periods of his life. Thus he still referred approvingly to Plekhanov and to his own earlier *Materialism and Empirio-Criticism* even *after* writing the *Philosophical Notebooks*.[76] Clearly Korsch's interpretation of Lenin's philosophy, while correct on some points, does not take into account all the complexities of Lenin's position, nor see it as a whole.

'The Materialist Conception of History' 129

How are we to interpret the significance of the *Anti-Critique* in Korsch's own work? After all, up until the mid-1920s he had been a fervent Leninist and now, at the end of the decade, he adopts the opposite position. It is very difficult to make judgements on such a transitional period in his work. But I think that Rusconi's judgement may be accepted:

> Standing on the letter of the writings of 1923–24, K. considers that Lenin rediscovered the true Marxist *praxis*, while in the *Anti-critique* of 1930 he has a diametrically opposed opinion. Besides a change of judgment and a partial self-criticism, it is a matter of correcting an initial ambiguity.[77]

Although during his phase of party-worship and 'orthodox Leninism', there are no reservations in his writings about his new position, we found that in *Labour Law for Factory Councils* Korsch's grasp of the basic ideas of 'Leninism' (the analysis of imperialism) was rather shaky and that in *Marxism and Philosophy* the political conclusions drawn were vague and indefinite. Throughout this period the relation between the organised activity of the party and the spontaneity of the working class had remained unclarified; now Korsch arrived at a much more definite position. He thought that the latter (which he saw as an essential component in the transition to socialism) was incompatible with the former. What his new position is will become clearer when we move on from his new view of Lenin's philosophy to his re-evaluation of Marxism itself. This has two aspects: a new periodisation of Marxism and a re-estimation of Russian Marxism; this new evaluation of Leninism leads to a rejection of the political theories of Marxism.

He now considered that the Marxism represented by Marxism-Leninism was no longer a progressive tendency in the labour movement. In all its historical phases of development Russian Marxism still had an 'ideological' character, and stood in contradiction to the real movement of history. This view was true both for the first period of Marxism in Russia, when it served to reconcile the Russian intelligentsia with the development of capitalism,[78] and for the second phase, which reached its high point with the Russian Revolution of 1905. In this period all revolutionary Russian Marxists declared themselves in complete solidarity with the Second International.⁷⁹ The same ideological character is shown in the third and latest phase in which

> it found its most vivid expression in Lenin's orthodox Marxist theory and his totally unorthodox practice; and it is now caricatured by the glaring contradictions between theory and practice in contemporary present-day 'Soviet Marxism'.⁸⁰

He does not go into more detail about the first phase, since it is not central to his argument; he had already written at some length about the second phase, more important for his argument, in the *Anti-Critique*. It was left to a later article, 'The Marxist Ideology in Russia' (1938) to explain in more detail what he meant by the third phase. In Western Europe, Marxism had developed as a theory *after* the bourgeois revolution had taken place; and it expressed a tendency to go beyond the goals of that revolutionary movement, to champion those of the new proletarian movement. In Russia, Marxism was from the beginning merely an ideological form assumed by the material struggle for carrying through the capitalist development of industry in a pre-capitalist country. It remained the ideology of industrialisation.⁸¹

Korsch continued to maintain, therefore, that the USSR was a new form of capitalism, a new way of carrying on the industrialisation of a backward country. Although in *Um die Tariffähigkeit* he had remarked on the similarities of Mussolini's Italy and the USSR in their repression of the trade union movement, he never went so far as to claim that the Soviet Union was itself fascist. To distinguish between the two regimes, he used a traditional Marxist criterion, that of the development of the productive forces. The difference between the Soviet Union and fascist regimes was:

> The fascist transformation [of a country] does not mean an economic revolution, nor a radical explosion of old relations of production and the liberation of new productive powers. This is ... the main difference between Fascism and Bolshevism.⁸²

Thus it can be seen that after 1926 his basic evaluation of the

Soviet Union remained the same—as state capitalism. What changed was the date from which this evaluation was supposed to apply. Initially he had thought that state capitalism began with the New Economic Policy (NEP) in 1921; then he dated its origin from almost immediately after the revolution. It must be said that there was nothing novel in this position, since it had been held by anarchists and even Social-Democratic critics of the Russian Revolution almost immediately after the seizure of power.[83] His new evaluation of the Soviet regime is not very original in itself. It is more significant for understanding Korsch's ideas in this period in that it puts forward a new position on the role of Marxism itself—a position which Korsch had not perhaps worked out fully in his writings on the Soviet Union, but which was made evident elsewhere.

Thus Korsch was coming to question the right of Marxism to dominate the revolutionary movement. In 1928, for example, he argued that 'for us the increasingly more vacuous competitive struggles between the present SPD and the present KPD already belong *historically* to a past period of the workers' movement',[84] which could be seen as an implied rejection of Marxism itself. This was soon to be made explicit at the level of abstract theory, and then concretised in his writings on the Spanish communes in the 1930s.

The first general exposition of his new conception of Marxism is to be found in the essay 'Das Problem Staatseinheit— Föderalismus in der französischen Revolution' (1930). The nub of his criticism was that, when formulating their theory of the 'dictatorship of the proletariat', Marx and Lenin had accepted the political forms of the 'bourgeois revolution'. When they declared the necessity of a new kind of state,

> the essential difference of this new state of the proletarian dictatorship from the bourgeois dictatorship of the Jacobins, according to the Marxist and Leninist conception, lay only in its aims . . . In short, only in its economic and social essence, not at all in any difference in its political form.[85]

During the transformation of capitalism into socialism, the political form of the state is to be modelled after the Jacobin dictatorship. This means that federalism is to be unconditionally rejected, and the unified centralised form of the state preferred.[86]

Even the lesson which Marx and Engels drew from the Paris commune, that the working class could not simply take possession of the old state machine and use it for its own purposes, but must be prepared to smash it, did not alter the fact that the Marxist state would also be centralised.[87] Although in constitutional terms it was a federation of councils, the 'Marxist-Leninist' state in Russia, the first example of the 'dictatorship of the proletariat', was in fact strongly unified and centralised in character.[88]

The rest of the article contains further reflections on federalism and a sympathetic account of Proudhon's position. This historical analysis was continued in a later article, in which he claimed that not only Lenin, but also Marx and Engels had falsified the experience of the Paris Commune. Marxism had had very little impact on the Commune, which took its inspiration from Proudhon, Bakunin and Blanqui. In fact, the Commune had essentially a federalist and not a centralised character.[89]

Korsch was now convinced that Marxism had a limited role to play in the class struggle, not because of any subsequent deformation of Marxism by Lenin or any of his successors, but because of the nature of Marxism itself. He expressed this view more clearly in an article written a few years later, which makes more explicit what is said above:

> Marx from the first to last defined his concept of class in ultimately political terms and in fact though not in words subordinated the multiple activities exerted by the masses in their daily class struggle to the activities exerted on their behalf by their political leaders.[90]

In this way, Marxism was itself transformed into an ideology. For example, in his struggle against social-democratic revisionism, Lenin, like Luxemburg,

> made use of a wholly *ideological platform* in that he sought the guarantee for the 'revolutionary' character of the labour movement not in its actual economic and social class content, but expressly only in the *leadership of this struggle by way of the revolutionary* PARTY *guided by a correct Marxist theory*.[91]

Thus using the distinction between ideology and theory mentioned earlier, Marxism itself can be shown to be an ideology.

Elsewhere Korsch even spoke of its being a myth of the Sorelian kind, to be judged by its usefulness in inspiring revolutionary movements. He disagreed with Sorel, however, in thinking that it was not the fate of all revolutionary theories to become merely inspirational myths.[92]

In summary, Korsch's view was that Marxism was only adequate to that stage of the class struggle at which the working class was fighting for 'bourgeois' demands; it was insufficient, even a hindrance, when it was necessary to advance the independent interests of the proletariat, and when it imposed upon the proletariat given political forms (of party, state, dictatorship) relevant to the bourgeois revolution; whereas,

> The real aim of the proletarian class struggle is not any kind of *state*, however 'democratic', 'communal' or even 'councils-based', but the classless and stateless communist society.[93]

It is perhaps unfortunate that although, during the period of his earlier writings about 'councils', he was writing about a contemporary experience in this period, there was no such movement in Germany, where the working class remained quite apathetic in the face of the growing Nazi threat, and was afterwards crushed. He was not able to test his ideas in the same way, because the only concrete situation in which 'councils' actually existed at this time was in Spain.

The articles Korsch wrote on the Spanish communes and the socialisation of industry in Catalonia do little more than describe the situation and graft on to this description the more abstract analysis which has already been presented.[94] But in doing so, he returns to an earlier theme, and, as it were, closes the circle. In referring to the collectivisation decree of the Catalonian economic council of 24 October 1936, he points out that this legislation was only the acknowledgement after the fact of an already completed change in the organisation of the transport and industrial system. He compares this attitude of the communes to the lengthy deliberations of the Socialisation Commission in Germany in 1918–19.[95] He believed that the organisation of the Spanish communes represented the form of struggle most suited to the goals of the working class. The communes preserved the spontaneous self-directing struggle for liberation which was at the heart of the struggle for the 'councils' in the immediate post-war period; and avoided the dangers of 'state politics', for the 'councils' could all too easily become merely the political instruments of a new kind of state. Korsch thus continues to emphasise the virtues of a spontaneous movement from below.

To sum up on the two main works examined in this chapter, *The Materialist Conception of History* and the *Anti-Critique*. It is not clear why Korsch took such pains over Kautsky's book. Perhaps it was because he considered him to be the most typical representative of 'Second International Marxism'. But since he claims that there is not so much difference between the 'orthodox' pre-war Kautsky, and the post-war 'renegade',[96] why did he not examine work from Kautsky's orthodox period? As G. Lichtheim has pointed out:

> Kautsky's standing as a theoretician must not be judged by this production [i.e. *Die materialistische Geschichtsauffassung*] of his declining years.[97]

Although Korsch's criticism is entirely correct from an 'activist' standpoint, requiring that Marxism provide a scientific basis for revolutionary politics, it does not take us very much further forward from *Marxism and Philosophy*. This is perhaps why very few writers on Korsch have paid any attention to *The Materialist Conception of History*. Those who have, have done so from rather an academic, non-political viewpoint.[98] One exception is L. Ceppa, who implies that Korsch makes a broader criticism of Kautsky than he actually does. He argues that

> For Korsch the *theoretical* inability [of Kautsky] to grasp the problem of epistemological constitution on the basis of social praxis was related to the practical and political inability to historicise—and thus revolutionise—the bourgeois capitalist state.[99]

Thus:

> According to Korsch, the positivistic aspects of Kautskian evolutionary materialism find their counterpart in the *idealist* aspects: the reformist over-emphasis of the bourgeois political state.

This argument is not to be found in Korsch's book, nor is it a construction which can be placed on it without exercising great ingenuity. *The Materialist Conception of History* is important not so much in itself as for the tentative formulation it offers of ideas much more fully developed in the *Anti-Critique*. Considering the narrowly philosophical case first of all, I do not think that Korsch has proved that in *Materialism and Empirio-Criticism* Lenin defended a mechanical version of materialism. This chapter has shown that the question is more complicated than that. When necessary, Lenin could make formally correct statements about the dialectical character of Marxist materialism which Korsch would have been bound to agree with. Although Lenin's *Philosophical Notebooks* had not yet been published, he had made public pronouncements about philosophical questions which were strongly 'Hegelian' and 'dialectical' in character.

In political terms, Korsch's 'ultra-radical' argument that Leninism was merely an ideological form assumed by the bourgeois revolution in an undeveloped country misrepresents and underestimates the force of Lenin's critique of Western Marxists such as Kautsky. Lenin's controversy with Kautsky was determined by specific political considerations—the necessity of exposing to the vanguard of the working class the fact that Kautsky's 'left-wing' opposition to the open reformists in the SPD was in essence quite fraudulent. By contrast, Korsch's analysis of Kautsky's general systematisation of historical materialism was, in fact if not in intention, rather academic in character. In the next chapter we shall see that Korsch was to go beyond his rejection of Lenin's version of Marxism to a more systematic revision of his conception of Marxism itself.

7 Karl Marx

In 1928 Korsch's mandate to the Reichstag expired (he did not stand again) and the *Kommunistische Politik* group dissolved itself. His main work was now to be the organisation of a Marxist study circle whose members were for the most part middle-class intellectuals. The circle he directed in the last few months before Hitler's seizure of power (from November 1932 to February 1933) the 'study circle for critical Marxism', had a study programme significantly entitled 'What is living and what is dead in Marxism'. Four of the eight meetings discussed philosophical questions such as the application of dialectical materialism to the natural and social sciences.[1] The circle held its meetings in an experimental school in Neukölln, Berlin, the 'Karl Marx School', at which Korsch's wife was a teacher.[2] The circle was attended by Lukács,[3] but probably the most well-known figures it influenced were Brecht and Döblin.

Although a former participant in the study circle, W. Rasch, has written, 'Korsch ... became Brecht's real teacher in the sphere of Marxist theory'.[4] Brüggemann has correctly noted that Brecht himself counted a diverse miscellany of people as his 'teachers', such as Sternberg, Tretyakov and Steffin.[5] This is too complex a question to enter into here, and in any case their relationship has been thoroughly examined in the literature.[6] Less well-known is Korsch's influence on Alfred Döblin, author of *Berlin, Alexanderplatz* and other novels which are only now becoming widely known in the English-speaking world. He was one of the most regular participants in the study circle immediately before Hitler's seizure of power.[7]

Hitler's seizure of power meant that any kind of oppositional politics, even of such a minimal type as the study circle which Korsch had been directing, was now a risky affair. Yet he did not flee the country immediately. He may have shared the illusions of many socialists and communists that Hitler's power could not last, but it became increasingly obvious that the apathy of the labour movement which had been an important factor in Hitler's victory still persisted. In fact, Hitler rapidly consolidated his position, which made even survival difficult for opposition groups. Korsch eventually found that it was no longer safe even to sleep in the huts on the workers' allotments where he had been taking refuge. As he was becoming a liability to his friends in Germany, he escaped to London via Denmark.[8]

In exile, he was to be even more isolated from political activity than during his last years in Germany. In his first period of exile he continued to write reviews for the *Zeitschrift für Sozialforschung*, as he had done since 1932. But as far as can be discovered, he never had a very close connection with the so-called 'Frankfurt School'. After 1934, he wrote only one review for their periodical, in 1938.[9] The articles he did write are all reviews of little importance: he did not contribute a full-length article. This is not surprising. A recent writer on the 'Frankfurt School' has stated that its one common characteristic was its relative autonomy from political movements,[10] which would hardly make much appeal to Korsch. At the same time, this lack of political commitment did have a positive side. It meant that Marxism could be applied critically and undogmatically without fear of party control. But, for Korsch, the problems of culture dealt with in this way were lacking in direct political relevance.

At any rate, he had little or no contact, either then or later, with this group.[11] The main political connections he formed were with the group around Anton Pannekoek, the International Communists of Holland, for whose journal he wrote one article;[12] and in America he associated himself with Paul Mattick's 'Councils' group.[13] The positions he supported on more immediate political questions are dealt with in the next chapter.

During the first years of exile, he was occupied with writing *Karl Marx*. This was to be part of a series 'Modern Sociologists', edited by Morris Ginsberg and A. Farquharson, in which studies of Tylor, Pareto, Comte and Veblen had already appeared.[14] This was obviously a more academic task than Korsch had ever undertaken before. For the previous twenty years he had been writing for a specific political audience; now he was being asked to write for a general audience, from a more academic point of view.[15] While he would have welcomed the project of writing a work on the content of Marxism which was still valid for the labour movement, it is doubtful if he would have put it in the form of an intellectual biography of Marx. There is little direct evidence of his views on the book, but apparently he thought of it as a textbook on Marxism, expressing his own interpretation, but not in itself an advance in Marxist research, nor a political statement.[16]

His views on other biographies of Marx are to be found in a review of recent biographical literature on Marx written for, but not published in, the *Zeitschrift für Sozialforschung*. He pointed out that the Soviet Union had performed a great service for the study of Marxism by bringing out uniform editions of the works of Marx and Engels, without which the work of E. H. Carr, Cornu and Mayer would not have been possible. It was no accident, however, that apart from the work of Riazanov, the Soviet Union had made no worthwhile contribution to the biographies of Marx. Korsch criticised E. H. Carr for various textual mistakes; took issue with Cornu for his formal, academic approach, remote from any political involvement; and found most to praise in Mayer's book on Engels, the only study comparable to Mehring's *Karl Marx: The Story of his Life*.[17]

While Korsch's criticism of the works mentioned is, in my opinion, quite valid, these books reflect the low ebb in Marxist theory at this point. It was a most unfavourable moment for rethinking the fundamentals of Marxist theory: the victory of Stalin in the Soviet Union meant the end of scientific analysis of Marx's works. Hitler's conquest of power in Germany meant that infinitely more pressing problems faced the Marxist movement in the West. The re-examination of Marxism in the light of the newly published *Economic and Philosophical Manuscripts* was to be postponed for two decades. At the time Marcuse accurately commented:

> The publication of the *Economic and Philosophical Manuscripts* must become a crucial event in the history of Marxist studies. These manuscripts could put the discussion about the origins and original meaning of historical materialism, and the entire

theory of 'scientific socialists', on a new footing. They also make it possible to pose the question of the actual connections between Marx and Hegel in a more fruitful and promising way'.[18]

Korsch knew of the *Manuscripts*, as he refers to them in *Karl Marx*, but he did not subject them to a rigorous analysis. This is rather disappointing, given that *Marxism and Philosophy* had drawn attention to the Hegelian antecedents of Marx's work, which were more prominent in the *Manuscripts* than in perhaps anything else Marx wrote.

Before analysing *Karl Marx*, it is necessary to resolve a problem of interpretation. Did the academic requirements of the 'Modern Sociologists' series impose a serious constraint? The answer is to be found in the Introduction to Korsch's book itself, which is very explicit about the practical-revolutionary message of Marxism, though admittedly its relevance to contemporary politics is left rather vague:

> Marx's revolutionary theory and practice formed at all times an inseparable whole, and this whole is what is living today of Marx. His real aim, even in this strictly theoretical work, was to co-operate in one way or another in the historical struggle of the modern proletariat.[19]

When the preparatory work for *Karl Marx* is examined, it becomes quite clear that no political points were suppressed. But the finished work is only a fragment of a much longer work envisaged by Korsch, who wanted to deal with a number of questions which simply could not have been compressed into one book. I shall now examine the series of drafts written for *Karl Marx*.

In general, the drafts gradually exclude all explicit criticisms of Marx and, at the expense of commentary on the subsequent development of Marxism, they focus more and more sharply on Marx's own work.[20] The first draft, in a letter dated 28 September 1934 from Korsch to Dr Rumney, the editor of the series, sets out Korsch's ideas for the main outlines of *Karl Marx*. This is perhaps only an exploratory first draft, rather than a definite proposal, for as it stands it covers an enormous range. For example, in the chapter 'Marx's concept of society', the second section is to deal with no less than: 'Kant, Fichte, Schelling, Schleiermacher, Hegel. The left Hegelians (Gans; Strauss, Feuerbach, Ruge; Bruno Bauer; Stirner; Moses Hess; Friedrich Engels)'.[21] In general, the material in this draft would be far too unwieldy for one volume.

The draft also covers subjects which are not dealt with in the finished work. Some of the proposed sections are more ambitious and more controversial in their interpretation of Marx: for example, on Marx's theory of ideology[22] or Marx's theory of social revolution.[23] The latter would have included criticisms of Marx's ideas: for example, in the sub-section 'Jacobinist traditions in Marx and Engels ...', in which Korsch would probably have made accessible to a wider public the ideas he had developed some time previously.[24] There would also have been sections of a more directly philosophical and political nature than anything which appeared in *Karl Marx*. A whole section of the fourth part was to be devoted to method, the most striking section under this heading being the third, a 'comparison of the Marxist method with empiricism, positivism, pragmaticism and with the empirical-axiomatic method of the modern natural sciences'.[25] In the third part, he intended to deal with the problem of reform and revolution, and, more generally, with the relation between economic and political action.[26]

On reflection, he decided that in the finished work he would adopt a less polemical approach, and refrain from criticising Marx.[27] The next series of drafts was written in 1935 while he was staying with Brecht in Denmark. Whereas the first draft was little more than a series of chapter headings, these are more substantive. But they are still condensed, which often makes them difficult to understand. In addition, they frequently deal with problems which he never subsequently wrote about at length, as in, for instance, his 'Theses on economics and politics'.[28] After explaining that Marxist theory and practice are fully materialist, that scientific socialism is directly opposed to utopian socialism, because it is an economic-materialist theory, he states: 'In this economic form consists on one side the advantage, on the other the limit of Marx's "materialist" theory of the development of society'.[29] He goes on to explain that this is not a theoretical limit, which could be overcome by a more sustained process of thought, but it is the result of historical conditions. The economic form of socialist theory developed by Marx is in itself neither

'Karl Marx' 141

positive nor negative, but in the course of history changes from a form of development to a barrier to knowledge; this makes the question of whether the maintenance of the economic form in Marxist theory is false or correct a senseless one.[30] The remaining sections do not make clear what this limitation is, although at one point Korsch does suggest that in some respects (especially in his critique of fetishism), Marx had gone beyond the framework of economic theory.[31] The rest of this draft examines the relations between the 'fetishism of commodities' as explained in *Capital*, and the concept of *Entfremdung*, from Marx's earlier *Economic and Philosophical Manuscripts*, but contains nothing that is not in the final version of *Karl Marx*.[32]

Another (untitled) draft deals with this point in more detail. only new feature it contains is his philosophical definition the kind of economics to be found in *Capital*: 'The normal and typical form of "critique" in *Capital* is neither the first (transcendent) nor the second (immanent), but the third "transcendental" form'.[33] This distinction, however, is used only as a pedagogical device for explaining the varieties of critique (theoretical-internal, practical-external ways of transcending categories) which Marx carried out: it does not lead to a more profound philosophical analysis.

The only other dated draft from this period which I shall remark on here is entitled *Economics, Politics: Social Forms of Consciousness (Ideologies)*.[34] In the main, this is another discussion of fetishism, but there is one interesting passage which shows a clear continuity with the ideas of *Marxism and Philosophy*: the economic concepts of the bourgeois mode of production

> themselves belong to the same bourgeois world, as a real object, as the real bourgeois relations of production, and in their structure, etc., can be determined, influenced, upheld and confirmed by that real [world]: they cannot be destroyed or considerably altered by a merely theoretical critique.[35]

After some difficulties with translation, the text was now ready. Let us turn to the published work.[36]

The first problem I shall consider is that of situating it in the rest of Korsch's writings. As a point of reference, I shall take Rusconi's opinion that

In the monograph on Karl Marx of 1938, Marxism is explicitly treated as a science of society in the sense of rigorous empirical research which does not require any philosophical foundation.[37]

Superficially, there is a striking impression that here Korsch does incline to a more scientistic view of Marxism than is to be found in the earlier, more 'philosophical' *Marxism and Philosophy*. This is especially evident in certain passages, for example when he says that 'Marx's new science is in its form above all a strictly empirical investigation'.[38] Here, Korsch takes a position much more oriented to a 'science of society' than he had done previously.

But the case for this assertion about *Karl Marx* obviously cannot be examined by looking at individual passages or remarks. Instead it is necessary to reconstruct the concepts of science and philosophy, and the relation between them, which inform the book as a whole. The reader will remember that the main thrust of the earlier *Marxism and Philosophy* was that the Second International version of 'orthodox Marxism' regarded Marxism as a descriptive science of society, and not as a guide to revolutionary action. The impulse to revolutionary action was to be found in the earlier philosophical writings of Marx, and to recover this revolutionary impulse it would be necessary to re-examine the philosophical foundations of Marxism to see how the more scientific elements of the later work still served the same end—revolutionary praxis.[39] It is at this basic epistemological level that any connection between *Karl Marx* and *Marxism and Philosophy* must be traced.

Examination of this problem is helped by the restriction of the book's content. It is confined to Marx's work and does not consider in detail any of the subsequent developments in the social sciences, either Marxist or non-Marxist, which have taken place since Marx. Even the original drafts, in which more substantial sections on the developments in Marxist thought were envisaged, contained very little on developments in non-Marxist thought.

What was the reason for this? Korsch might reasonably have argued that lack of space prevented an assessment of post-Marxist developments, but he did not. One contemporary reviewer, in criticising the book, actually mentioned the correct reason:

> Korsch is convinced that during the seventy years since Marx

published the first volume of *Capital*, nothing of basic importance has happened in the science of man ... Generally speaking, Marxism in Korsch's view has nothing to learn from modern sociology.[40]

This is a reasonable comment, because Korsch himself had said that

> In Ricardo's economic system and in Hegel's philosophy, bourgeois society had reached the highest grade [sic] of critical self-consciousness of which it was capable without violating its own principles.[41]

Marx himself had thought that after Ricardo, economics lost all pretensions to being a science and descended to the level of 'vulgar apologetics'.[42] Korsch simply extends this view to all post-Marxian social sciences. He makes the further claim that, while 'bourgeois economics' was becoming increasingly 'apologetic', Marxism was gaining in scientific relevance:

> It was this combination of sustained energy and wide ranging vision that lent to *Capital* the extraordinary vitality by virtue of which it remains entirely 'topical' in the present day. One might even say that in many respects it is only now beginning to come into its own.[43]

While not discussing subsequent developments in non-Marxist thought he does not examine changes in Marxist thought either. As he wrote in the introduction to *Karl Marx:*

> It is the purpose of this book to restate the most important principles and contents of Marx's social science in the light of recent historical events and of the new theoretical needs which have arisen under the impact of those events. In so doing we shall deal throughout with the original ideas of Marx himself rather than with their subsequent developments brought out by the various 'orthodox' and 'revisionist', dogmatic and critical radical and moderate schools of the Marxists on the one hand, and their more or less violent critics and opponents on the other hand.[44]

None the less Korsch does introduce a number of his views on the changes which have taken place in Marxism—albeit in rather a compressed and oblique manner. In particular, Engels is supposed to have made some changes to the original Marxist doctrine.[45]

The first part of this argument is that Engels' early philosophical development was quite different from Marx's. The latter, coming from a free-thinking background, reached materialism via the philosophy of Democritus and Epicurus, the seventeenth- and eighteenth-century materialists, and, finally, through an independent critical evaluation of Hegel; whereas Engels, who had suffered under the pressure of the pietistic hypocrisy of his early family life, came to materialism through religion, Strauss, critique of the gospels, Hegel and Feuerbach.[46]

Clearly this is a correct description of the early development of Marx and Engels, but what influence did this have on their later work? Korsch insists that there is a continuity between Marx's early philosophical writings and *Capital*. But without Marx's guiding hand, did Engels have such a clear grasp of the new materialist position they had developed together? Korsch's position is ambivalent. In one passage which discusses how the critical materialist principle derived by Marx from the determinate historical form of bourgeois society is, in the later development of Marxism, changed into a dogmatic principle applicable to any other historical epoch, he argues that

> Marx . . . does not lay down any general propositions as to the essential nature of all society but merely describes the particular conditions and developmental tendencies inherent in the historical form of contemporary bourgeois society.[47]

The blame for making a general philosophy of society or sociological theory from 'historical materialism' rests only on the 'epigones of Marxism', whom Korsch does not mention by name here.[48] He seems to imply that, while Marx was alive, Engels' formulation of ideas was, if not actually erroneous more easily capable of misinterpretation. After Marx's death, Engels began to reveal more clearly a tendency to *mistaken* formulations:

> in his last period Friedrich Engels no longer adhered on every point to the great scientific advance, the materialist conception

'Karl Marx' 145

of history worked out by him in conjunction with Marx.[49]

This applies particularly to Engels' theory of the reciprocal relations (*Wechselwirkungen*) between 'base' and 'superstructure' which he expounded in a series of letters at the end of his life.[50] In attempting to defend Marxist materialism against the charge of being 'vulgar' or 'one-sided' materialism, he had conceded too much to the revisionists who wanted to blunt the revolutionary impulse of Marxism.[51] Engels' attempts to defend dialectical materialism by discussing 'base' and 'superstructure' in terms of 'primary' and 'secondary' are certainly clumsy and confusing, but Korsch's strictures are surely too severe—or at least are not sufficiently proved.

The other references to post-Marxist developments within the socialist movement are oblique, but quite consistent with positions set out in greater detail elsewhere; for example his estimation of revolutionary anarcho-syndicalism, his critique of politics (Leninism) as leading to totalitarianism, Lenin's rejection of 'left communism'.[52]

Another argument which Korsch uses to support his rather dogmatic, *a priori* rejection of subsequent sociology seems at first sight to be more valid:

> in confronting the general principles of the Marxian theory with bourgeois science we shall not so much refer to the more recent displays of contemporary social thought in which their persisting difference has already been modified to a certain extent by mutual interaction. We shall rather try to bring out the contrast in the pure form in which it originally appeared in classical and post-classical bourgeois writers of the 18th and early 19th centuries on the one hand, and in the writings of Marx and Engels on the other.[53]

But it is only an 'assumption' that Marxism is 'modified' rather than refuted.

Perhaps the most satisfactory way of resolving this problem will be to bring out the differences in 'pure form' between Marxism and 'bourgeois science'. The difficulty is that, just as in *Marxism and Philosophy* his concept of philosophy remained implicit, so here the concept of science is not made explicit. In the earlier work, he had concluded a long footnote on the relation of philosophy to science in Hegel and Engels thus: 'The important question this raises is, of course, what Marx and Engels really mean by the concept of science or positive sciences'.[54] But the question remained unanswered in the earlier work, and the deficiency is not remedied in *Karl Marx*. It is, in my opinion, the central question to discuss.

To do so, I shall compare Korsch's ideas with a positivist conception of science.[55] He refers to Marx's criticisms of Comtean positivism on the opening page of *Karl Marx*, but does not discuss positivism in general at any point. I now aim to show that, although he still apparently rejects positivism, his ideas are in fact ambivalent. It can be said that there are two aspects of positivism: firstly, its conception of the object and methods of the natural sciences; secondly, its conception of the relation between the natural and social sciences. I shall consider each of these in turn.

Positivism considers the object of science to be a 'Nature' held to be rigidly separate from human intervention, a naturalistic 'natural' order. Korsch has the basis for a strong attack on positivism, since he contests its very notion of the object of science. Insisting that natural science does not deal with a 'natural' order,

> Marx started from an altogether different viewpoint [from Hegel] from the outset. Physical nature according to him does not directly enter into history. It does so by indirection [*sic*] i.e., as a process of material production which goes on not only between man and nature, but at the same time between man and man.[56]

This means that Korsch rejects the notion of a 'dialectics of nature'. He was wrongly accused of doing so when he wrote *Marxism and Philosophy*,[57] in which, although he was in general disagreement with the undialectical concept of nature which was to dominate Soviet Marxism, he did not deal with this question.[58] Nor did he discuss the 'dialectics of nature' directly in his critical writings on Lenin's *Materialism and Empirio-Criticism*.[59] By the time *Karl Marx* was written, Soviet Marxism held the dialectic of nature as an article of faith and argued that any deviation must inevitably be in the direction of idealism.[60]

It is perhaps significant that in the above passage, Korsch refers only to Marx and not to Engels. The Soviet arguments for the 'dialectics of nature' (in particular, Stalin's *Dialectical and Historical Materialism*) rely heavily on certain passages in the later Engels.[61] At the time of the earlier controversy, Lukács had sharply criticised Engels:

> But Engels' deepest misunderstanding consists in his belief that the behaviour of industry and scientific experiment constitutes praxis in the dialectical, philosophical sense. In fact, scientific experiment is contemplation at its purest. The experimenter creates an artificial, abstract milieu in order to be able to *observe* undisturbed the untrammeled workings of the laws under examination eliminating all irrational factors both of the subject and the object.[62]

Korsch does not criticise Engels' concept of nature at such a level of abstraction. But in the passage quoted above (p. 146), his ideas clearly differ from these of Engels. Elsewhere, this is even clearer when he draws the logical conclusions of his concept of nature: 'Being "social", nature has a specifically historical character varying in the different epochs. As an historical and social nature it has above all a class character'.[63] He cites examples from Marx to show that the cherry trees growing in front of the philosopher's window are not of 'natural' origin; modern food, and likewise the knife and fork it is eaten with, are not 'natural' products.[64] But these examples only show that Nature is modified by Society, not much more. The real problem is, what is the relation between the laws of nature (e.g. the law of gravity) and the society which has 'discovered' them? Because Korsch avoids this much more complicated question, his arguments against the positivist conception of Nature are valid only to a limited extent. He has not shown that the positivist notion of the object of science is fundamentally incorrect.

What he has to say on the positivist conception of scientific method is more diffuse. But here he implicitly accepts a number of positivist views, For example, in his emphasis on the role of quantification in science. In *Karl Marx*, this appears as an oblique reference. In discussing the relations between 'base' and 'superstructure', he mentions the view that such relations are reciprocal (*Wechselwirkungen*) and that the 'superstructure' can produce reactions (*Rückwirkungen*) in the 'base'. He comments:

As long as there is no sufficiently exact determination of the quantitative amount of action and reaction and of the precise conditions under which at a given time the one or the other will take place, the original statement of the materialistic principle will be in no way clarified or improved by the super-addition of so-called 'interactions' ... It is on the contrary deprived of all precise meaning by that utterly meaningless addition and thus transformed into a scientifically useless phrase.[65]

By implication Marxist science is 'quantitatively adequate' in this sense. In his later work with Lewin on field theory and its application to the social sciences, his position was more explicit:

The new principle formulated by the great Galileo three hundred years ago—measure all that can be measured and make measurable what as yet cannot be measured—is valid not only for physical science in the narrower sense, but just as much for ... the various branches of the social sciences.[66]

Consistently with this, Korsch suggests that the investigation of society will be on a scientific basis when it rests on observation and experiment.[67] This raises the question of causality, which has at least traditionally stood at the centre of debates about 'scientificity'. He suggests that the concept can be modified in the light of new discoveries in science:

Twentieth century natural science is aware that the 'causal' relations occurring in a particular field of knowledge are not to be defined by a general concept of 'law' of causality, but must be determined specifically for each separate sphere.[68]

Perhaps not very much can be read into this. But in one respect he does adopt a position very much closer to positivism. I am referring to his ideas on how a theory and its concepts should be verified, which is what I now wish to discuss.

Korsch insists that Marxism, as a strictly empirical science, has concepts which are

not new dogmatic fetters or pre-established points which must be gone through in a particular order in any 'materialistic' investigation. They are an undogmatic guide for scientific research and revolutionary action. 'The proof of the pudding is in the eating'.⁶⁹

In particular, for example, in arguing that Marx did not accept a naïve pseudo-Darwinist metaphysical concept of evolution, he makes the methodological point that

> From an *a priori* valid axiom, it [development] is reduced to a working hypothesis which must be empirically verified in each case ... Thus the path is made free for a strictly empirical research.⁷⁰

Here, Korsch does seem to accept a crudely dualistic position: *either* metaphysical *a priori* constructions *or* empirically verifiable propositions. This dualism is even rather reminiscent of the cruder formulations of the verification principle.⁷¹

The positivist notion of verification also involves the idea that reality manifests itself immediately in appearances, and that to distinguish between appearance and reality leads to metaphysics. Here, too, Korsch takes a somewhat ambivalent position. In his discussion of fetishism he shows himself perfectly well aware of Marx's way of distinguishing appearance and reality—indeed this is the focal point of his exposition. He thus appears to accept Marx's dictum that 'all science would be superfluous if the outward appearance and the essence of things directly coincided'.⁷² Elsewhere his position is much more positivist. In discussing the material of Marxist economic analysis, he points out that whereas Ricardo begins his system with the general concept of 'value', Marx begins his critical investigation into the theory and reality of present-day bourgeois economics with the analysis of an external object a '.... palpable things ...',⁷³ the commodity. This is quite indisputable; but he then goes on to say:

> Value then in all its denominations, like other economic things or relations such as 'commodity', 'money', 'labour power', 'capital', etc., means to Marx a *socio-historical fact* or something which though not described in physical terms is still empirically given in a strictly verifiable manner.⁷⁴

The commodity may be actual and tangible, but the existence of value and capital, the fundamental categories of Marxist economics, are certainly not 'given in a strictly verifiable manner'.[75] Korsch's remarks indicate a rather confused understanding of the question.

In sum, Korsch's refutation of the positivist notion of the object of science is inadequate; and he shows a tendency to accept a positivist conception of scientific method.

Now consider the second aspect of positivism—the idea that the way forward for the social sciences is by the application of the procedures and methods of the natural sciences. Korsch certainly does not hold the idealist view that there are certain features of human action which make the method of the natural sciences inappropriate to a scientific study of society. What was his position on the relation between natural and social sciences?

He states quite clearly that

> Bourgeois materialism has revolutionised the natural sciences. The proletarian materialism of Marx and Engels proposed from the outset to subject the historical and social world to the same materialistic principle.[76]

This is very evidently a positivist view, and the passage quoted is, from a Marxist standpoint, rather curious in two respects. Firstly, in the Marxist conception, surely it was not 'bourgeois materialism' which itself brought about a revolution in the natural sciences; was it not rather the presence of certain social conditions which was the basis for the rise of both 'bourgeois materialism' and natural science? Secondly, are there not also certain preconditions for the full development of the social sciences—namely a rational, planned, society which has the necessary regularity and consistency for scientific method to be applied to it?[77] I find that here, too, as on other aspects of positivism, Korsch's position is ambivalent. He can state the case against positivism formally: 'positivism could not move with freedom in the new field of social science, but remained tied to the specific concepts and methods of natural science',[78] but in fact his own exposition of Marxism as a science does make a number of assumptions about the nature of science which are definitely positivist in character.

I would now like to analyse his exposition of Marxism as a science. The new materialistic science is said to have three basic principles. The first is that of historical specification:

> Marx comprehends all things social in terms of a definite historical epoch. He criticises all the categories of the bourgeois theorists of society in which that specific character has been effaced.[79]

This principle is not only of theoretical significance:

> The principle of historical specification, besides its theoretical significance as an improved method of sociological analysis and research, becomes of first-rate importance as a polemical weapon in the practical struggle waged against the existing conditions of society.[80]

For example, the first objection of the bourgeoisie against communism is that the communists want to do away with property. Korsch quotes the answer of the *Communist Manifesto*, that the abolition of the previously existing property relations is not a characteristic peculiar to communists. They only wish to abolish a specific form of property, i.e. bourgeois private property in the instruments of production, itself a historical product of a different kind of property-relations, which had been destroyed by capitalism. He shows how Marx deals in a similar manner with bourgeois objections to communism on the questions of personality, freedom, education, the state, law, the family, patriotism, eternal truths, religion and morality.[81]

The second of the 'basic principles' of the Marxist sciences is that Marxism is not positive but critical:

> The description of existing bourgeois conditions as specific conditions of a transitory phase in an historical process assumes a further importance as a theoretical basis for a critical examination of the structure of present society as a particular historical type of socio-economic formation.[82]

In dealing with this, the principle apparently most opposed to positivism, Korsch does not make use of the opportunity to criticise positivism explicitly. He simply shows that bourgeois thought was critical when the bourgeois class was fighting against feudalism, but this critical feature of bourgeois thought disappeared when the victory over feudalism had been achieved. After this point, real progress in social science is to be made not by a further positive development of bourgeois principles, but by a critique of them. Long before this critique was carried out by socialists, it had to a surprising extent been anticipated by the last great representatives of the classical period of political economy (Ricardo) and German idealist philosophy (Hegel). Marx owed, and recognised, a great critical debt to these thinkers who had perceived that bourgeois society is inherently contradictory. His attitude to the historical school was quite different, because its critique was romantic and reactionary.[83]

The third principle is the orientation to practical transformation. The connection with a practical social movement is not a distinguishing feature of Marxism. After all, in its ascendant phase the bourgeois theory of society was in the service of a practical movement. The victory of the bourgeoisie was followed by a transformation of this theory into a supposedly pure science, without presuppositions or value judgements.[84] By analogy, Marxist theory 'is not only a theory of bourgeois society, but at the same time a theory of the proletarian revolution'.[85] The content of the science based on these principles is the materialist critique of political economy, and the 'so-called' materialist conception of history and the class struggle.[86]

Before I examine the principles themselves in more detail, a few basic problems about them need to be stated. Such problems are not really dealt with in the text itself. The first concerns the status of the principles: do they constitute the logical basis of Marxism, or are they merely a pedagogical device for presenting the ideas of Marxism simply? As a convenient classification, they do succeed in putting forward complex ideas in an easily comprehensible form. This is admitted even by those who are otherwise unsympathetic to the book.[87] From a logical point of view, the principles are much less satisfactory. Is the list of principles supposed to be exhaustive and exclusive? Do the three principles derive from or exemplify one basic principle, which is not explicitly stated? Is there any logical ordering among the three?

Perhaps the most fundamental objection concerns the very idea of presenting Marxism as a set of principles, because this implies a new conception of the relation between form and content. One of the strong points of *Marxism and Philosophy* was its insistence that it would be incorrect to separate form from content and to exhibit the formal properties of the Marxist system as distinct from its content. This point does not need to be re-examined here: the best criticism of this new feature of *Karl Marx* can be found in Korsch's own earlier work.[88]

I shall now examine the principles as they stand. It is not necessary to give them equal attention. The principle of practical application has the corollary that the Marxist theory reflects certain aspects of society: 'The materialistic theory of the social revolution of the proletarian class is at the same time a powerful lever in that same social revolution';[89] which is merely a restatement of the notion of the reality of ideology which was already fully discussed in *Marxism and Philosophy*.[90] Nothing new is added here to that discussion.

Whatever its relevance to social science, the principle of 'criticism' is rather obvious as a principle of Marxism. Korsch's analysis of the critical features of the last great thinkers of bourgeois society, Ricardo and Hegel, and of the different kind of 'criticism' to be found in the historical school cannot, I think, be faulted. The only aspect of this principle at which one might cavil is whether the notion of 'critique' (*Kritik*) and the related concept of '*Aufhebung*' (a crucial component of the Hegelian dialectic) is adequately dealt with. In *Karl Marx*, there is an explicit reference to 'critique'. There it is noted that

> Not only Marx and Engels but all revolutionary Hegelians of the '40s and '50s of the last century, had used the word 'critique' in this large historical sense [i.e. as referring not merely to further development, but to total transformation].[91]

In describing the basic Marxist view of the relation between present capitalist society and future socialist society, the notion of *Aufhebung* is clearly implied:

> He [Marx] sees in the modern capitalistic mode of production with its immense unfolding of productive powers far exceeding with all earlier epochs, an indispensable material foundation for that more highly developed form of communal life which will be inaugurated by the social revolution of the working class.[92]

In 'Why I am a Marxist', Korsch tries to use the notion of critique to show that Marxism is neither a 'positive materialistic philosophy' nor a 'positive science':

> From beginning to end it is a theoretical as well as a practical *critique* of existing society ... 'Critique' is to be understood not in a merely idealistic sense but as a materialist critique. It includes from the point of view of the *object* an empirical investigation 'conducted with the precision of a natural science', of all its relations and development, and from the point of view of the *subject* an account of how the impotent wishes, intuitions and demands of individual subjects, develop into an historical effective class power leading to 'revolutionary practice' (Praxis).[93]

But the principle of criticism states such obvious facts of Marxism that it was hardly worth stating as a principle of Marxism. Whatever other distortions Marxism may have suffered at the hands of its interpreters (hostile or otherwise) and critics, no-one has seriously doubted that it is pre-eminently critical of bourgeois society. Even the Marxists of the Second International who showed the greatest tendency to use Marxism as a descriptive science of society did not forget to take a critical stance at the appropriate moments.

The most important principle in terms of the significance Korsch ascribes to it is that of historical specification, and the associated criticism of theories of evolution. This idea appears very early in his Marxist days. In an unpublished review of M.N. Roy's *Indien*, written in 1922, he had drawn attention to the specificity of Marxism:

> It is well known that Marx expressly rejected the idea that one could convert his historical survey of Western Europe into a universal philosophico-historical theory, which could, without any more ado, be valid for other countries.[94]

The principle is also applied to itself in *Marxism and Philosophy*. But it is most prominent in the later work. Korsch explains how Marx shows that concepts such as ground rent and capital have expressed different historical realities at different times, and how the Marxist analysis of economics refers specifically to modern bourgeois production and the productions of commodities in specific production-relationships.[95] He applies this principle quite consistently. In *Marxism and Philosophy*, he had applied it to the periodisation of Marxism itself, but here he carries it through to the very origins of Marxism. The Marxist version of materialism could only arise when material production is socialised, when 'the realm of material production is, formally speaking, completely separated from all other realms of the life of society'.[96]

Korsch dealt with two objections to the concept of historical specification. One is that bourgeois social scientists do investigate other societies, and do accept that the notion of evolution applies to society. Korsch replies that

> Even where bourgeois investigators speak of an historical 'development' of society, they do not step beyond the magic circle of bourgeois society. They consider all the earlier forms as 'preliminary stages' leading up to its present fully developed form.[97]

As opposed to this, Marx argues that the specific kinds of society (Asiatic, antique, feudal and bourgeois) represent not different, but higher or lower forms of social life. The categories of bourgeois society are a key to understanding earlier epochs of the economic formation of society.

The other objection he considers is:

> How does that emphasis on 'specification' which we have shows to be the very foundation of Marx's materialistic criticism and research, conform to the equally fundamental demand for some degree of generalisation which is necessarily bound up with every attempt at a truly scientific statement, and is certainly recognised by Marx.[98]

Which he answers as follows:

> Just as in modern natural science the general law has no independent existence outside the collection of the particular cases covered by its application, so the social law exists only in the historical development through which a particular form of society proceeds from its particular state in the past to its par-

ticular state in the present and from that to the social forms brought about by its further change.[99]

He bases this point on the procedure of modern science, which starts from the analysis of the single stone (in the case of the falling stone and the law of gravity).

What are the merits of this principle? It gives a firm injunction to empirical research into specific cases, which seems to be the best safeguard against the ossification of Marxism into a set of scholastic and dogmatic principles. But it still remains one-sided. Korsch's answer to the objection about generality and abstraction is not really adequate at the level of complexity Marx himself had reached. In the Introduction to the *Contribution to a Critique of Political Economy*, Marx had considered not only the conventional method of abstraction (that of simple ommission), but also his own more complex solution, which involves an intricate set of relations between abstract and concrete.[100]

This is only a criticism of the extent to which Korsch had made use of Marx's ideas. More generally, there are serious problems with the principle. A principle must be specific within limits: but how are these limits known? In other words, what is the basis for the specification? There is a great danger of circularity here: if one says that Marx's analyses are only valid for a specific historical period, i.e. capitalism, then what justifies the claim that this specific period is capitalism? The force of this criticism is that specificity cannot be an independent or primary principle, since it depends on a prior specification of periods. When this has been done, it may form an important component of an analysis, but it cannot be a prior investigating principle. What conception of laws as applied to social science does it give rise to?

Arguing that, in modern natural science, the general law only applies to the whole class of specific cases governed by it, Korsch adds: 'Thus the only genuine laws in social science are the laws of historical change.'[101] The same objection about specificity applies here too, but there are also further problems. This notion may seem more attractive than the static and mechanical conception of laws held by e.g. Bukharin: 'in nature and society there is a *definite* regularity, a fixed natural law'.[102] Gramsci's objection to such a position shows a greatly superior understanding of the issues involved:

Vulgar evolutionism is at the root of sociology, and sociology cannot know the dialectical principle with its passage from quantity to quality ... But this passage disturbs any form of evolution and any law of uniformity understood in a vulgar evolutionist sense.[103]

Korsch's position appears to supply a satisfying solution to the problem of the differences between laws of society and laws of nature, but ultimately it is vacuous. We are not told what the laws of development are, nor how they are to be investigated. Perhaps what is meant as a 'law of development' is to be found in the well-known passages from the Foreword to the *Critique of Political Economy* which Korsch himself quotes:

> At a certain stage of their development, the material productive forces of society come into conflict with the existing relations of production ... From forms of development of the productive forces, these relations turn into their fetters. Then begins an epoch of social revolution.[104]

While his 'specificity' remains without content, it also lacks a further dimension, which is to be found in Engels. Korsch states the principle that there are no naturalistic laws of society:

> There is, from the historical and social principle of Marxian science, no absolute and predetermined limit beyond which an apparently 'naturwüchsige' [original] foundation of all social life might not in future be discovered to be no more than an historical and historically changeable form, and thus a form which can be modified and overthrown by a conscious action.[105]

But Engels argues that the very notion of 'naturalistic' laws of society is rooted in a specific kind of society—capitalism—and is not simply a 'mistaken' idea which must be countered by a 'correct' idea. By contrast, Korsch tends to treat this as merely an ideological mistake. Engels argues thus:

> the production of commodities ... has its peculiar, inherent laws ... They reveal themselves in the only persistent form of social interrelations, i.e. in exchange, and here they affect the

individual producers as compulsory laws of competition. They are, at first unknown to these producers themselves ... They work themselves out, therefore, independently of the producers and in antagonism to them as inexorable natural laws of their particular form of production. The product governs the producers.[106]

In sum, the principle of historical specification may be useful negatively—as a means of criticising false generalisations—but it does not seem to have very much creative power.

This concludes the examination of the individual principles. Before I go on to look at the content of the science to be founded on the principles, one important question still remains. What was Korsch's view of the need for a philosophical foundation for Marxism? In *Marxism and Philosophy*, he had seen philosophy as making an indispensable contribution to the formal side of Marxism. Does his partial acceptance of positivism mean that he also has a positivist hostility to philosophy?

In *Marxism and Philosophy*, he had objected to the 'scientific socialism' of the Second International Marxists and had argued for a re-examination of the philosophical foundations of Marxism. In *Karl Marx*, his position has definitely changed. He does not hold an avowedly positivist position, and therefore simply reject philosophy out of hand. He still maintains that Marx and Engels carried through the critical and revolutionary principle contained in the Hegelian dialectic, and that 'Even more distinctly than in its contents, the critical element inherent in Hegel's philosophy manifests itself in his *method*'.[107] Stating that Marx's materialist science does not need the kind of philosophical foundation provided by the materialism of the eighteenth century, he goes on to say that 'the materialistic science ... embodied in Marx's empirical investigation of society is not only far in advance of all idealistic philosophy but of all philosophical thought whatever'.[108]

In fact, in the whole section on philosophical materialism, he attacks the 'epigones' of Marx, for making 'historical materialism' a general philosophy of history; and criticises the attempt to patch up the materialist theory of Marx with a philosophical system, be it that of Kant, Mach, Spinoza or anyone else. More positively, he states:

'Karl Marx'

The only reason why the materialistic philosophers Marx and Engels, up from a certain point in their development, turned their backs upon philosophy . . . is the fact that they wanted to go one step further and to outbid the materialism of philosophy by a direct materialistic science and practice.[109]

None the less, Marx and Engels always considered it important to combat any non-materialist standpoint, in whatever guise it might appear. Korsch concedes that eighteenth-century materialism was of lasting significance for Marxist theory in as much as it stood for enlightenment and progress, and opposed mysticism and obscurantism.[110] But he criticises Feuerbach's naturalistic materialism on the grounds that it does not allow of a true social-scientific investigation, because it excludes the historical process.[111]

As has already been seen, Korsch conceived of bourgeois materialism as applying to the natural sciences; proletarian materialism extended its methods to the social sciences. The position which is emerging is exactly the same as that so sharply criticised in *The Materialist Conception of History*—i.e. it displaces the accent in 'dialectical materialism' from dialectic to materialism.[112] His new position is much more clearly expressed in his Introduction to the 1932 edition of *Capital*:

The dialectic may be compared with the modern axiomatic method of the mathematical sciences, insofar as this method uses an apparently logical-constructive procedure to deduce from certain principles the results already arrived at through detailed research.[113]

In an unpublished manuscript of the same year, *Dialectics of Everyday Life*, he had even argued that 'basically, the dialectic is something quite simple and everyday'.[114] In *Karl Marx*, he hardly discusses the dialectic at all, nor the significance of the early philosophical phase of Marx's writing. He merely commented on this earlier period: 'this new critical insight [into economics] was couched in a highly philosophical language',[115] and made the connection more explicit:

What Marx here [in *Capital*] terms the *Fetishism of the World of Commodities* is only a scientific expression for the same thing that he had described earlier, in his Hegel-Feuerbach period, as 'human self-alienation'.[116]

In both these passages, he does refer, however, to the *Economic and Philosophical Manuscripts*, published for the first time in 1932, which in their strongly Hegelian character confirmed the more philosophical nature of Marx's preoccupations in his earlier period. It is rather paradoxical that when the material supporting a more philosophical conception of Marxism was not yet available he held a more Hegelian version of Marxism (i.e. in *Marxism and Philosophy*); whereas when such material was available, he virtually ignored its philosophical implications.

The real shift which took place compared to *Marxism and Philosophy* becomes more apparent when what he has to say about Hegel is examined. His ideas on Hegel are anticipated in works written earlier in the 1930s, the 'Theses on Hegel and the Revolution' (1932) and 'Empiricism in Hegelian Philosophy' (1931).[117] In the former, he pushes his practical conception of philosophy to its extreme limits in arguing that 'Hegelian philosophy and its dialectical method cannot be understood except in its connection with revolution',[118] and that Hegel's is the philosophy not of the revolution as a whole, but of the period of restoration. While this concept cannot be discussed extensively here, Korsch takes far too simple a view. As Lukács has convincingly demonstrated in *The Young Hegel*, Hegel's conception of the dialectic in the early theological writings is markedly different from that which appears in the *Philosophy of Right*.[119]

What is Korsch's new estimation of Hegel? In the first place, Hegel is valued for non-philosophical reasons:

> Marx found hidden beneath the idealistic speculative forms of Hegel's Philosophy of Law, History, Aesthetics, Religion, etc. of Logic and History of Philosophy, just that which he had not been able to find anywhere else in the whole of past and contemporary philosophy and science: namely, a methodical starting-point for an empirical investigation of the so-called 'spiritual nature of man'.[120]

Hegel is given a much more 'materialist' reading than is customary. Korsch finds that Hegel gave unexpectedly realistic empirical knowledge of the nature of bourgeois society, which he had derived from the 'enquirers into the nature of social man'—the Scottish and English social thinkers of the seventeenth and eighteenth centuries.[121] He also argues that this was how Marx himself evaluated Hegel:

> He [Marx] adhered in truth, from the very beginning only to the 'natural scientist' of society whom he had discovered beneath the mystifying disguise of the philosophical explorer of the human mind.[122]

Korsch now adopts a new position on the relation of Marx and Hegel—a position which he had earlier rejected. The great difference between them is now said to be that Hegel glorifies the existing institutions of society and argues for moderate progress within the narrow limits of the contemporary Prussian state. Thus he explicitly limited the application of the dialectic to the *past* development of society.[123] Marx, on the other hand, argued that the dialectic should not be limited in this way, and should be applied to the *future*. Korsch now thinks that Marx 'In actual fact ... completely broke with the whole of Hegel's speculative philosophy'.[124]

He takes his criticism to its logical conclusion. He argues that, in the Marxist system, the real historical development of society founded on the unfolding of the forces of production replaces the timeless development of the Hegelian philosophy. The Hegelian 'contradiction' is replaced by the struggle of social classes; dialectical 'negation' by the proletariat; and the 'dialectical synthesis' by the proletarian revolution, and the transition to a higher stage of development of society.[125] In his final summary, however, he does say that the new Marxist materialism offers a new method (and, by implication, not just a new set of results), a *novum organon* for the discovery of scientific truths. Here again his position is somewhat ambiguous. He makes points about form and content similar to those he had made in *Marxism and Philosophy*: 'Until today, the Marxist method is, in its formal side, still not very developed';[126] and in yet more positivist vein continues:

> Its [the Marxist analysis of society's] partly philosophical form has not prevented it from attaining a series of important and, up to the present, valid scientific results.[127]

This surely means a reinterpretation of Hegel. Whereas in *Marxism and Philosophy* Hegel was valued for his dialectical conception of reality, with its emphasis on an active relation to reality (as opposed to a naïve realist standpoint which simply reflects reality passively), here Hegel is valued not as a philosopher of 'dialectics' but as an empirical scientist.

This new view has two aspects. Firstly, there is a much greater stress on the empirical character of Hegel's writings. Despite all 'speculative mystifications', Hegel stands out from his idealist contemporaries, the theorists of the organic state and the historical school. Hegel had grasped the material relation between men and things, but had concealed this under the apparently speculative connection between concepts.[128] It certainly is true that Hegel's works do contain an extraordinary amount of empirical material. This holds for both the more 'concrete' works, such as the *Philosophy of Fine Art*, and the *Philosophy of History*, where the empirical material is more fully presented, and also for the more 'abstract' works such as the *Logic*, which clearly draws on a vast body of empirical knowledge. As Korsch pointed out, perhaps the most direct references to modern society, and the proletariat, are to be found in the *Philosophy of Right*, in which Hegel realistically described how the proletariat lived in dependence and need, was excluded from the advantages of 'bourgeois society' and was continually threatened with falling into degradation.[129]

The second aspect of Korsch's evaluation of Hegel concerns the empirical legacy of Hegel to Marx. He now considered that Marx drew on Hegel not for a method, but for certain empirical concepts. In general terms, in discussing the way in which Marx transcended bourgeois political economy, Korsch states that Marx 'confronts the concepts of economics with those of Hegelian philosophy'.[130] The crucial concept here is that of '*bürgerliche Gesellschaft*' (civil society). Referring to Marx's Preface to *A contribution to the Critique of Political Economy*, Korsch writes:

> We see here the decisive significance which the concept of civil society had gained for the young Marx, who was then just passing from Hegelian idealism to his later materialistic theory.[131]

'Civil society' was a concept taken by Hegel from the earlier seventeenth- and eighteenth-century thinkers—the 'enquirers into the social nature of man' who

> in the preceding centuries, had first set up the new idea of Civil Society as a revolutionary slogan, and had even unearthed, in the new science of political economy, the material foundations of that new and 'civilised' form of society.[132]

In this interpretation of Hegel, there is a remarkable parallel between Korsch and Lukács. While the similarities between the earlier *Marxism and Philosophy* and *History and Class Consciousness* have often been discussed, the connection which also exists at this period has not, as far as I know, been commented upon. In his *The Young Hegel* written in 1938, Lukács gives a similarly 'materialist' reading of Hegel, stressing his dependence on Smith and Ricardo, and the fact that Hegel was the only serious thinker to have busied himself with the problems of the German revolution. He stated that the aim of his study was to demonstrate that

> during one crisis in his [Hegel's] life, at a time when he had become estranged from the ideals of the great contemporary revolution, he found his way out of the labyrinth and back to dialectics with the aid of a compass provided by political economy and in particular the economic condition of England.[133]

Although Korsch and Lukács interpret Hegel in a more 'materialist' fashion than they had done in 1923, the parallel cannot be carried too far. In particular their political views diverged widely; nor at that time did Lukács express such a positivist conception of Marxist science as Korsch held.

This concludes the discussion on the principles put forward in *Karl Marx*, the philosophical basis for the principles (or more correctly the lack thereof), and the kind of science which they were meant to support. By far the largest part of the discussion so far has concerned the 'formal' side of the problem, because this is *Karl Marx's* distinctive feature; that is, its conception of philosophy and science. It now remains to examine the content of the Marxist science as it is there presented.

Korsch argues that Marxism has a twofold content: the materialist conception of history, and political economy. The former has to a large extent been discussed already in connection with the question of philosophy. It will be more useful to discuss the single general statement made in the last chapter of *Karl Marx* which subsumes them both. He states that the most important contributions made by Marx to the investigation of society consist in that he

(1) related all phenomena of the life-process of society to economics; (2) conceived of economics itself as a social science; (3) defined all social phenomena historically.[134]

What does he mean by 'economics'? He argues that Marxism is not economics in the conventional sense at all:

political economy, as distinct from the adulterations of the 'vulgar' economists of the nineteenth century and from the more recent attempts at an entirely new start, originated historically as an integral part of the *new science of civil society*, created by the bourgeoisie in its revolutionary struggle to establish this very society.[135]

He insists that the concepts Marx uses are not economic ones in the narrowest sense, but concern the social relations between men. Thus in Marx's hands political economy becomes the science of social labour (*gesellschaftliche Arbeit*).[136]

With the exception of one chapter (Chapter 7, 'The fetishism of commodities') his exposition of Marx's critique of political economy is unremarkable. Only a brief outline, therefore, will be given here. He begins by establishing the relation between Marxism and classical political economy (Chapters 1–3). In his early period, Marx's critique was still couched in philosophical terms (Chapter 4). The next chapter departs from the main argument to make the rather confusing claim that, during his further study of political economy, Marx laid a greater stress on economic theory itself. Returning to a presentation of the central argument, Korsch confines himself to what Marx had designated as the three fundamentally new elements of *Capital*: the treatment of the general form of surplus value; the twofold nature of the commodity labour-power; wages as an irrational manifestation of some other relation (Chapter 6). Marx was able to make this advance because, unlike bourgeois economists, he regarded the most general category of economics no longer as value or quantity of value, but the form of the commodity itself (Chapter 7).

The brief analysis of the theory of commodity fetishism forms the most original and rewarding chapter in this section. Korsch succeeds in relating this theory internally to the rest of Marx's argument[137] and in showing that commodity fetishism is the basis for the 'self-alienation of humanity'. The following two chapters (8 and 9) explain how, given that commodity fetishism conceals from the producers their mutual social relations, the social organisation of labour is still achieved. The final chapters are by comparison rather uninteresting. Chapter 10 deals rather vaguely with 'Common misunderstandings of the Marxian doctrine of value and surplus-value', without specifying (apart from an incidental reference to Walras and Pareto) who has been prey to such misunderstandings, or what their significance is. The concluding chapter merely repeats the claim that later in life Marx took an increasingly positive attitude towards economic science.

It is in the sense of economics specified above that we must understand Korsch's argument that 'Marx's materialistic social science is not sociology, but economics'.[138] This raises the question of the relation of Marxism to sociology. In fact, Korsch asks this question at the very beginning of his work, perhaps as a token gesture to the fact that his book was appearing in a series on 'Modern Sociology' and insists that

> The science of socialism as formulated by Marx, owed nothing to this 'sociology' of the nineteenth and twentieth centuries, which originated with Comte and was propagated by Mill and Spencer.[139]

The reason for this is that Marxism stands much closer to the problems placed on the order of the day by modern historical development. In fact, Marxism is related not to sociology as it subsequently developed, but to

> another body of social thought which descended from an earlier time when the name of 'sociology' had not yet been invented, but 'society' had already been discovered and recognised along with physical nature as an equally material and important realm of human knowledge and human action.[140]

Korsch's point about the relation between Marxism and its earlier 'sociological' counterparts is valid. But his explanation of the subsequent development of sociology is too simplistic:

> It would be more correct to say that since ... [Comte] bourgeois social thought has been a reaction against the theory and thus also the practice of modern socialism. Up to the present day 'sociologists' have endeavoured to submit to another way of answering the embarrassing questions first raised by the proletarian movement. From this standpoint only is it possible to understand the essential unity of the manifold theoretical and practical tendencies which during the last hundred years have found their expression under the common denomination of Sociology.[41]

Korsch states this point in a little more detail in the Paris manuscript. Quite a few of the most significant figures in the later development of sociology emerged in direct confrontation with the Marxist theory of society. He names from the preceding two generations Tönnies, Stammler, Max Weber, Troeltsch, Scheler and Mannheim.[142] It is perhaps surprising that he does not have more sympathy for the last-mentioned, whose work on ideology was concerned in some respects with questions similar to those dealt with in *Marxism and Philosophy*.[143] Among economists a typical representative of such opposition to Marxism was Werner Sombart, whose career Korsch traced in some detail to prove his point.[144]

But there are two exceptions to Korsch's refusal to consider the ideas of modern (or at least post-Marxist) sociology. He did remark on the fate of one of its founding concepts, namely progressive evolution. Spencer had wished to present the investigation of society in this sense as ' "the study of evolution in its most complex form" '.[145] But in its later development, sociology ridiculed the naïvety of this original bourgeois idea of progress:

> Spencer himself although still adhering to the idea of a general progress involving as its inevitable consequence a higher moral development, formulated at the same time the far more neutral definition of development as 'a progress from a simple to a complex form'.[146]

As capitalist society loses its dynamic, its theoretical reflection assumes completely static forms. Some of the ideas Korsch puts forward here are more philosophically expressed in Gramsci's critique of Bukharin. The latter, it will be remembered, was the prime exponent of a mechanical and rigid materialism. Thus in his *Historical Materialism*, he had aimed to expound a general theory of society:

> Sociology is the most general (abstract) of the social sciences ... history furnishes the material for drawing sociological conclusions ... making sociological generalisations ... sociology in its turn formulates a definite point of view, a means of investigation ... a method for history ... The working class has its own proletarian sociology, known as *historical materialism*.[147]

Gramsci gave a very convincing answer to this conception of sociology as method, at a much more abstract level than Korsch had succeeded in doing:

> Sociology has been an attempt to create a method of historical and political science in a form dependent on a pre-elaborated philosophical system, that of evolutionist positivism, against which sociology reacted, but only partially. It therefore became the philosophy of non-philosophers, an attempt to provide a schematic description and classification of historical and political facts, according to criteria built up on the model of natural science.[148]

In *Karl Marx*, however, Korsch did not discuss Bukharin's work at all. His strictures on founding a 'general' theory of society, 'historical materialism' or sociology were adequately expressed in his principle of specification.

The other exception is mentioned in a draft written in 1935. It relates to the materialist theory of consciousness and ideology which he was not able to examine in *Karl Marx* to the extent that he would have liked. Had he done so he would no doubt have removed the rather confusing impression left by this passage:

> The treatment of the economic concepts in the materialist critique of Marx contains the key to understanding the materialist theory of consciousness, therefore to the Marxist

theory of ideology, or as the same area has recently been called by Marx's imitators, the 'sociology of knowledge' (Mannheim).[149]

These remarks on the conception of sociology in *Karl Marx* conclude my exposition of its argument.

My overall assessment of *Karl Marx* is that it is Korsch's least satisfactory major work. Admittedly Korsch was not given a completely free hand in terms of length (assuming that he would have wanted to write an intellectual biography of Marx, and not an evaluation of Marx's contribution to the socialist movement). I have shown, however, that, despite the restrictions he was working under, he does manage to make quite a number of political points about Marx and his successors, and his analysis of Marxism itself is quite consistent with what he was writing in other less restricted publications. The main value of the book today is still as a model textbook of one crucial aspect of Marxism (political economy) which is also the most difficult. Beyond this point, the interpretation given to Marx's work tends to have a positivist bias. While there is a fairly explicit rejection of the positivist conception of the object of science, there is in fact an implicit acceptance of some features of positivist method (e.g. verificationism). This tendency toward positivism is particularly evident in his attitude towards philosophy.

In denying that Marxism needs to be supported by the kind of materialist philosophy evolved in the seventeenth and eighteenth centuries, he seems to deny that Marxism needs to have any kind of philosophical basis. The contrast with *Marxism and Philosophy* is very striking. The direction he was taking there—towards a re-examination of the epistemological bases of Marxism—is, in my opinion, one that opened up greater possibilities for the creative application of Marxism. The attempt to do so directly, as in *Karl Marx*, without any philosophical prolegomena (instead he rejects philosophy)—leads to the vacuity of the principles of Marxism Korsch proposes.

It cannot be denied that the principles have a certain validity as a way of presenting Marxism, as a useful heuristic device.[150] But the claim that they are *the* principles of Marxism cannot be supported. Indeed, the whole conception of presenting Marxism as a set of principles is rather formalist. It begs many philosophical questions about the status of such principles. The dualism of for-

'*Karl Marx*'

mally valid universal principles—empirically verified concrete application is not satisfactorily resolved even if 'concrete application' is considered to be a principle. The unsatisfactory nature of such a principle does not emerge in *Karl Marx*, where the limitations of space prevented Korsch from being able to show how this principle could be applied to the world situation post-Marx.

Thus there is a marked difference between *Karl Marx* and *Marxism and Philosophy*. The former lacks the philosophical subtlety which distinguished the earlier work, and shows a trend towards a more positivist conception of Marxism as a science. Apparently this would make Korsch's approach more open and less dogmatic, giving greater possibilities for empirical analysis, but, for the reasons indicated, it does not do this.

This is, however, one important continuity between the two works. This is the continued stress on revolutionary praxis. In the opening sections of *Karl Marx*, Korsch writes:

> As a materialistic science of the contemporary development of bourgeois society, Marxian theory is at the same time a practical guide for the proletariat in its struggle to realise proletarian society.[151]

He closes the book with the last of Marx's *Theses on Feuerbach*: 'Philosophers have only *interpreted* the world differently; the important thing, however, is to change it';[152] just as he had closed *Marxism and Philosophy* with another of the theses, of similar import: 'Philosophy cannot be abolished without being realised'.[153]

Karl Marx is Korsch's last extended theoretical statement. Although he was not able to present a full interpretation of Marxism, a reasonably clear picture of the direction he was taking does emerge. In the concluding chapter, I shall follow this development through the much more fragmentary writings of the last period of his life.

8 Beyond Marxism?

The previous chapter ended with the publication of *Karl Marx* in 1938. This was to be Korsch's last major work, although until 1946 he continued to write a certain number of articles each year, but no more books. Thereafter, he published very little, his last article appearing in 1954, seven years before his death. This whole period covers twenty-three years, longer than that between *What is Socialisation?* (1919) and *Karl Marx* (1938), yet to deal with it fully requires a much shorter chapter than any previous one. Why was this period so barren? There are, I feel, two main reasons for this: the difficulties he encountered in emigration, and the lack of an influential Marxist movement during his years in the USA. I shall deal with these factors before examining his writings of this period.

Owing to a combination of circumstances (political intrigue against him by the Communist Party and an incident involving another refugee being contributory factors), he had been unable to get a residence permit for England.[1] In any case, the opportunities in England for the refugee scholars who began to stream out of Germany in 1933 were strictly limited,[2] so that in 1936 Korsch finally decided to move to the United States of America. Conditions for émigrés were not much easier there because in the late 1930s America was suffering from the effects of the Depression. This was still being felt by the colleges and universities, which were forced to make cuts in their expenditure, resulting in unemployment even for American academics. Thus it was estimated that, in 1933, 5000 American PhDs, many of whom would in the normal course of things have gone into academic life, were still unemployed.³

The problem was further complicated by the fact that in the German emigration quite a high proportion belonged to the academic professions.⁴ Further, as Lazarsfeld has pointed out, the foreign intellectual was, by comparison to today, comparatively rare in America in the 1930s.⁵ Up to 1945, Korsch applied for a number of university posts, but did not get a permanent appointment. He held appointments for an occasional semester, and a visiting assistant professorship at an obscure university in the South, but this was all. During the war, he gave occasional lectures on Germany in connection with military training programmes, but this did not lead to a more permanent position.⁶

He also applied to the Guggenheim Foundation for support for a project on the 'Sociology of speech and thought'. This was to develop an idea first put forward in his 'Thesen über Ökonomie und Politik' one of the first drafts for *Karl Marx*, that

> every language, and every successive form of a language is at first a necessary instrument of thought and action: a form for the development of thought which only changes into a restriction on thought in its recorded form, which is inevitable.⁷

He also appeared at two academic congresses—a sociologists' congress in Detroit in 1938, and the Fifth International Congress of the Unity of Science, at Cambridge, Massachusetts, at which he gave a paper on 'Mathematical Constructs in Psychology and Sociology'. He had worked on this paper with his old friend Kurt Lewin.⁸ This, too, was of no avail in getting him a post.

The main lifeline for exiled Marxists or Marxisants was the Institut für Sozialforschung, which had moved to New York City in 1934, to become the International Institute for Social Research. Due to the continued generosity of Hermann Weil, and a timely transfer of its funds, the Institute was relatively well off. But, as I have already noted,⁹ although Korsch had earlier written some articles for its journal, the *Zeitschrift für Sozialforschung*, he and the Institute had little sympathy for each other. Apparently he did participate in some of its seminars, but he was never offered a full membership. As late as the Institute's 1944 unpublished history *Ten Years on Morningside Heights*, Korsch was listed as a 'Fellow', but this seems to have meant little.[10]

Besides being unable to find employment or financial support (although the financial problem was relieved by his wife's finding a job teaching German at a college near Boston),[11] Korsch was further isolated because he seems to have found great difficulties in making the necessary cultural adjustment. Although he did not publish anything about his experiences in the USA, he made some very revealing comments in a letter to Paul Partos in 1939. He had found that America was really quite different from the 'old' Europe in which he had lived, worked and fought. Even after two and a half years, in increasing measure, he said, it

> seems to the European that ... everything is too large, too broad, too incoherent, too difficult to have an overall view of ... so that it is impossible to take a uniform position on it.[12]

He summed up his feelings in a classic, if somewhat Teutonic, verdict of the émigré: 'The indivdual feels that he is tiny, powerless, ignorant, in the face of the breadth, variety and changeability of general existence and events'.[13] Even in 1956, after almost twenty years in his land of exile, he could write of 'my desolation [*Wüste*] in the US'.[14] He seemed to find it difficult to apply to American society the traditional categories derived from the European experience: 'In the European sense, there is neither a state, nor a definite arrangement of society according to interests, classes, or relevant ideas, to be found in America'.[15] This lack of an orientation relates to the second reason for the difficulties in his years in America: that the political scene was very different and confusing for a European, particularly a Marxist.

Although the Depression years were times of widespread unemployment and mass poverty, the American working class seemed to make little positive response. There was not even a reformist socialist party on the lines of the English Labour Party, let alone a large Marxist party such as the SPD or the KPD in Germany. The group Korsch felt closest to was the 'Council Communist' group founded in 1935 by Paul Mattick. As its founder admitted, this could not be regarded as a party—only as a propaganda organisation advocating self-rule by the working class.[16]

Korsch's work with this group was the main political activity he carried out in emigration. What was its character? Mattick later described the politics of the group as follows:

> the group was equally far removed from the traditional Socialist party, the new Communist party and the various 'opposition' parties that these movements brought forth. It rejected the ideologies and organisation concepts of the Second and Third Internationals, as well as those of the stillborn 'Fourth International'. Based on Marxist theory, the group adhered to the principle of working class self-determination through the establishment of workers' councils for the capture of political power and the transformation of the capitalist into a Socialist system of production and distribution.[17]

The attraction this group had for Korsch was obvious. It held to the positions he had already reached before going into exile: on the Jacobinist traits still present in Marxism and Leninism, and the rejection of 'Trotskyism' along with 'Stalinism'. I have examined these positions in a previous chapter, so there is no need to do so here.[18] What I now propose to do is to examine his ideas on the main political question of the day—that of the rise of fascism and the outbreak of the Second World War.

When Korsch was a member of the KPD, he held the orthodox Marxist view that the twentieth century was the imperialist epoch of wars and revolutions.[19] Now, by contrast, he inclined to a more pessimistic view: 'More than any preceding period of recent history and on a much vaster scale, our period is a time not of revolution, but of counter-revolution'.[20] This meant revising his views on the earlier period of his political activity. Thus his attitude to the German revolution of 1918–19 changed radically:

> [The workers' revolution] was in reality nothing but an elementary explosion ... it was a mere accident that this rebellion was experienced by its participants as an attempt at a socialist revolution.[21]

He now thought that the workers' councils were:

> a spontaneous experiment of the German workers in a new form of democracy ... Looking backward, we may say that this was the very last chance for the survival of a genuine

democratic self-government under conditions of a rapidly increasing monopoly and state capitalism in post-war Europe.[22]

Korsch also argued that the formation of the KPD was a mistake. When the USPD accepted the twenty-one conditions for joining the Comintern, it did not listen to the warnings of the 'left communists' on the Liebknecht-Luxemburg tradition who emphasised the spontaneity of rank-and-file mass action as against the supremacy of leadership from above. He even went further, to argue that this leadership was acting on secret orders received from the 'often suspicious agents of unknown superiors'.[23]

Returning to the present the most obvious sign of the counterrevolutionary nature of the epoch was the rise of fascism. Korsch recognised, as he had perhaps been unwilling to recognise immediately after Hitler's seizure of power, a fact that many Marxists still refused to face—that fascism had genuine popular support:

> Although Nazism is neither socialist nor democratic, yet by feeding upon the failures and omissions of the so-called 'system politicians', it enrolled in the long run the support of the majority of the nation, and in both the economic and political fields solved a number of concrete problems that had been neglected or frustrated by the unsocialist attitude of the socialists and the undemocratic behaviour of the democrats.[24]

His own view of fascism was that it was revolutionary in its political form, but evolutionary in its objective social content:

> The transition to a new type of capitalistic society, that could no longer be achieved by the democratic and peaceful means of traditional socialism and trade-unionism, was performed by a counter-revolutionary and antiproletarian yet objectively progressive and ideologically anti-capitalistic and plebeian movement that had learned to apply to its restricted evolutionary aims the unrestricted methods developed during the preceding revolution.[25]

Thus there was a certain room for evolution in capitalist society. In a paradoxical way, this evolutionary process was being carried forward by the fascist counter-revolution:

> a certain part of the tasks that 'normally' would have been fulfilled by a genuinely progressive and revolutionary movement were fulfilled in a distorted but nevertheless realistic manner by the transitory victory of a non-socialist and undemocratic but plebeian and anti-reactionary counter-revolution.[26]

Korsch emphasised that Nazi Germany was still a capitalistic society, but of a new type.[27] In its basic economic aspect, it appeared to represent a transition from the private and anarchic form of competitive capitalism which was the rule in the nineteenth century, to a system of planned and organised monopoly capitalism or state capitalism.[28] This was a historically necessary transition and it would be quite unmaterialistic and unscientific to expect that the historical progression from competitive capitalism to planned economy and state capitalism could be repealed by any power in the world. Even America could not escape this development. Here he rather exaggerates to make his case:

> There is no essential difference between the way the New York Times and Nazi press publish daily 'all the news that's fit to print' ... There is no difference in principle between the eighty-odd voices of capitalist mammoth corporations—which over the American radio recommend to legions of silent listeners the use of Ex-Lax, Camels and Neighbourhood grocerys [sic], along with music, war, base-ball and domestic news and dramatic sketches—and the one suave voice of Mr Goebbels who recommends armaments, race-purity, and the worship of the Fuehrer.[29]

While Korsch argues for the need for an economic analysis of fascism, the nearest he gets to this is contained in the arguments above. A more substantial analysis of the economy of fascist societies never emerges. Admittedly this would be a very difficult task, and he is rightly critical of well-researched investigations into this new and (for a Marxist) puzzling phenomenon, e.g. Franz Neumann's *Behemoth*.[30] Korsch still maintained that although Marxism could offer no political guide to action for the working class because of its basically faulty appreciation of politics, its economic analysis remained sound:

> There is no doubt today less than at any former time in history that the Marxian analysis of the working of the capitalist mode of production and of its historical development is fundamentally correct.[31]

It is interesting to note, in view of the conception of laws of society which he had put forward in *Karl Marx*, but which he had not given instances of, that he claims that his analysis explains the 'law of the fully developed counter-revolution of our time', which is:

> After the complete exhaustion and defeat of the revolutionary forces, the Fascist counter-revolution attempts to fulfil by new revolutionary methods, and in widely different form, those social and political tasks which the so-called reformistic parties and trade unions had promised to achieve but in which they could not succeed in the given historical conditions.[32]

This counter-revolutionary character of the epoch was complemented by similar developments in the 'communist' world. Thus in political terms there is little difference between the Soviet Union and the fascist states. In fact,

> Through the comprehensiveness of its anti-democratic and totalitarian development it has often anticipated the so-called fascist characteristics of the openly counter-revolutionary states of Europe and Asia.[33]

What he was referring to was the fact that in internal Russian politics the punishments given for the smallest deviations from the prescribed patterns of opinion exceeded in violence even the measures used in fascist countries. Russia is also fully involved externally in 'imperialist politics', the game of power politics using international alliances.[34]

His explanation of this similarity depends on the estimation of Marxism itself which he had arrived at as early as 1930. Here he draws the consequences of this position for the analysis of the Soviet Union:

Beyond Marxism?

If the political concepts of Marxism were derived from the great tradition of the bourgeois revolution, if the umbilical cord between Marxism and Jacobinism was never cut, it seems less paradoxical that the revolutionary Marxist state in its present development should reflect that great historical process of decay by which today the leading sections of the bourgeoisie in every country of Europe abandon their previous political ideals.[35]

At the outbreak of the war, then, he was, given the nature of his analysis, understandably very pessimistic about the outcome:

> in the present war, the victory of either party will result in a further gigantic step towards the fascisation of Europe if not of the whole European, American, Asiatic world of tomorrow.[36]

Given that this was the likely outcome, could the working class adopt any political position which would lead it in the direction of socialism? Korsch argued that none of the revolutionary slogans of the First World War could be immediately applied to the present situation, because

> There is no longer a need for the revolutionary workers of 1941 to bring about by their own consistent effort that 'transformation of the capitalist war into a civil war' that was described as the ultimate aim of the working class by the most daring revolutionary slogan of 1914. The present war from its very outset ... has been a veritable civil war on both a European and a world-wide scale.[37]

The reason for this is that the bourgeoisie in all the 'democratic' countries was itself divided into pro- and anti-Hitler factions, unlike the unity of the ruling class which had prevailed during the earlier war. Under such conditions, the slogan 'Down with the imperialist war!' fitted in too perfectly with the tendencies of the bourgeois appeasers and isolationists. The same applied to the slogan 'Defeat of one's own country!', which was a practical policy to which substantial sections of the ruling class in several European countries subscribed, because they preferred the victory of fascism to the loss of their supremacy.[38] After criticising the conduct of the 'democratic' nations, such as Great Britain and the USA, he puts forward his view of the policy necessary for the working class, if it is to defeat Hitler and fascism. This is to be achieved by

> the independent fight of the working class for its most elementary, most narrowly defined, most concrete class aims. Not Great Britain, not 'democracy', but the proletarian class is the world champion in the revolutionary fight of humanity against the scourge of fascism.[39]

This is hardly a very specific political directive to the working class. Indeed it seems questionable whether it would lead to political action in the traditionally revolutionary sense at all—a fight for the 'most narrowly defined, most concrete class aims' would seem to indicate the trade union struggle as the area in which the working class must concentrate its efforts. This perhaps reflects the narrowing opportunities (never very great) for revolutionary politics in the USA.

From this point onwards (1941), Korsch's political activity declined considerably. His main contribution had been to the journal *Living Marxism*. But in the autumn of 1942, in the face of increasing reaction, it was obliged to change its name to the more neutral *New Essays: A Quarterly Devoted to the Study of Modern Society*, and a year later it had ceased publication entirely. During the war Korsch's main activity which had a political bent was his work in connection with military training programmes, which he assisted by giving lectures on German politics.[40]

While he was a regular contributor to *Living Marxism*, his work had focused fairly consistently on the political problems of the day, especially fascism. Now that he no longer had such a focus for his work, it began to grow more diffuse in direction. I shall now examine the various lines of thought which he started but was unable to finish.

In March 1945, his old friend and collaborator Bertolt Brecht wrote to him about his proposed verification of the *Communist Manifesto*. He asked Korsch to loan him a copy of *Kernpunkte der materialistischen Geschichtsauffassung*, so that he might remain on the right lines theoretically. In his reply, Korsch seemed more intent on telling his friend about a lecture he had been invited to give on the economic and social structure of the Soviet Union, to the faculty of the State University of Louisiana, Baton Rouge, only adding incidentally, 'Your [Brecht's] 380 sheets are a masterwork'.[41]

During this period, Korsch's published writings on more abstract questions virtually ceased, with the exception of a review of Vernon Venable's *Human Nature: The Marxian View*.[42] It has already been noted in connection with his work with Lewin on field theory that he was prepared to go much further in the direction of positivism than he was at the time of writing *Karl Marx*, as the following passage shows:

> the historical and sociological approach of Marx and Engels to the phenomena of knowledge has resulted in the accumulation of a vast and as yet (pace Scheler and Mannheim) almost entirely untapped reservoir of pregnant thought that is only waiting for its complete disentanglement from the residue of a now obsolete philosophical language. The first vigorous steps in this direction were already taken by Marx himself, and, in a less penetrating manner, by Engels. Yet this important development was not continued by Marxian scholars of the two subsequent generations. They either ignored and forgot these problems or, if they were aware of them, tended to reverse the whole process by reading Hegelian philosophy back into the scientific and pragmatic theory of Marx.[43]

At the same time, however, he maintained that the early philosophical phase of Marx's writing could not be simply set aside as merely an 'idealist prelude' to their later materialist and socialist theories:

> It is not possible to dissect the development of the Marxian thought into two entirely independent phases. The manifold forms in which the philosophical language of the earlier phase still survives in the later development of the theoretical and practical activities of Marx and Engels must be considered in any attempt at the interpretation of the Marxian theory.[44]

Clearly a book review was an inadequate place for explaining his new views, but unfortunately Korsch never did succeed in doing this at any greater length. For a time he toyed with the idea of rewriting *Karl Marx*. In September 1947, he went to Mexico to visit Brecht. There he was shown a German text of his book.

Although he made a substantial number of corrections, it is difficult to read into these any great change of ideological position. Anyway, in 1947 Brecht took a copy with him to Europe in order to find a publisher for the new version. In April 1948 he reported to Korsch that he had been unsuccessful. By this time, in any case, Korsch's interests had changed and he had decided that he did not want to have it published.

He had now become interested in something quite different—in the developments in colonial countries, the liberation movements which began at the end of the Second World War. His interest in this area of the world was first signalled by his article 'The World Historians: From Turgot to Toynbee' (1942), in which he pointed out:

> how illusory were the dreams of the classical philosophers and historians of the bourgeois epoch who imagined that in some way they were dealing with the Universe when all the time they dealt with an exceedingly small sector of that Universe.[45]

His interest in this question grew after the war. In the European countries there were immense social conflicts. Germany in particular saw the re-emergence of factory councils (*Betriebsräte*) and their eventual absorption under the system of '*Mitbestimmung*' (co-determination).[46] How unfortunate it was that Korsch with his immense wealth of experience from the early 1920s did not comment on this!

Instead, from as early as 1946, he showed greater attention to the colonial situation, in his article 'Independence Comes to the Philippines'.[47] He shows how the Western domination of the colonies has to assume new forms. Independence was now recognised as inevitable and the Western powers were concerned about how to make the colonies 'mature' enough for independence. He warns, however, that this independence

> will . . . be used as a further link in the chain of economic oppression and exploitation. So it appears that the struggle for and against independence, and the various positions which different groups and interests adopt in this struggle, at the moment in fact have a radically altered significance.[48]

The old-style colonial politics of Western imperialism were made obsolete by the great Depression of the 1930s and by the rise of Japan, Hitler and Mussolini. The new style of imperialist politics to be seen in the counter-measures of the expansionist Western countries against the independence movements which arose both during and after the war, had its roots in determinate political and cultural developments.[49] Korsch recommends a concrete materialist investigation of this new imperialism, but only gives one result of his studies here:

> The new form of imperialism depends ... [more] than all previous varieties ... on 'friendly governments', puppets, quislings and all possible kinds of collaborators, including certain kinds of so-called resistance movements.[50]

The remaining fragmentary drafts he wrote on this question in the following eight years testify to his continuing interest, but do not allow an evaluation of any position much more advanced than the one reached in the article above.

It was perhaps the failure of the working-class movement in the West which gave an impetus to the 'Ten Theses on Marxism Today', the final summary of Korsch's position in these years. Before reviewing that work, I would like to mention briefly the events of his final years. It has not been possible to discover very much about the last years before his mental collapse in 1957. One interesting connection one would have liked to know more about is that with Roman Rosdolsky. In 1952 and 1953, Korsch worked with the latter on Marx's *Grundrisse*. This was hardly known at the time, as there were only three or four copies in the West before the appearance of the 1953 Berlin edition. Rosdolsky later completed a brilliant analysis of the *Grundrisse*, but unfortunately we do not know if Korsch played any part in this.[51] The rest of this period is the familiar story of the later years of unfulfilled projects. The most important of these apparently is the *Buch der Abschaffungen*, a rewriting of *Karl Marx*, which has not yet been made available. In 1957, after a period of poor health, Korsch had a final breakdown, and was not able to work again before his death.

The 'Ten Theses on Marxism Today' were the basis of a lecture Korsch gave on his journey to Europe in 1950, among other places at Zürich.[52] In view of the fact that they were unpublished and fragmentary, I think it would be unwise to place too much reliance on them.[53] They are not in any case significantly new in terms of the ideas they state. It would be quite erroneous to hold that they mark Korsch's first break with Marxism. For example, his view that Marxism accepts the political forms of the bourgeois revolution (Theses 6,7);[54] the notion that Leninism is the form in which Marxism is applied to Russia and Asia (Theses 8,9); the need for workers' direct determination of production (Thesis 10), are, as earlier chapters have shown, all ideas which he had begun to formulate in the late 1920s and to expound at greater length in the 1930s. What is most striking is the sharpness with which Marxism is generally attacked. Here I would like to quote at some length, as it is this feature which is novel in the 'Theses':

> 1. It no longer makes sense to ask to what extent the teaching of Marx and Engels is, today, theoretically acceptable and practically applicable.
> 2. Today, all attempts to re-establish the Marxist doctrine as a whole in its original function as a theory of the social revolution of the working class are a reactionary utopia.
> 4. The first step in re-establishing a revolutionary theory and practice consists in breaking with that Marxism which claims to monopolise revolutionary initiative as well as theoretical and practical direction.[55]

Admittedly, this is qualified by the third thesis:

> 3. Though basically ambiguous, there are, however, important aspects of Marxian teaching which in their changing function and applying to different locations have until today retained their effectiveness ... [56]

Such a decisive rejection would seem to call for a new *content* to Korsch's criticism of Marx, but this is not indicated at all here, as all his objections had been voiced previously. He now situates Marx as 'one among the numerous precursors, founders and developers of the socialist movement of the working class'.[57] Of equal importance with Marx are the utopian socialists from Thomas More to the present day; Marx's great competitors Blanqui, Proudhon and Bakunin; and also the further development of Marxism by German revisionism, French syndicalism and Russian Bolshevism.

• • •

Beyond Marxism? 183

Ten Theses is Korsch's last published comment on Marxism. Whereas he himself thought that he had gone beyond Marxism, in my view he had returned to a political position very similar to the one he had held in his pre-Marxist days. His acceptance of the 'correctness' of Marx's economic analyses while rejecting the validity of Marx's concept of politics led him to an essentially eclectic position, in which the syndicalist and 'spontaneist' elements predominated. Let us look more closely at the features of his thought which remained constant throughout his changes of political allegiance.

What remained consistent throughout his active political life was the stress on practice. In his pre-Marxist phase, he had thought that the active will necessary for social change should act at the level of psychology, rather than at that of politics. His position in this period is admirably expressed by Rusconi:

> direct action is considered [by Korsch] primarily as an expression and stimulus of moral and psychological energies indispensable for the creation of a socialist economy. It is a pedagogic, not a political, operation. In these direct actions, we are still a long way from specifying what subjects and what political forms will push the revolution forward.[58]

In his 'Leninist' period as a leading member of the KPD, Korsch seemed to have specified the subjects (the revolutionary party and its subordinate organisations) and the political forms (the revolutionary workers' councils) which would push the revolution forward. The two major works of this period are *Labour Law for Factory Councils* and *Marxism and Philosophy*, in which he attempted to apply the theory of Marx and Lenin, as he understood it, to the problems of law and ideology. I add the qualification 'as he understood it' because it is important to realise that Korsch's understanding of Lenin in particular was seriously at fault. His own conviction that ideology must express the conditions of the existing class struggle is shown to be quite erroneous. During this period, Korsch was associated with the broadest revolutionary working class movement yet seen in Europe, but in itself this did not confer correctness on either his or the KPD's theories. Although contact with such a movement gave his work an immediacy and coherence which it often otherwise lacked, his stress on practice and his failure to understand the nature of ideological struggle persisted despite his undoubtedly sincere adherence to Leninism. Thus we have shown that both *Labour Law for Factory Councils* and *Marxism and Philosophy* aimed to apply Lenin's ideas to contemporary problems facing the revolutionary movement—and that both embodied fundamental errors. The former showed a misunderstanding of Lenin's conception of imperialism as a transitional epoch—it argued that this notion could be applied not only to changes in the economic structure of society but also to its ideological features. In the latter, Korsch argued that, just as Lenin had 'restored' Marx's teaching on the state and applied it creatively, he himself would carry out a similar restoration of Marx's ideas on philosophy. Yet unlike Lenin's work, the end result is rather insubstantial: it provides neither a concrete analysis of specific ideologies nor definite political perspectives based on this analysis.

During such a period, the stress on 'practice' at least meets a response in the situation and activity of the working class. But Korsch applied Lenin's idea that the present (imperialist) epoch was one of 'wars and revolutions' rather too literally. Trotsky, who also accepted Lenin's conception, introduced the necessary qualification:

> A recognition of the fact that the war and October opened an epoch of world revolution does not mean, of course, that at every given moment we have on hand an immediately revolutionary situation ... The epoch of world revolution will have its periods of rise and fall.[59]

This raises the question which Korsch was soon to face, after the defeat of the German revolution in October 1923: What is to happen in non-revolutionary situations? If Marxism is merely the expression of the general conditions of the actually existing class struggle, does it become non-revolutionary when the working class turns away from revolutionary struggle? Korsch's argument is then open to the following objection. For him, Marxism as a theory of revolution derives its truth value not from its representation of total social practice nor from the interests of the proletariat within the total system of capitalist society but from the contingent turns of the organised class struggle. The historical verification of the Marxism theory is then reduced to the im-

Beyond Marxism? 185

mediacy of its contingent practical success. Thus Marx's theory loses its necessary character. It also loses its anticipatory character. Korsch's reconstruction of the development of Marxism does not give sufficient weight to the anticipatory content of Marxism which occurs thanks to its scientific analysis of society, and which enables it to foresee the conditions under which the class struggle will take place, and thus anticipate the forms of the emerging class positions, instead of simply reflecting them after they have formed.

When Korsch applied his criterion of practice consistently outside of a revolutionary movement it led him to reject Lenin and finally Marx as a political guide. This did not become immediately apparent after his expulsion from the KPD. His first major work after this point was his critique of Kautsky's *The Materialist Conception of History*. His main objection to Kautsky was that

[His] conception of history is ... a 'purely scientific theory' which can only be considered 'proletarian' in so far as today it is as a matter of fact recognised only in the circles of the proletariat and its intellectual representatives.[60]

For the most part, this work contains nothing which could not have found a place in *Marxism and Philosophy*. But it contains an anticipation of Korsch's criticism of Leninism which was to be more fully elaborated in the *Anti-Critique* to *Marxism and Philosophy*. There he made a distinction between 'theory'—that is, the expression of the conditions of the actually existing class struggle—and 'ideology', which he applied to Lenin's concept of the party and revolution. He came to the conclusion that Lenin's famous proposition about class consciousness being brought to the working class from the outside by socialist intellectuals indicated that 'Leninism' like 'Kautskyism' was an ideology. It served a different purpose (the development of capitalism and then state capitalism in Russia) but it was an ideology none the less.[61]

Given this view of Marxist theory, there is a certain logic in Korsch's progression from seeing Leninism as an ideological distortion of Marxist theory to seeing Marxism itself as an ideology:

Marx, from the first to the last, defined his concept of class in ultimately political terms, and in fact though not in words, subordinated the multiple activities exerted by the masses in their daily class struggle to the activities exerted on their behalf by their political leaders.[62]

Yet this did not mean a total rejection of Marxism, as was made clear in Korsch's last major work, *Karl Marx*. His view of Marxism is that it does not need *any* philosophical supports (cf. *Marxism and Philosophy*)—indeed, is anti-philosophical; he lays much greater emphasis than in any previous work on the scientific character of Marxism:

> Marx's new socialist and proletarian science which, in a changed historical situation, further developed the revolutionary theory of the classical founders of the doctrine of society, is the genuine social science of our time.[63]

Yet in no sense does Korsch argue that Marxism has *no* practical thrust. For instance, his concluding chapter states that

> Marx ... defined all social phenomena historically and, indeed, as a revolutionary process which results from the development of the material forces of production and is realised by the struggle of the social classes.[64]

Thus in Karl Marx we find an uneasy co-existence between a 'practical' conception of the class struggle, to which Marxism has made great contributions, and a 'theoretical' conception, coloured by positivism, of Marxism as a social science.

The non-revolutionary period which began in the mid-1920s was to continue for the rest of Korsch's life. He himself summed up the dilemma of the revolutionary activist in a non-revolutionary period in an article written in 1946:

> It is useless to discuss the controversial aspects of a theory of society ... when such a discussion does not form part of a real social struggle. There must be various possibilities of action for the party, group or class, which the theory in question can relate to.[65]

The positive side of Korsch's Marxism, which makes it superior to most varieties of 'Western Marxism', is that it attempted to place

Marxism in the service of the revolutionary working class movement; its weakness was that, because it failed to realise the importance of theoretical preparation for the resurgence of such a movement and the necessity for a Leninist party to lead such a movement if it was to be victorious, it was condemned to passivity even at the height of a revolutionary movement, as Korsch's own experience in the German revolution showed. The last word must be left to Lenin:

> Without revolutionary theory there can be no revolutionary movement.[66]

Notes

In the quoted material in the text and within these Notes, except where indicated all the translations are my own.

All emphases are in the original, except where stated; square brackets indicate my interpolation.

References to Korsch's works are given to the most easily available editions (see the Bibliography, pp. 217–28) and the principal works discussed in the text are abbreviated in these Notes as follows:

Was ist Sozialisierung? (*What is Socialisation?*) *WS*. Unless otherwise stated, references are to E. Gerlach (ed.) *Karl Korsch: Schriften zur Sozialisierung* (1969).
Arbeitsrecht für Betriebsräte (*Labour Law for Factory Councils*) *AFB*. Unless otherwise stated, references are to the 1968 edition.
Marxismus und Philosophie (*Marxism and Philosophy*) *MP*. Unless otherwise stated, references are to the English translation by F. Halliday (London, 1970).
Die materialistische Geschichtsauffassung (*The Materialist Conception of History*) *MG*. Unless otherwise stated references are to the 1971 German edition (Frankfurt-am-Main).
Karl Marx KM. References will usually be given to the English text (1938), denoted by (E). The German edition (1967), denoted by (G), will be referred to where it differs significantly from the English edition.

The above criterion applies to the works of Marx, Engels and Lenin, and wherever possible references are to Marx and Engel's *Selected Works in One Volume* (London, 1968) (given as *MESW*), the *Marx-Engels Werke* (East Berlin, 1964–) (given as *MEW*), and to Lenin's *Collected Works* (London: Lawrence & Wishart, 1960–) (given as *CW*).

The International Institute for Social History, Amsterdam, where many of Korsch's manuscripts are to be found, is abbreviated as IISG.

A list of abbreviations used in the Bibliography for periodicals appears on p. 217.

INTRODUCTION

1 See chapter 4 below.
2 See chapter 5 below.
3 Ernst Lohagen, 'Erhöht die Festigkeit und Aktivität der Partei', Pressedienst SED, 30 January 1951:

> [Before 1933] the history of the Communist Party of Germany was filled with bitter struggles against right and 'left' opportunists. In the course of these struggles, not a few 'leaders' were removed from the party, like... Korsch... who all, if they are still alive, serve American imperialism as agents [H. Weber, *Der deutsche Kommunismus*, p. 588].

See also: I. Hildebrandt's entry on Korsch in *Geschichte der deutschen Arbeiterbewegung: Biographisches Lexikon* (East Berlin, 1970), pp. 250–2. For example:

> His further political work [i.e. after expulsion from the KPD] and his activity as a journalist were characterised by anti-communism and hatred for the Soviet Union... Since 1933, he has lived in the USA and shown himself to be a bitter opponent of Marxism-Leninism and the revolutionary movement.

4 See e.g. *Geschichte der deutschen Arbeiterbewegung*: vol. 4, 1924—January 1933 (Berlin, 1966), which does not mention Korsch.
5 Korsch, 'The Present State of the Problem of *Marxism and Philosophy*—An Anticritique', *MP*, p. 89.
6 Perry Anderson, *Considerations on Western Marxism*, p. 48.
7 Ibid., pp. 56, 75.
8 Cf. S. Carillo, '*Eurocommunism*' *and the State* (London, 1977), esp. pp. 7–10.

1 KORSCH'S EARLY YEARS

1 Biographical details are taken from an interview with Hedda Korsch by Fred Halliday, who generously made a complete transcript available. This appears in a shortened version in *New Left Review*, no. 76 (November–December 1972), pp. 34–45. Hereafter, the transcript is referred to as *Interview with HK*. Here, p. 2.
2 Ibid., pp. 2, 3; for an interesting comparison of the social class of revolutionary leaders born at this time, see Perry Anderson, *Considerations on Western Marxism*, p. 7.
3 *Interview with HK*, pp. 4, 5; also M. Buckmiller, 'Zeittafel zu Karl Korsch' in C. Pozzoli (ed.), *Über Karl Korsch*, p. 103.
4 Korsch, *Die Anwendung der Beweislastregeln im Zivilprozess und das qualifizierte Geständnis*, Einleitung, pp. 1–2.
5 *Interview with HK*, p. 8.
6 See Buckmiller, op. cit., pp. 104, 105.
7 W. Hausenstein and A. Kranold, *Der deutsche Student einst und jetzt*, p. 5.
8 See e.g., W. Z. Laqueur, *Young Germany: A History of the German Youth Move-

ment. On p. 117, he refers to Korsch as an example of the way in which some earlier prominent members of the youth movement went in a socialist direction.
9 Hausenstein and Kranold, op. cit., p. 5.
10 *Interview with HK*, p. 5.
11 He became editor in 1909. See Buckmiller, 'Marxismus als Realität', in Pozzoli (ed.), op. cit., p. 23.
12 Editorial (anon.), *Jenaer Hochschulzeitung*, no. 1 (December, 1908), p. 1.
13 Max Weber (Bern), 'Zum Begriff der Sozialpolitik', in V. F. Wagner and F. Marbach (eds), *Wirtschaftstheorie und Wirtschaftspolitik*, pp. 167–76.
14 See R. Bendix, *Max Weber: An Intellectual Portrait*, pp. 14–16.
15 See Bibliography of Korsch's writings, section C, nos. 4, 6, 11.
16 See editorial statement about the need to bring students and workers together, *Jenaer Hochschulzeitung* (25 May 1909), p. 1. Korsch was editor from February 1909.
17 *Interview with HK*, p. 6.
18 Ibid., p. 5.
19 See K. Sontheimer, *Der Tatkreis*, p. 231; E. Diederichs, *Aus meinem Leben*, pp. 38–64, discusses his activity in Jena. Also I. Deak, *Weimar Germany's Left-wing Intellectuals*, p. 286.
20 See Bibliography of Korsch's writings, section C, nos. 23, 32, 38.
21 It was: E. Schuster, *Die bürgerliche Rechtspflege in England*. Part of this appeared in Korsch, 'Beiträge zur Kenntnis und zum Verständnis des englischen Rechts', *Zeitschrift für Internationales Recht* (1914), pp. 273–301. See also *Interview with HK*, p. 8.
22 A. M. McBriar, *Fabian Socialism and English Politics, 1884–1918*, p. 166. The Nursery was founded in 1906 (p. 182).
23 Engels to Kautsky, 4 September 1892. In *Marx-Engels on Britain, MEW*, vol. 38, pp. 446–8. See also Engels to Sorge, 18 January 1893, *MEW*, vol. 39, pp. 7–10.
24 Bo Gustaffson, *Marxismus und Revisionismus. Eduard Bernsteins Kritik des Marxismus und ihren ideengeschichtlichen Voraussetzungen*, p. 180. See also chapter 4, 'Bernstein und die Fabier', pp. 127–80. Also P. Gay, *The Dilemma of Democratic Socialism* pp. 93–9, for a similar view.
25 A. M. McBriar, op. cit., p. 6.
26 Korsch, 'Die Fabian Society', *Die Tat* (1912–13), pp. 426–7.
27 Letter to J. A. Dawson, Southern Advocate of Workers' Councils, July-August 1948. In E. Gerlach and J. Seifert (eds), *Karl Korsch, Politische Texte*, p. 388.
28 Korsch, 'Die Fabian Society', p. 423.
29 Ibid., p. 426.
30 Ibid., p. 426.
31 See below, pp. 22ff.
32 Korsch, 'Die Fabian Society', p. 424.
33 Korsch, 'Die Freiheit in England', *Die Tat* (1913), p. 670.
34 Korsch, 'Die Fabian Society', p. 426.
35 Fabian Tract no. 70, 'Report on Fabian Policy', p. 5.
36 Korsch, 'Die Freiheit in England', p. 668.
37 Korsch, 'Die Technik der öffentlichen Debatte in England', *Die Tat* (1913),

pp. 714, 716.
38 Korsch, 'Vom englischen Zeitungswesen', *Die Tat* (1913), p. 462.
39 Ibid., p. 465
40 Korsch, 'Die Fabian Society', p. 426.
41 Korsch, 'Das Examen als politisches Problem', *Die Tat* (1913), p. 771.
42 Korsch, 'Rassenhygiene und Volksgesundheit', *Die Tat* (1913), p. 760.
43 Fabian Society, *Committee of Inquiry on the Control of Industry*, memorandum by Mrs Webb, p. 1.
44 Ibid., p. 3. See this passage in Korsch, 'Die sozialistische Formel für die Organisation der Volkswirtschaft', *Die Tat* (1912), p. 508.
45 Fabian Society, *Committee of Inquiry on the Control of Industry*, pp. 4-5.
46 See Fabian Tract no. 150, *State Purchase of Railways;* Fabian Tract no. 171, *The Nationalisation of the Mines and Minerals Bill*.
47 Korsch, 'Die sozialistische Formel für die Organisation der Volkswirtschaft, pp. 507-9.
48 Korsch, 'Grundsätzliches über Sozialisierung', in E. Gerlach (ed.), *Schriften zur Sozialisierung*, p. 74.
49 Korsch, 'Die sozialistische Formel...', p. 507.
50 Ibid., p. 507.
51 Ibid., p. 509.
52 E. Gerlach, 'Die Entwicklung des Marxismus von der revolutionären Philosophie zur wissenschaftlichen Theorie proletärischen Handelns bei Karl Korsch', Introduction to *MP* (Frankfurt-am-Main, 1966), p. 9, takes this view. Buckmiller, *Marxismus als Realität*, pp. 29 ff., quite rightly disputes it.
53 Korsch, 'Die sozialistische Formel...', p. 508.
54 Fabian Society, *Committee of Inquiry on the Control of Industry*, p. 3.
55 Letter to Union Leage (sic), IISG MS. (1950 or 1951).

2 *WHAT IS SOCIALISATION?*

1 *Interview with HK*, pp. 9-11.
2 See e.g. P. Broué, *La révolution en Allemagne, 1917-23*, pp. 188 ff.
3 Korsch, *Revolutionäre Friedensbedingungen*, IISG MS (1919), pp. 1-2.
4 See G. Ritter and S. Miller (eds), *Die deutsche Revolution—Dokumente*, pp. 248-99, 'Die Berufungsurkunde vom 4-2-1919'.
5 Ibid., 'Erklärung der Sozialisierungskommission über ihren Arbeitsplan, 11 Dezember 1918'.
6 See 'Robert Wilbrandts *Sozialismus*', *Die Tat* (1920), pp. 782-7; 'Praktischer Sozialismus', *Die Tat* (1920), pp. 735-41; R. Wilbrandt, *Sozialismus*, pp. 184, 311, where he refers approvingly to Korsch.
7 Korsch was scientific assistant to Robert Wilbrandt; see *Verhandlungen der Sozialisierungskommission über den Kohlenbergbau im Winter 1918-19* (Berlin, 1921), p. 77. He was present on 6, 7 and 9 January, but is not reported as having spoken. Without quoting any sources, Halliday claims that Korsch was a member of the Commission: see F. Halliday, Introduction to *MP* (London, 1970), p. 8.
8 F. L. Carsten, *Revolution in Central Europe, 1918-19*, pp. 154, 165.
9 'Tätigkeitsbericht der Sozialisierungskommission von 7 January 1919', Ritter

192 Notes to pp. 19–21

and Miller (eds), op. cit., pp. 239–40.
10 In a statement of resignation, it complained that it had expected better provision of information and assistance; see 'Rücktrittserklärung der Sozialisierungskommission von 7 January 1919—Schreiben an die Reichsregierung vom 3 February 1919', in ibid., p. 247.
11 In H. Müller-Franken, *Die Novemberrevolution* (Berlin, 1931), p. 210.
12 Korsch, *WS*, p. 37.
13 *WS* is reprinted in E. Gerlach (ed.), *Karl Korsch: Schriften zur Sozialisierung*, and all references here are to this edition.
14 The others in this series of 'Sozialpolitische Schriftenreihe' are: (2) G. B. Shaw, *Der Sozialismus und die geistig Begabten* (Berlin, 1919), translated by Hedda Korsch; (3) M. Luserke, *Warum arbeitet der Mensch?* (Hanover, n.d. [?1919]); (4) K. Lewin, *Die Sozialisierung des Taylor-Systems* (Berlin, n.d. [?1920]).
15 Advertisement for *Freies Deutschland*, 1 Jg., Hft. 4 (Hanover, 1919), inner cover.
16 This argument is based on the textual evidence of *WS*. It has secondary confirmation in, e.g., Korsch's pencilled note on the LSE library copy of *WS*: 'To Sidney Webb Esq. In sincere respect from the author'. Buckmiller, 'Marxismus als Realität' in Pozzoli (ed.), op. cit., p. 35, footnote 50, claims that in April 1919 Korsch called for the foundation of a Fabian Society, but goes not give any evidence for this. Halliday's unsupported statement that Korsch had joined the USPD in 1917 is definitely false: see Halliday's introduction to *MP*, p. 8. In his preface to *Der Sozialismus und die geistig Begabten* (see note 14 above), Korsch wrote that the Fabian Tracts are '... the unsurpassed model for political tracts ... inexhaustible sources of economic and cultural knowledge'. (1 April 1919, p. 7).
17 Korsch, *WS*, p. 22.
18 Ibid., p. 22.
19 Ibid., p. 22.
20 Korsch, 'Praktischer Sozialismus', in *Kommentare zur deutschen 'Revolution' und ihrer Niederlage*, p. 33.
21 Korsch, *WS*, p. 15.
22 Ibid., pp. 15, 23.
23 For example, ibid., p. 33; 'Die Sozialisierungsfrage vor und nach der Revolution', ibid., p. 50.
24 Korsch, 'Grundsätzliches über Sozialisierung', ibid., p. 69. He is referring to E. Dühring, *Kursus der Philosophie* (Leipzig, 1875), p. 7. Korsch does not mention the famous passage in *Capital*:

> The transformation of scattered private property ... into capitalist private property is ... a process incomparably more protracted, violent and difficult than the transformation of capitalistic private property resting on socialised production into socialised property [Marx, *Capital*, vol. 1 (Dona Torr edition, London, 1938), p. 789]. *MEW*, vol. 23, p. 790, speaks of '*Vergesellschaftung der Arbeit*'.

25 Korsch, 'Grundsätzliches über Sozialisierung', *Schriften zur Sozialisierung*, pp. 77–82.

Notes to pp. 21–8 193

26 Ibid., p. 69. footnote 1; no reference is given. Cf. Fabian Tract no. 70, p. 4: '... the socialisation of industry'.
27 Ibid., p. 34 makes it clear that *Kommunalisierung* is merely a form of *Verstaatlichung*.
28 'Die Sozialisierungsfrage vor und nach der Revolution'. *Der Arbeiterrat* (1919), p. 14, makes this point more explicitly than does *WS*; cf. *Schriften zur Sozialisierung* pp. 51, 52.
29 *WS*., pp. 25, 26.
30 Ibid., p. 20.
31 Ibid., p. 38.
32 Ibid., p. 52.
33 Ibid., p. 58.
34 Ibid., p. 38.
35 Ibid., p. 50.
36 Ibid., pp. 50–1.
37 Ibid., p. 72.
38 R. Seidel, *The Trade Union Movement of Germany*, p. 35.
39 *WS*, p. 25.
40 In *Schriften zur Sozialisierung*, p. 55.
41 *WS*, p. 23.
42 Ibid., p. 23. Kautsky's proposals were put forward in: *Richtlinien für ein sozialistisches Aktionsprogramm*.
43 *WS*, p. 34.
44 Ibid., p. 35.
45 Ibid., p. 41.
46 Ibid., p. 42.
47 See Fabian Tract no. 51, *Socialism: True and False*, pp. 12–16.
48 *WS*, pp. 15, 18.
49 Ibid., p. 26.
50 Ibid., pp. 15–21.
51 E.g. Gerlach, in his introduction to *Schriften zur Sozialisierung*, pp. 6, 11; Buckmiller, 'Marxismus als Realität', in Pozzoli (ed.), op. cit., p. 33.
52 *Schriften zur Sozialisierung*, p. 72; cf. also p. 84.
53 Ibid., p. 70; see also p. 87, where he refers to the 'petit-bourgeois' nature of the majority SPD, and to the conflict between its reform programme and genuine Marxist socialism.
54 Ibid., pp. 78, 79. He is referring to the idea that capitalism prepares the way for socialism not only negatively but also positively.
55 Ibid., p. 51.
56 Korsch, 'Praktischer Sozialismus', in *Kommentare zur deutschen 'Revolution' und ihrer Niederlage*, p. 21.
57 Ibid., p. 21.
58 Korsch, *Schriften zur Sozialisierung*, p. 70.
59 W. Greiling, *Marxismus und Sozialisierungstheorie*, pp. 53–4.
60 Korsch, 'Praktischer Sozialismus', p. 20.
61 Korsch, 'Die Sozialisierungsfrage vor und nach der Revolution', *Schriften zur Sozialisierung*, p. 54.
62 Korsch, *Schriften zur Sozialisierung*, pp. 80–1; cf. his article 'Die Verwaltung der Produktion durch die Arbeiter in Sowjetrussland', *Neue Zeitung* (29

Notes to pp. 29–35

January and 1 February 1920) described the work of the Russian councils.
63 Korsch, *Schriften zur Sozialisierung*, p. 70.
64 V. Lenin, 'The Question of Co-operative Societies at the International Socialist Congress in Copenhagen', *CW* (London, 1963), vol. 16, p. 280.
65 Korsch, *Schriften zur Sozialisierung*, pp. 77, 78. For 'war socialism' see G. D. Feldman, *Army, Industry and Labour in Germany, 1914–18*, p. 115 ff.
66 Gerlach, introduction to *Schriften zur Sozialisierung*, p. 9, footnote 6.
67 *Critique of the Gotha Programme*, Section 4, *MESW*, p. 327; *MEW*, vol. 19, p. 28.
68 See above, pp. 21 ff.
69 Korsch, *Schriften zur Sozialisierung*, p. 51.
70 Ibid., p. 52.
71 C. B. Burdick and R. H. Lutz, *The Political Institutions of the German Revolution*, pp. 213–15 (Ebert's speech).
72 See above, p. 30.
73 *WS*, pp. 80, 81.
74 Lenin, 'Our Programme', *CW*, vol. 4, pp. 210–14, especially p. 211.
75 Lenin, *State and Revolution*, *CW*, vol. 25, pp. 385–497.
76 This is well described in E. H. Carr, *A History of Soviet Russia, The Bolshevik Revolution 1917–23*, vol. 2, pp. 64–80.
77 E.g. Korsch, 'Stinnes Kostgänger Staat: Eine kritische Würdigung der Goldkreditvorschläge der Industrie', *Neue Zeitung* (19 September 1921).
78 For the USPD's view, see E. Praeger, *Geschichte der USPD.*, pp. 182, 183.
79 Adler, *Demokratie und Rätesystem*, p. 65.
80 O. Bauer, *Der Weg zum Sozialismus*, especially pp. 9 ff; cf. also *Schriften zur Sozialisierung*, Appendix 2, 'Aus einem Aufruf der deutschösterreichischen Sozialdemokratie', pp. 45–8. In ibid., p. 79, Korsch claims that this was written by Bauer, but I have not been able to verify this.
81 Bauer, op. cit., p. 10.
82 E. Preobrazhensky, *The New Economics*, pp. 150–53.
83 A. Gramsci, *Selections from the Prison Notebooks*, p. 245 ff.
84 Korsch, *Schriften zur Sozialisierung*, p. 29.
85 Ibid., pp. 55 and 57 respectively.

At any early time (before 1914) I was particularly attracted by the Syndicalist tendency within the workers' movement in France, Italy, Spain, England, Australia and the USA (as well as by de Leone's [sic] principal writings). This line led me into the revolutionary 'Councils' Movement during and after World War I, and at a later time, into contacts with the then existing Syndicalist and Anarchist groups in various European countries [Letter to Union Leage (sic), IISG MS. (1950 or 1951)].

87 Korsch, *Schriften zur Sozialisierung*, pp. 79–80.
88 Ibid., p. 79.
89 G. D. H. Cole, *A History of Socialist Thought*, vol. 4, part 1, pp. 452, 453.
90 G. D. H. Cole, *Guild Socialism Re-stated*, p. 27.
91 Ibid., pp. 46–7.
92 Ibid., pp. 48, 137.
93 Ibid., p. 180.
94 Fabian Tract no. 192, G. D. H. Cole, *Guild Socialism*, p. 4.

95 G. D. H. Cole, *A History of Socialist Thought*, vol. 3, part 1, p. 246.
96 Korsch, *Schriften zur Sozialisierung*, p. 74.
97 Ibid., p. 72:

> during the period of the... 'Second International', the majority of the leaders of revolutionary socialism sought to establish the 'scientific' character of Marxist theory in such a way that they rejected any concern about the clarification of... how the socialist demand 'socialisation of the means of production' could be realised in practice, as a relapse into pre-Marxist ideology and utopianism.

3 LABOUR LAW FOR FACTORY COUNCILS

1 Korsch, 'Wandlungen des Problems der politischen Arbeiterräte in Deutschland', *Neue Zeitung* (7 March 1921).
2 Ibid.
3 Votes in Reichstag elections:

USPD	2,315,000	4,895,000
SPD	11,466,000	5,614,000
	(19 January 1919)	(6 June 1920)

Sources: Braunthal, *History of the International*, vol. 2, pp. 213, 214. USPD membership: 300,000 (March 1919); 800,000 (June 1920); also Broué, *La révolution en Allemagne*, p. 323: Broué, p. 291, discusses the sociological basis of the voting.
4 M. Buckmiller, 'Zeittafel zu Korsch – Leben und Werk' in C. Pozzoli (ed.), *Über Karl Korsch*; p. 103, gives the date as June 1919, without, however, substantiating this. But it is unlikely that it would be much before this: see p. 19.
5 In the June 1920 election, the KPD received only 441,000 votes, according to Braunthal, op. cit., p. 213. On 1 October 1919 there were 106,000 members; in July 1920, 66,000 members. See H. Weber, *Die Wandlung des deutschen Kommunismus*, vol. 1, pp. 363–4.
6 144,000 to 91,000 votes. Korsch appears as delegate 253 (Kersch) from Jena: see *Protokoll über die Verhandlungen des ausserördentlichen Parteitags in Halle*, p. 286. Korsch had stood for election to this conference on the basis of unconditional acceptance of the conditions for joining the Third International: see *Neue Zeitung*, 5 October 1920.
7 M. Buckmiller, op. cit., says that Korsch entered the KPD in December (p. 103). There is no record of his having attended the USPD-KPD unity conference on 3 December 1920. See list of delegates, pp. 273–6 of *Bericht über die Verhandlungen des Vereinigungsparteitages der USPD (Linke) und der KPD (Spartakusbund)* (Berlin, 1921).
8 A. Eberlein, *Die Presse der Arbeiterklasse und der sozialen Bewegung*, p. 1987, gives it as the newspaper for the KPD, Thüringia.
9 See above, p. 19.
10 C. W. Guillebaud, *The Works Council*, p. 4.

11 S. W. Halperin, *Germany Tried Democracy*, p. 163. The paragraphs following (2–4) provided for a complicated structure of *Bezirksarbeiterräte* (district workers' councils) and *Reichsarbeiterräte* (workers' councils of the Reich) to realise the aim of this plan. This is explained and diagrammatically presented in Korsch, *AFB*, pp. 115–16.
12 Cited in Korsch, *AFB* (Berlin and Leipzig, 1922), p. 1, as Anlage.
13 The official criticism of the March Action by the Comintern and the new line are to be found in 'Speech on Comrade Radek's report on "Tactics of the Comintern"'. (Third Congress), in L. Trotsky *The First Five Years of the Comintern*, vol. 1, pp. 269–82. As far as I can ascertain, Korsch did not comment on the March Action at the time. Much later he wrote:

[The March Action] was the first of a long series of events in which the elite of the most valiant and the most devoted workers was sacrificed for an insane enterprise that was not based on a spontaneous movement from below nor on a critical condition of the existing economic and political system ['Revolution for What? A Critical comment on Jan Valtin's *Out of the Night*', *Living Marxism* (1941), pp. 27–8].

14 The Comintern had defined its attitude on this question, even before the March Action. Cf. a 1920 resolution:

wherever industrial organisation ... such as the shop stewards, the factory councils ... are formed with the aim of fighting the counter-revolutionary tendencies of the trade union bureaucracy, the communists will naturally support them with all their energy ['Le Mouvement syndical, les comités de fabriques et d'usines', Second Comintern Congress, in *Thèses, manifestes et résolutions adoptés par les premiers quatre congrès de l'Internationale Communiste 1919–23*, p. 55].

15 Out of over 900 delegates, only 100–150 voted for the left resolution. See Max Schippel, 'Betriebsrätekongress (Deutschland)', *Sozialistische Monatshefte* (1921), p. 39.
16 Broué, op. cit., p. 587.
17 Korsch, 'Die Betriebsrätebewegung im Reich', *Neue Zeitung* (21 September 1922).
18 See below, pp. 73 ff.
19 Korsch, *Quintessenz des Marxismus*, Vorwort (pages unnumbered).
20 See below, pp. 43 ff.
21 *Quintessenz des Marxismus*, parts 2–5.
22 Ibid., p. 1.
23 Cf. the review of *Quintessenz des Marxismus* by H. Duncker, *Die Internationale* (1922),
24 *Quintessenz des Marxismus*, p. 4.
25 Buckmiller, op. cit., p. 42.
26 His professional lecture was entitled, 'Ius belli ac pacis im Arbeitsrecht' (Antrittsvorlesung, Mai 1924).
27 Korsch, reviews of E. Paschukanis, *Allgemeine Rechtslehre und Marxismus*, and K. Renner, *Die Rechtsinstitute des Privatrechts und ihre soziale Funktion*, Grünberg-

Notes to pp. 43–52

Archiv (1930), pp. 301–10.
28 Ibid., p. 303.
29 Korsch, *Quintessenz des Marxismus*, p. 6.
30 Ibid., p. 6.
31 K. Marx, *Critique of the Gotha Programme, MESW*, p. 320; *MEW*, vol. 19, p. 21.
32 K. Marx, 'Preface to *A Contribution to the Critique of Political Economy*', *MESW*, p. 181; *MEW*, vol. 13, p. 8.
33 See F. Engels, *Ludwig Feuerbach and the end of Classical Philosophy, MESW*, pp. 612, 613; *MEW*, vol. 21, pp. 301, 302.
34 Marx, 'Class Struggles in France', in *Surveys from Exile, Political Writings*, vol. 2 (Harmondsworth: Penguin, 1973), pp. 69–70; *MEW*, vol. 7, p. 42.
35 See e.g. the review by H. Dersch, *Archiv für Sozialwissenschaft* (1924), pp. 505–16.
36 *AFB*, p. 141, footnote 3.
37 Ibid., p. 141, footnote 2.
38 Ibid., p. 139.
39 Ibid., p. 197.
40 Ibid., p. 108.
41 Ibid., p. 59.
42 Ibid., p. 60.
43 Ibid., pp. 59–61.
44 Ibid., p. 125.
45 Ibid., pp. 125–6.
46 *AFB* (1922 edn.), p. 184.
47 *AFB*, p. 117.
48 Ibid., p. 110.
49 Ibid., p. 26.
50 Ibid., pp. 32, 33.
51 Lenin, *Imperialism, the Highest Stage of Capitalism, CW*, vol. 22, pp. 187–304.
52 Ibid., p. 205.
53 V. Lenin, *The Junius Pamphlet, CW*, vol. 22, pp. 309–10.
54 G. Lukács, *Lenin*, p. 11.
55 Korsch, *MP* (London, 1970), p. 48.
56 Korsch, *AFB*, p. 129.
57 Ibid., p. 141.
58 Korsch, 'König Kapital und seine Hofnarren' *Neue Zeitung* (7 October 1922). At this period, Stinnes was one of the most powerful German capitalists, with vast monopoly interests.
59 *AFB*, p. 36.
60 Ibid., p. 36. This is a question on which he later changed his opinions radically, when he considered the political methods of the bourgeois and proletarian revolutions to be essentially quite different. See pp. 131 ff. below.
61 Ibid., p. 38.
62 Ibid., pp. 37–9.
63 Ibid., p. 39.
64 Ibid., p. 40.
65 Ibid., p. 40.
66 Ibid., p. 43.
67 Ibid., p. 49.

68 Ibid., pp. 55–7.
69 Ibid., pp. 15 ff.
70 Ibid., pp. 46–7; 86–8.
71 Ibid., p. 47; pp. 89–107.
72 Ibid., p. 26.
73 Ibid., pp. 51 ff.
74 Ibid., p. 149.
75 Korsch, 'Ius belli ac pacis im Arbeitsrecht', pp. 6–7.
76 Ibid., p. 9.
77 *AFB*, p. 50.
78 Ibid., pp. 46–8.
79 Ibid., p. 49.
80 Ibid., pp. 55–6.
81 Ibid., p. 57.
82 Ibid., p. 131 ff.
83 Ibid., p. 28.
84 Ibid., p. 29.
85 K. Marx, *Capital*, ed. Dona Torr (London: Allen & Unwin, 1957), pp. 511–12. *MEW*, vol. 23, p. 526.
86 *AFB*, p. 36.
87 Ibid., p. 34.
88 Ibid., p. 36.
89 Ibid., pp. 29, 33.
90 *Protokoll der Verhandlungen des elften Kongresses der Gewerkschaften Deutschlands* (Leipzig and Berlin, 1922), p. 421.
91 S. and B. Webb, *Industrial Democracy*, p. 84.
92 O. Bauer, *Der Weg zum Sozialismus*, p. 19.
93 Cf. L. Goldmann's attempt to demonstrate the 'social' character of literature in the imperialist epoch in his *Human Science and Philosophy*, p. 67.
94 *AFB*, p. 150.
95 Ibid., p. 135.
96 Ibid., pp. 110–14.
97 Ibid., p. 139.
98 Bibliography of Korsch's writings, section C, nos. 69, 73.

4 MARXISM AND PHILOSOPHY

1 Unless otherwise stated, quotations from Korsch, *MP*, are from the English translation by F. Halliday (London, 1970). See the Bibliography, p. 218, for details of the first edition and the other translations of the work.
2 Korsch, *MP*, p. 42.
3 Ibid., p. 39.
4 Ibid., p. 39.
5 See Chapter 6 below.
6 *MP*, p. 29.
7 Ibid., p. 31. In his otherwise rather non-committal review, Marcuse praises *MP* for its historical account of Marxist conceptions of philosophy; see 'Das

Problem der geschichtlichen Wirklichkeit', *Die Gesellschaft* (1931), p. 350
8 *MP*, p. 37.
9 Ibid., p. 42.
10 Ibid., p. 41; my emphasis.
11 Ibid., p. 45.
12 Ibid., p. 48.
13 Ibid., pp. 50–1.
14 Ibid., pp. 51–8. Cf. R. Hilferding, *Das Finanzkapital*, p. viii. Quoted in *MP*, pp. 54–5.
15 *MP*, p. 58.
16 Ibid., pp. 58–61.
17 Ibid., p. 63.
18 Ibid., p. 66. He added: 'this will be studied further in a later work'. But he was not to return to this point until his views had changed substantially (see pp. 162 ff.).
19 Ibid., pp. 68–9.
20 Ibid., pp. 75–9.
21 Ibid., p. 84.
22 Ibid., p. 29.
23 *AFB*, p. 33.
24 Ibid. p. 76.
25 See above, pp. 48 ff.
26 *MP*, p. 63.
27 Ibid., p. 63.
28 Ibid., p. 61.
29 Ibid., p. 50.
30 Ibid., p. 29. See V. Lenin, 'On the Significance of Militant Materialism', *CW*, vol. 33, p. 233.
31 '... first published in *Lenin Miscellanies IX and XII* in 1929–30', Preface to vol. 38, *CW*, p. 13.
32 V. Lenin, 'Conspectus of Hegel's Science of Logic', *CW*, vol. 38, p. 180.
33 V. Lenin, 'Once Again on the Trade Unions.' *CW*, vol. 32, pp. 70–107; 'On the significance of militant materialism', *CW*, vol. 33, pp. 227–36.
34 See I. Meszaros, *Lukács' Concept of Dialectic*, pp. 159–60.
35 M. Jay, *The Dialectical Imagination*, pp. 5, 10. Weil's monograph was *Sozialisierung: Versuch einer begrifflichen Grundlegung (Nebst einer Kritik der Sozialisierungspläne)* (Berlin-Fichtenau, 1921).
36 See below, pp. 90 ff.
37 *MP*, p. 48.
38 A. Gramsci, *Selections from the Prison Notebooks*, p. 238.
39 See, e.g., L. Trotsky, *Lessons of October*, p. 94.
40 *MP*, p. 63.
41 Ibid., p. 73.
42 Ibid., p. 74.
43 Korsch, *Kernpunkte der materialistischen Geschichtsauffassung*, p. 9.
44 G. Rusconi, *La teoria critica della società*, p. 111.
45 G. Lukács, *History and Class Consciousness*, p. 27.
46 Korsch, *Kernpunkte* ..., p. 9.
47 Ibid., p. 53.

48 Ibid., p. 72.
49 Marx, *MESW*, p. 181; *MEW*, vol. 13, p. 8.
50 Korsch, *15 Thesen über wissenschaftlichen Sozialismus*, IISG MS. (1923), p. 2.
51 *MP*, p. 83.
52 This was to be more of a problem in connection with his later critique of the Lenin of *Materialism and Empirio-Criticism*; see pp. 124 ff.
53 *MP*, pp. 84–5.
54 Korsch, *Kernpunkte* . . ., p. 17.
55 Korsch, 'The Marxism of the First International', *MP*, p. 153.
56 Ibid. p. 153.
57 Kautsky, 'Review of *Marxism and Philosophy*', *Die Gesellschaft* (1924), p. 312. This point is repeated by S. Marck. 'Neukritizistische und neuhegelsche Auffassung der marxistischen Dialektik', *Die Gesellschaft* (1924), p. 576.
58 Kautsky, op. cit., pp. 312, 313.
59 L. Althusser, *For Marx*. The epistemological 'coupure' in Marx's writings is discussed on pp. 33–8.
60 Korsch, *MP*, p. 54.
61 Korsch, *Kernpunkte* . . ., p. 10.
62 Ibid., p. 10.
63 Ibid., p. 8.
64 'The economists explain to us how production is carried on in the . . . given conditions; but they do not explain how these conditions are themselves produced: i.e. the historical movement which calls them to life [K. Marx, *The Poverty of Philosophy*, chapter 2, 'First Observation' (Moscow, 1973), p. 91; *MEW*, vol. 4, p. 126.
65 Korsch, *MP*, p. 54.
66 Korsch, 'Über materialistische Dialektik', in *MP* (Frankfurt-am-Main, 1966), p. 172.
67 Korsch, *MP*, p. 54.
68 Ibid., p. 57.
69 N. Bukharin, *Theory of Historical Materialism*, p. xv.
70 See below, pp. 144 ff.
71 Korsch, *AFB*, p. 28.
72 Ibid., p. 29.
73 Bukharin, op. cit., p. 143.
74 Korsch, *Kernpunkte* . . ., p. 22.
75 G. Lukács, 'Review of Wittfogel', *Political Writings, 1919–1929*, p. 144.
76 Lukács, *History and Class Consciousness*, p. 24, footnote 6.
77 For the reviews see *Arbeiterliteratur* (1924): articles by Rudas, 'Orthodoxer Marxismus?' (pp. 493–517), 'Die Klassenbewusstseinstheorie von Lukács' (pp. 669–97, 1064–89); Deborin; 'Lukács und seine Kritik des Marxismus' (pp. 615–40). Rudas discusses Lukács' restriction of the dialectic to society on p. 499; Deborin does on p. 616. Cf. 'Lukács already has his followers, and in a certain sense is the leader of a whole tendency which includes: Comrades Korsch, Fogarasi, Revai et al.', p. 618.
78 Korsch, 'Ein Nachwort statt Vorwort', *MP*, p. 71.
79 Korsch, 'Über die Zeitschrift *Die Internationale*', *Neue Zeitung* (21 March 1925).
80 Korsch, *MP*, p. 92.

Notes to pp. 82–94

81 Korsch, 'Der junge Marx als aktivistischer Philosoph', *Geistige Politik* (1924), p. 43.
82 Korsch, *MP*, p. 82.
83 Kautsky, op. cit., p. 311.
84 Lukács, *Lenin*, p. 9.
85 Kautsky, op. cit., p. 311.
86 Korsch, *Kernpunkte* ..., p. 16.
87 Korsch, *MP*, p. 74.
88 Marx, Letter to Engels, 14 January 1858, *MEW*, vol. 29, p. 260.
89 Lukács, *History and Class Consciousness*, p. 1.
90 G. Vacca, *Lukács o Korsch?*, pp. 90–1.
91 F. Engels, *Dialectics of Nature* (London, 1964), section entitled 'Dialectics', p. 63; *MEW*, vol. 20, p. 348.
92 S. Marck, 'Neukritische und neuhegelsche Auffassung der Marxsche Dialektik', *Die Gesellschaft* (1924), p. 576.
93 Korsch, *MP*, p. 79.
94 Korsch, 'Die Marxsche Dialektik', *MP* (Frankfurt-am-Main, 1966), p. 169.
95 Cf. Korsch, 'Über materialistische Dialektik', ibid., p. 173.
96 Korsch, *MP*, p. 63.
97 Ibid., p. 44.
98 Korsch, *Kernpunkte* ..., p. 13.
99 Ibid., p. 13.
100 Korsch, *MP*, p. 49.
101 Ibid., pp. 50–1.
102 Kautsky, op. cit., p. 306.
103 Korsch, *MP*, pp. 51–2.
104 Korsch, 'Der junge Marx ...', *MP* (Frankfurt-am-Main, 1966), p. 41; also *MP*, p. 64.
105 Bukharin, op. cit., p. x.
106 Korsch, *MP*, p. 34.
107 Marx, *The Eighteenth Brumaire of Louis Bonaparte, MESW*, p. 120; *MEW*, vol. 8, p. 142.
108 Korsch, *MP*, p. 37.
109 Hegel, *Logic*, p. 15.
110 Cf. H. Lefebvre, *Dialectical Materialism*, especially Section I, 'The dialectical contradiction', pp. 21–113.
111 Kant, *Critique of Pure Reason*, 'Transcendental Doctrine of Elements: 2nd Part: Transcendental Logic', p. 99.
112 Korsch, *MP*, p. 52.
113 Kant, op. cit., 'The Antinomy of Pure Reason, Third Conflict of the Transcendental Ideas: 2nd part: Transcendental Logic', p. 409.
114 Ibid. This is the Third Antinomy.
115 Lukács, *History and Class Consciousness*, pp. 83–222.
116 Ibid., pp. 110–11.
117 Korsch, *MP*, pp. 84–5.
118 Lukács, 'Towards a methodology of the Problem of Organisation', *History and Class Consciousness*, pp. 295–342.
119 F. Jakubowski's *Ideology and Superstructure in Historical Materialism*, (first published as *Der ideologische Überbau in der materialistischen Geschichtsauffassung*

[Danzig, 1936] was the first work to attempt to revive interest in Korsch and Lukács, but it passed virtually unnoticed at the time. Cf. M. Merleau-Ponty, *Les aventures de la dialectique*, pp. 81–99.
120 Jan Sten, 'Die Grundaufgaben der propagandistischen Arbeit', pp. 499–502; here p. 501.
121 R. Hilferding, 'Die Aufgaben der Sozialdemokratie in der Republik' (Sozialdemokratischer Parteitag in Kiel, 1927); *Protokoll*...(Berlin, 1927), p. 165.
122 Max Adler, 'Die Beziehungen des Marxismus zur klassischen deutschen Philosophie', In H. J. Sandkühler and R. de la Vega (eds), *Austromarxismus*, pp. 155–90; here p. 158.
123 F. Engels, *Ludwig Feuerbach and the End of Classical German Philosophy*, *MESW*, p. 590.

5 POLITICAL DEBATES, 1923–8

1 See *Verhandlungen des deutschen Reichstags* (Berlin, 1928), vol. 396, p. 79 for a list of topics on which Korsch spoke. Of these, 'revaluation' (*Aufwertung*) was the most frequent (thirty-three times).
2 *Bulletin of the Fourth Congress of the Communist International*: 'the Tactics of the Communist International', p. ix, 'the Workers' Government', p. 14.
3 Ibid., p. 14.
4 Korsch, 'Um die Arbeiterregierung', *Kommentare zur deutschen 'Revolution' und ihrer Niederlage*, p. 95.
5 Ibid., p. 96.
6 See *Bericht über die Verhandlungen des III (8) Parteitages der Kommunistischen Partei Deutschlands*, Leipzig 28 January–1 February 1923 (Berlin, 1923), pp. 422–24.
7 J. Braunthal, *History of the International*, vol. 2, p. 281; also A. Neuberg, *Armed Insurrection*, pp. 81, 82.
8 P. Broué, *La révolution en Allemagne 1917–23*, pp. 666 ff.
9 Quoted in *Die Lehre der deutschen Ereignisse: Das Präsidium des EKKI zur deutschen Frage*, January 1924 (Hamburg, 1924), p. 60 (Zinoviev's speech).
10 Broué, op. cit., p. 758, gives 13 October; O. Flechtheim, *Die KPD in der Weimarer Republik*, pp. 93–4, gives 16 October.
11 *Stenographische Berichte über die Sitzungen des 2. Landtags von Thüringen*, vol. 5 (Weimar, n.d.), pp. 5486–9.
12 Flechtheim, op. cit., p. 124.
13 G. Witzmann, *Thüringen von 1918–33: Erinnerungen eines Politikers*, p. 97.
14 Neuberg, op. cit., p. 83; also W. T. Angress, *Die Kampfzeit der KPD, 1921–23* (Dusseldorf, 1973), especially Chapter 13, 'Eine Revolution scheitert', pp. 462–511.
15 Broué, op. cit., p. 775.
16 Witzmann, op. cit., p. 102.
17 *Interview with HK*, p. 14.
18 *Die Lehre*..., EKKI resolution (19 January 1924), p. 104.

Notes to pp. 101–4

19 *Die Lehre . . .*' p. 67.
20 Weber, *Die Wandlung des deutschen Kommunismus*, p. 68.
21 'Der Faszismus ist tot—nieder mit dem Faszismus', *Neue Zeitung* (6 November 1924).
22 Korsch, 'Kritisches und Positives zur Frage der Taktik der Kommunistischen Partei, II', *Neue Zeitung* (3 April 1924).
23 See his 'Leninismus und Trotzkismus', *Neue Zeitung* (28 February 1925) in which he argues that it is necessary to root out Trotskyism and Luxemburgism within the party. See also, 'Trotzki als Geschichtsschreiber', *Neue Zeitung* (4–5 December 1924) which is similarly critical.
24 See e.g. M. Buckmiller, 'Marxismus als Realität', in Pozzoli (ed.), *Über Karl Korsch*, pp. 60–2, which does not come to any definite conclusions. Also 'Die Entwicklung des Marxismus von der revolutionären Philosophie zur wissenschaftlichen Theorie proletarischen Handelns bei Karl Korsch', *MP* (Frankfurt-am-Main, 1966), p. 17: 'The immediate consequence of the theoretical "restoration" of Marxism was for Korsch the praxis of the revolutionary party . . . but Korsch never justified the domination of a party apparatus'. Cf., by contrast, G. Rusconi's Introduction to *MG* (Milan, 1971), p. xxvi.
25 E.g. Korsch, *KM*, p. 243.
26 In *Kommentäre* . . . p. 132, the (unnamed) editor says of Korsch's review of Stalin's *Lenin und der Leninismus* in a footnote that 'in fact his argument defensively yet critically lay at the extreme of what was possible within the party'. To support his claim, it is argued that, while Korsch gives Stalin's book the most fulsome praise, he also argues that its function will only be fulfilled if proper use is made of it by: ' "specially trained course-leaders" '. To suggest that this implies a criticism of Stalin seems highly contrived. The only article I have seen which makes similar points to mine is Douglas Kellner, 'Korsch's Revolutionary Historicism', *Telos*, no. 26 (Winter 1975/76), pp. 70–93; in particular pp. 71–81.
27 Korsch, 'Lenin und die Komintern', *Die Internationale* (1924), pp. 320–27. Review of Stalin, *Lenin und der Leninismus*, *Die Internationale* (1924), pp. 668–70.
28 Korsch, 'Lenin und die Komintern', p. 320.
29 Korsch, 'Stalin, *Lenin und der Leninismus*', p. 669.
30 Ibid., p. 669.
31 Korsch, 'Lenin und die Komintern', p. 327.
32 Ibid., p. 322.
33 *Bericht des Gen. Zinovievs über die 'Tätigkeit des Exekutivkomitees der Kommunistischen Internationale'*, p. 968. The amalgam technique of bracketing together opponents who had little in common apart from their heterodoxy is here shown quite clearly. Graziadei had written an openly 'revisionist' book, *Preis und Mehrpreis in der kapitalistischen Wirtschaft. Kritik der Marxschen Werttheorie* (Berlin, 1923). Korsch never rejected the Marxist theory of value. Cf., against Graziadei, Korsch, 'Die gesellschaftliche Wirklichkeit des Werts', *Der Ring* (1926), p. 139.
34 *Bericht* . . . p. 969.
35 See above, pp. 77, 82, 85.
36 An exception is the favourable review by A. Fogarasi, *Die Internationale*

(1924), pp. 414–16.
37 *Inprekorr* (1924), p. 1796.
38 See D. Joravsky, *Soviet Marxism and Natural Science*, p. 114. I was not able to consult the Russian edition of *MP*.
39 Korsch, *Anti-critique*, *MP*, p. 91.
40 Quoted in ibid., p. 109.
41 Quoted in ibid., p. 109. Cf. M. Merleau-Ponty, *Les aventures de la dialectique*, p. 81.
42 *Bericht* . . ., p. 969.
43 H. Weber, *Die Wandlung des deutschen Kommunismus. Die Stalinisierung der KPD in der Weimarer Republik*.
44 'Über die Zeitschrift *Die Internationale*: Auszug einem Schreiben der Agitprop Abteilung des EKKI an die Zentrale der KPD', *NZ* and *Inprekorr* (1925).
45 Ibid.
46 Korsch's name appears for last time as editor in the volume for February 1925. Thereafter he was replaced by E. Schneller.
47 Weber, *Die Wandlung des deutschen Kommunismus*, vol. 1, pp. 110, 111.
48 See 'Offener Brief: Brief der EKKI an alle Organisationen und die Mitglieder der KPD', in H. Weber, *Der deutsche Kommunismus*, pp. 234–6, for the new line on the SPD and the trade unions.
49 'Der historische Umschwung in der KPD', by DM (Moscow), *Inprekorr* (1925), p. 2354.
50 Weber, *Die Wandlung*, vol. 1, pp. 18, 19.
51 Korsch, 'Der Wortlaut des Dawes—und McKenna—Berichts', *Die Internationale* (1924), pp. 283–4; 'Die Durchführung des Dawes-Gutachtens und der Kampf um den Achtstundentag', *Die Internationale* (1924), pp. 547–60; 'Der Bericht des Agenten über das erste Jahr des Dawesplans', *Die Internationale* (1926), pp. 27–31.
52 'Nieder mit dem kleinbürgerlichen anti-Bolschewistischen Geist', Beilage, *Rote Fahne* (22 September 1925).
53 See Korsch's reply, 'Konkrete Erklärung über meine angeblichen antibolschewistischen Ausführungen in Frankfurt am Main', *Neue Zeitung* (6 October 1925).
54 Weber, op. cit., vol. 1, pp. 138–40. Also, S. Bahne, 'Zwischen "Luxemburgismus" und "Stalinismus", die Ultralinke Opposition in der KPD,' *Vierteljahreshefte für Zeitgeschichte* (1961), pp. 359–83; pp. 370–79 are on the Korsch group.
55 'Plattform der Linken' (Appendix to *Der Weg der Komintern*).
56 Ibid., p. 17.
57 Ibid., p. 18.
58 Ibid., pp. 19, 20.
59 Ibid., p. 21.
60 Ibid., p. 21.
61 Ibid., p. 22.
62 Ibid., p. 22.
63 Cf. the complaints of other oppositionists, e.g. Trotsky, *The Third International after Lenin*, pp. 156–7.
64 Korsch, *Der Weg der Komintern*, p. 3.
65 Ibid., p. 6.

Notes to pp. 109–14

66 The discussion of Bauer's position is on pp. 9–13.
67 Korsch, *Der Weg der Komintern*, p. 9.
68 Weber, op. cit., vol. 1, p. 151.
69 Ibid., p. 153. S. Bahne, 'Zwischen "Luxemburgismus" und "Stalinismus": Die Ultralinke Opposition in der KPD', *Vierteljahreshefte für Zeitgeschichte* (1961), p. 371. Korsch and Schwarz were expelled from the KPD on 3 May; this was confirmed by the EKKI on 22 June.
70 Weber, op. cit., vol. 1, pp. 154, 155.
71 Ibid., p. 164. The 'left communists' included R. Fischer, Katz, Korsch, Schlagewerth, Scholem, Schwan, Urbahns, Schutz, Tiedt; see also ibid., p. 82.
72 Korsch, 'Zehn Jahre Klassenkämpfe in Sowjetrussland', *Kommunistische Politik* (October 1927) (like all *KP* articles, pages unnumbered; 'Aufruf für Mjasnikow', *Die Aktion* (1929), p. 85. Trotsky censured Urbahns for publishing 'Korschist' articles. See *La défense de l'URSS et l'opposition: Écrits*, vol. 1 (Paris, 1955), pp. 223–72, especially pp. 147, 232, 262, 264.
73 Korsch, 'Zehn Jahre'. Also I. Deutscher, *The Prophet Unarmed 1921–29*, pp. 431, 432.
74 Korsch, *Der Weg der Komintern*, p. 16. Bordiga had spoken up for Korsch, but mainly about the way 'ideological terror' had been used against him. See *Protokoll der 6 EKKI: February-March 1926* (Hamburg and Berlin, 1926), p. 577.
75 'Brief von A. Bordiga an Korsch' (28 October 1926). First published in 1928 in *Prometeo 1928*, organ of the French and Belgian sections of the Italian left communists. In C. Pozzoli (ed.), *Über Karl Korsch*, p. 247.
76 E.g. 'La gauche marxiste en Allemagne et les tâches des révolutionnaires marxistes dans l'Internationale', *Le Réveil communiste* (Lyon, 1928); 'Avant les élections de 1928', *Contre le Courant: Organe de l'opposition communiste* (Paris, 1928).
77 *Verhandlungen des deutschen Reichstags: Berlin, 1926* (10 June 1926), p. 7444.
78 Korsch, 'Zehn Jahre . . .'.
79 *Verhandlungen . . .*, p. 7444.
80 Korsch, 'Die zweite Partei', *Kommunistische Politik* (December 1927).
81 Ibid.
82 I have been unable to find out anything about this union. There is no mention of it in H. M. Bock, 'Bibliographischer Versuch zur Geschichte des Anarchismus und Anarcho-Syndikalismus', in Pozzoli, op. cit., pp. 295–334.
83 *AFB*, pp. 74–6; see above, pp. 48 ff.; *Um die Tariffähigkeit*, p. 3.
84 *Um die Tariffähigkeit*, p. 5.
85 Ibid., p. 9.
86 Ibid., p. 19.
87 Ibid., respectively pp. 22–4; 26–9; 30–6.
88 Ibid., p. 43.

6 THE MATERIALIST CONCEPTION OF HISTORY

1 'Aufruf für Mjasnikow' appeared in *Die Aktion* (May 1929), signed *'Kommunistische Politik'*, but the last issue of the periodical appeared, as far as can

be ascertained, in December 1927.
2 Korsch, 'Gutachten über Antonio Labriola', IISG MS. (1929), p. 2.
3 Ibid., p. 2.
4 Korsch, *MG*, (Frankfurt-am-Main, 1971), p. 106. References are to this edition.
5 Ibid., pp. 76–7.
6 Ibid., pp. 60–80.
7 Ibid., p. 61.
8 Ibid., p. 60
9 K. Kautsky, *Die materialistische Geschichtsauffassung*, vol. 1: *Natur und Gesellschaft*; vol. 2: *Der Staat und die Entwicklung der Menschheit*. Cf. the preface, p. xii: '[This book] is the quintessence of my life's work. It represents the method upon which I have based a half century's work ... it is not merely the foundation, but the result of the work of my life'. See also Korsch, op. cit., p. 1.
10 Kautsky, op. cit., p. xiv.
11 *MG*, p. 11.
12 Ibid., p. 16.
13 Ibid., p. 12.
14 See Chapter 4, p. 101 below.
15 *MG*, pp. 20–37.
16 Ibid., p. 20.
17 Ibid., pp. 36, 37.
18 Ibid., p. 101. See also Section V, 'Klasse und Klassenkampf', pp. 81–100.
19 See p. 82 above.
20 *MG*, p. 53.
21 Ibid., p. 55.
22 Ibid., p. 4.
23 Ibid., pp. 4–5. Cf. F. Jakubowski, *Ideology and Superstructure in Historical Materialism*, p. 68:

> Kautsky wrote *The Materialist Conception of History* at a time when he was no longer generally recognised as the standard marxist theoretician. Nevertheless, it still typifies the ideas of the Second International both in the prewar period and today.

24 *MG*, p. 4.
25 Ibid., p. 4.
26 Ibid., pp. 24, 25, 48, 76.
27 Ibid., p. 80. Cf: 'The views held by Kautsky and his like are a complete renunciation of those same revolutionary principles of Marxism that writer has championed for decades.' V. Lenin, 6 July 1920 Preface to *Imperialism*, *CW*, vol. 22, p. 192.
28 *MG*, pp. 81, 82.
29 V. Lenin, 'The Proletarian Revolution and the Renegade Kautsky', *CW*, vol. 28, pp. 227–325.
30 *MG*, p. 7.
31 Ibid., p. 126.
32 Ibid., pp. 125–6, 130.

Notes to pp. 119–27

33 Ibid., pp. 129–30.
34 Ibid., p. 30.
35 V. Lenin, 'On the significance of militant materialism', *CW*, vol. 33, p. 231. Cf. Korsch, *MG*, p. 31.
36 F. Engels, 'Flüchtlingsliteratur: II: Programme der blanquistischen Kommuneflüchtlinge', *MEW*, vol. 18, p. 532. For Marx's rejection of eighteenth-century materialism see *The Holy Family*, Chapter 6, Section 3C: 'Critical battle against French Materialism' (Moscow: Progress Publishers, 1975) pp. 140–6.
37 Korsch, *MG*, pp. 31, 111.
38 Ibid., p. 111. For the whole argument, see pp. 109–11.
39 Kautsky, *Ethik und materialistische Geschichtsauffassung*. Reviewed by O. Bauer, 'Marxismus und Ethik'. *Die neue Zeit* (1906), pp. 485–99.
40 Korsch, *MG*, p. 113, footnote 125.
41 In ibid., there is no mention of Bukharin.
42 Ibid. pp. 114–17 for the whole argument: here, p. 115.
43 Ibid., p. 107.
44 Ibid., p. 129.
45 Ibid., p. 114.
46 Lukács, 'Bernstein's Triumph: Notes on the Essays Written in Honour of Karl Kautsky's Seventieth Birthday', *Political Writings, 1919–1929*, p. 130. Originally in *Die Internationale* (1924); my emphasis.
47 V. Lenin, 'Imperialism and the split in socialism', *CW*, vol. 23, p. 119.
48 Korsch, *MP*, p. 91.
49 Ibid., p. 91.
50 Ibid., pp. 97–8.
51 Marx, *Communist Manifesto*, *MESW*, p. 46; *MEW*, vol. 4, p. 475.
52 Ibid., p. 102.
53 Lenin, *What is to be Done?*, *CW*, vol. 4, p. 375.
54 *MP*, p. 113.
55 Ibid., pp. 110–11.
56 Ibid., p. 112.
57 N. Krupskaya, *Memories of Lenin* (London, 1932) vol. 2, pp. 28, 29.
58 Korsch, *MP*, p. 98.
59 Ibid., p. 114.
60 Ibid., pp. 115 ff.
61 Ibid., p. 116.
62 Korsch, 'Lenin's Philosophy', *Living Marxism* (1938), p. 141.
63 Lenin, 'What the "Friends of the People" Are and How They Fight the Social Democrats', *CW*, vol 1, pp. 129–360; here, pp. 165, 167; The section on Hegel and the dialectical method is at pp. 165–74. See also Korsch, 'Lenin über den historischen Materialismus', *Zeitschrift für Sozialforschung* (1932), pp. 423, 424.
64 Lenin, *Materialism and Empirio-Criticism*, *CW*, vol. 14, p. 69.
65 Engels' *Dialectics of Nature*, which would also have offered much support to Lenin's position, did not appear until 1925; I. Deutscher, *The Prophet Unarmed*, vol. 2, p. 172.
66 Lenin, *CW*, vol. 14, p. 41.
67 Ibid., pp. 98ff. Cf. Engels, *Ludwig Feuerbach and the End of Classical German*

Philosophy: 'The most telling refutation of this as of all other philosophical crotchets is practice, namely, experiment and industry' (*MESW*, p. 595; *MEW*, vol. 21, p. 276).
68 N. Bukharin, *Theory of Historical Materialism* (New York, 1925), p. 56.
69 Lenin, *CW*, vol. 14, p. 240.
70 Ibid., p. 329.
71 Lenin, *One Step Forward, Two Steps Back*, Section R, 'A Few Words on Dialectics', *CW*, vol. 7. pp. 410–16.
72 See K. Kautsky, *Bernstein und das sozialdemokratische Programm*, pp. 20–33. There is a review of this in Lenin, *CW*, vol. 4, pp. 193–204.
73 See Lenin's review of Kautsky's *Die Agrarfrage*, *CW*, vol. 4, pp. 94–100. For his acknowledgement of Hilferding's contribution to *Imperialism*, see *CW*, vol. 22, p. 195. Cf. T. Perlini, 'A proposito di Korsch', *La critica sociologica* (Rome, 1970), p. 37.
74 Z. A. B. Zeman, *The Merchant of Revolution*, pp. 64–8.
75 'I am fully aware of my unpreparedness in this sphere [i.e. of philosophy] which prevents me from speaking about it in public' [Letter to Gorki, 7 February 1908, *CW*, vol. 34, p. 381].
76 E.g. 'Let me add in parenthesis for the benefit of young Party members that you *cannot* hope to become a real intelligent Communist without making a study ... of all Plekhanov's philosophical writings, because nothing better has been written on Marxism anywhere in the world' ('Once Again on the Trade Unions', *CW*, vol. 32, p. 94). See also 'Preface to the second edition of *Materialism and Empirio-Criticism*', 2 September 1920, recommending the earlier work, in *Materialism and Empirio-Criticism* (New York, 1927), p. 11. I have been unable to find this in the Collected Works.
77 G. Rusconi, *La teoria critica della società*, pp. 119–20.
78 Cf. A. Pannekoek, *Lenin als Philosoph*. The material base of Lenin's Marxism 'in Russia ... was the struggle against Tsarism, to a great extent comparable with earlier struggles against absolutism in Europe' (p. 109).
79 Korsch, *MP*, p. 123.
80 Ibid., p. 124.
81 Korsch, 'The Marxist Ideology in Russia', *Living Marxism* (1938), p. 45.
82 K. Korsch, 'Thesen zur Kritik des faschistischen Staatsbegriffs', *Gegner* (1932), p. 20.
83 See P. Lösche, *Der Bolschewismus im Urteil der deutschen Sozialdemokratie 1903 bis 1920*, p. 250 ff.
84 Korsch, 'Der Weg der Henriette Roland Holst', *Die Aktion* (1928), p. 238.
85 Korsch, 'Das Problem Staatseinheit—Föderalismus in der französischen Revolution', in *Revolutionärer Klassenkampf* (Berlin, n.d.), pp. 52–3. (See bibliography for original reference).
86 Ibid., p. 53.
87 Ibid., p. 55.
88 Ibid., p. 56
89 Korsch, 'Revolutionäre Kommune—2', in *WS*, pp. 103–5 in particular.
90 Korsch, 'Marxism and the Present Task of the Proletarian Class Struggle', *Living Marxism* (1938), p. 118.
91 Korsch, 'The Passing of Marxian Orthodoxy', *International Council Correspondence* (1937), p. 11. Also:

[Lenin saw that] the guarantee of the revolutionary character of the workers' movement was to be sought not in its real, and in particular in its economic class content, but expressly only in the subjective leadership of this struggle by the revolutionary party directed by a correct Marxist theory [Von der bürgerlichen Arbeiterpolitik zum proletarischen Klassenkampf', *Kampf-Front* (1930), p. 24].

92 Korsch, 'Über einige grundsätzliche Voraussetzungen für eine materialistische Diskussion der Krisentheorie', *Proletarier* (1933). In *Korsch, Mattick, Pannekoek. Zusammenbruch des Kapitalismus oder Revolutionäres Subjekt* (Berlin, 1973), p. 98. See also Korsch, 'The Marxist Ideology in Russia...', p. 47.
93 Korsch, 'Revolutionäre Kommune—2' in *Schriften zur Sozialisierung*, p. 107.
94 See 'Revolutionare Kommune—1, 2'; 'Ökonomie und Politik im revolutionären Spanien'; 'Die Kollektivierung in Spanien', in *Schriften zur Sozialisierung*, pp. 91–108, 109–17 and 118–26 respectively.
95 Ibid., p. 121.
96 Korsch, *MG*, p. 5.
97 G. Lichtheim, *Marxism* p. 265.
98 Alfred Schmidt, *The Concept of Nature in Marx*, p. 47, merely observes: 'Karl Korsch, one of the few authors in the extensive literature on Marx who understood the complex dialectic of nature and history, emphatically criticised Kautsky's distortion of the Marxist theory of history'.
99 L. Ceppa, 'Korsch's Marxism', *Telos* (Winter-Spring 1975/76), p. 99.

7 KARL MARX

1 The programme of the study circle was: (1) What does the restoration of Marxism mean? (2) The historical Marx. (3) Marx as a politician. (4) Marx as an economist. (5) Marx as a philosopher. (6) Dialectical materialism in the natural sciences. (7) Dialectical materialism in the social sciences. (8) Dialectical materialism in practice. See the IISG MS., 'Studienzirkel Kritischer Marxismus. Karl Korsch: Lebendiges und Totes im Marxismus. November 1932–February 1933'
2 *Interview with HK*, pp. 19–20.
3 Ibid., p. 20.
4 W. Rasch, 'Der marxistische Lehrer von Brecht', p. 998.
5 H. Brüggemann, 'Bert Brecht und Karl Korsch, Fragen nach Lebendigem und Totem im Marxismus', in C. Pozzoli (ed.), *Über Karl Korsch*, p. 178.
6 Ibid., pp. 177–88.
7 L. Kreuzer, *A. Döblin*, pp. 143, 192.
8 *Interview with HK*, p. 21.
9 Korsch, 'Review of *Collectivisations: L'oeuvre constructive de la révolution espagnole, Recueil de documents'*, *Zeitschrift für Sozialforschung* (1938), pp. 469–74.
10 M. Jay, *The Dialectical Imagination*, p. 4. Cf. Phil Slater,' *The Origins and Significance of the Frankfurt School* (London, 1977), pp. iv, xv.
11 See below, pp. 171 ff. A balanced view of Korsch's connections with the Frankfurt School is to be found in Phil Slater, *The Origins and Significance of the*

Frankfurt School, pp. 38, 68, 69, 74, 153.
12 Korsch, 'Zur Neuordnung der deutschen Arbeitsverfassung', *Rätekorrespondenz* (1934), pp. 1–20.
13 See pp. 172, 173.
14 By R. Marett; F. Borkenau; F. S. Marvin and J. A. Hobson respectively. All London, 1936.
15 *Interview with HK*, p. 22. See the publisher's blurb for the 'Modern Sociologists' series: 'It is hoped that these books will serve not only as textbooks in the Universities and Adult Education classes ... but also as a systematic introduction to any intelligent reader to the best of modern thinking about the social world in which we live and work' [flyleaf; not paged].
16 *Interview with HK*, p. 22.
17 Korsch, *Neuere Marxbiographische Literatur*, IISG MS. (1934). A pencilled note, signed 'KK 1946' in the IISG MS. may explain why Korsch's relations with the Institut für Sozialforschung were not very close. Against a remark on the tricks used by E. H. Carr in his biography of Marx, Korsch wrote (in German): 'This remark was then "taken over" by Marcuse, without citation, from my unprinted MS., in his review of the book in the Zfs ...' [p. 8]. See. H. Marcuse's review of these books in *Zeitschrift für Sozialforschung* (1935), pp. 103–5. The remark referred to is on p. 104; The books reviewed are: Riazanov, *Marx and Engels*; E. H. Carr, *Karl Marx: A Study in Fanaticism*; A. Cornu, *Karl Marx, l'homme et l'oeuvre; de l'Hégélianisme au matérialisme historique, 1818–1845*; G. Mayer, *Friedrich Engels*. The subtitle of Carr's book gives a fairly clear indication of his approach; Cornu's book was an original piece of research into the early philosophical years of Marxism. The book referred to is F. Mehring. *Karl Marx, The Story of his Life* (London, 1936).
18 H. Marcuse, 'The Foundations of Historical Materialism', pp. 1–48 of *Studies in Critical Philosophy*; here p. 1. The essay was first published in *Die Gesellschaft* (1932).
19 Korsch, *KM* (E), pp. 10–11. (See p. 188 above for list of abbreviations.)
20 The drafts are to be found in the IISG. They are appended to the 1967 German edition of *Karl Marx*, edited by G. Langkau of the IISG. For references to the German text, I shall use this edition, rather than the original drafts.
21 Korsch, Letter to Rumney, 28 September 1934, in Korsch, *KM* (G), p. 211.
22 Ibid., part 2, section III, 2, p. 213.
23 Ibid., part 3, section III, p. 213.
24 Ibid., part 3, section Ib, p. 212. See above, p. 131.
25 Ibid., part 4, section II, 3, p. 214.
26 Ibid., part 3, sections II, III, p. 213.
27 Letters to Paul Mattick, 29 August 1935, 7 December 1938: cited in ibid., p. viii. Dr Rumney's thoughts on Korsch's original proposal are unfortunately not documented.
28 Korsch, *KM* (G), Appendix II, pp. 214–20.
29 Ibid., p. 216.
30 Ibid., p. 217.
31 Ibid., p. 218.
32 Cf. ibid., pp. 218 ff. and 95 ff.
33 Ibid., p. 221.

34 Ibid., Appendix VI, pp. 229–32. Appendix IV, 'Economics and Politics (the Problem of Sociology)', pp. 222–5, is dated mid-December 1935, but contains nothing notable; Appendix V, 'Economics and Sociology', pp. 226–9, is undated, probably from this period, and equally unremarkable.
35 Ibid., p. 232.
36 Alternative versions of the text are found in ibid., pp. 241–76. These concern the original Paris text (1946) and the American text (1947). The text reproduced in (G) is a version of the 1947 text revised by Korsch. Dr Langkau's work on these versions of the text is most thorough.
37 G. Rusconi, *La teoria critica della società*, p. 128. Cf. T. Perlini, 'A proposito di Korsch', *La critica sociologica* (1970), p. 33, which makes the same claim more forcefully.
38 Korsch, *KM* (E), p. 234.
39 See pp. 77 ff., 83 ff., above.
40 F. Borkenau, 'Review of Karl Marx', *Sociological Review* (1939), p. 118.
41 Korsch, *KM* (E), pp. 61–2.
42 K. Marx, *Capital*, Afterword to the second edition, vol. 1 (London: Allen & Unwin, 1957) p. xxiv. *MEW*, vol. 23, p. 21.
43 Korsch, 'Introduction to *Capital*' (1932), in *Three Essays on Marxism*, p. 61.
44 Korsch, *KM* (E), pp. 10–11. The introduction is not in (G).
45 In the pre-publication drafts, letter to Dr Rumney (28 September 1934), there was a section entitled 'Specific differences in the concept of society held by Marx and Engels' (*KM* (G), part 1, Section 3, p. 211).
46 Korsch, *KM*, pp. 172 ff.
47 Ibid., p. 168.
48 Ibid., p. 169.
49 *KM* (G), p. 193. Not in (E).
50 Ibid., pp. 221–2 (drafts). See Engels to Mehring, 14 July 1893, *MEW*, vol. 39, pp. 96–100; to Borgius, 25 January 1894, ibid., pp. 205–7; to J. Bloch, 21 September 1890, *MEW*, vol. 37, pp. 462–5; to C. Schmidt, 27 October 1890, ibid., pp. 488–95.
51 *KM* (E), p. 222.
52 Ibid., pp. 216–18. Korsch was sympathetic to anarcho-syndicalism, but not without reservations. The opposite view is argued by Roberto Paris, 'Gramsci e la crisi teorica del 1923', *Nuova rivista storica*, nos. 1/2 (1969), p. 178.
53 *KM* (E), p. 45. A very similar passage occurs in 'Leading Principles of Marxism: A Restatement', in *Three Essays on Marxism*, pp. 11–12, 54; see also Korsch, *MP*, p. 47.
54 Korsch, *MP*, p. 46, footnote 25.
55 The following discussion has been greatly influenced by L. Kolakowski, *The Alienation of Reason: A History of Positive Thought*, and A. Schmidt, *The Concept of Nature in Marx*.
56 Korsch, *KM* (E), pp. 190–1.
57 See above p. 81.
58 D. Joravsky, *Soviet Marxism and Natural Science*, pp. 233 ff., describes this process.
59 See above, pp. 124 ff.
60 See H. Marcuse, *Soviet Marxism*, p. 143: 'the emphasis on the dialectic of

nature is a distinguishing feature of Soviet Marxism—in contrast to Marx and even Lenin'.
61 See Engels, *Anti-Dühring, MESW*, Introduction, section 1, p. 38. 'Nature is the proof of dialectics . . . in the last instance [it] operates dialectically and not metaphysically'. The passage is in *MEW* at vol. 20, p. 22. For J. Stalin, see *Dialectical and Historical Materialism*, pp. 6 ff.
62 Lukács, *History and Class Consciousness*, p. 132.
63 Korsch, *KM* (E), p. 191.
64 Ibid. p. 191.
65 Ibid., p. 226.
66 Korsch, 'Mathematical Constructs in Psychology and Sociology', IISG MS., p. 2.
67 Korsch, *KM* (E), p. 79.
68 Ibid., p. 227. See also 'Review of P. Frank', *Zeitschrift für Sozialforschung* (1932), pp. 404–5, although this does not make any general points. In 'Notes to a Lecture by Einstein on Causality', IISG.MS. (1930), p. 11, he records the point that modern physicists believe in statistical, but not strong determinism.
69 Korsch, *KM* (E), p. 229.
70 Ibid., p. 52.
71 E.g. A. J. Ayer, *Language, Truth and Logic*, pp. 36 ff.
72 Marx, *Capital*, vol. 3, *MESW*, p. 817; *MEW*, vol. 25., p. 825.
73 Korsch, *KM* (E), p. 30.
74 Ibid., p. 34.
75 See my article, 'The Law of Value and Marxist Method', *CSE Bulletin* (Autumn 1973), pp. 64–70.
76 Korsch, *KM* (E), p. 178.
77 See E. Preobrazhensky, *The New Economics*, pp. 48 ff., for a brilliant discussion of this point.
78 Korsch, *KM* (E), p. 231.
79 Ibid., p. 24. In 'Leading Principles of Marxism', (*Marxist Quarterly*, 1937), quoted here from *Three Essays on Marxism*, pp. 25–9 he puts forward the principle of concrete application, clearly a gloss on this principle.
80 *KM* (E), p. 38.
81 Ibid., pp. 38–44.
82 Ibid., p. 57. In 'Why I Am a Marxist' in *Three Essays on Marxism*, he adds a fourth principle, that: 'Its [Marxism's] subject matter is not *existing* capital in its affirmative state but declining capitalist society as revealed in the demonstrably operative tendencies of its breaking-up and decay' (p. 61). Clearly this is not a separate principle, but a corollary of the second principle.
83 Korsch, *KM* (E), pp. 65–7.
84 Ibid., p. 86.
85 Ibid., p. 82.
86 Ibid., p. 73.
87 See e.g. F. Borkenau, 'Review of *Karl Marx*', p. 117, which admits that it is a 'model text-book' of Marxism.
88 See above, pp. 90 ff.
89 Korsch, *KM* (E), p. 84.

Notes to pp. 153–62   213

90 Ibid., p. 215; *KM* (G), p. 185: where Korsch refers to his earlier work. See above, pp. 69 ff.
91 *KM* (E), p. 108.
92 Ibid., p. 68.
93 Korsch, 'Why I Am a Marxist', *Modern Monthly* (April 1935), pp. 65–6.
94 Korsch, 'Indiens Erwachsen', IISG MS. (1922).
95 Korsch, *KM* (E), pp. 24–8.
96 *KM* (G), p. 144; not in (E).
97 *KM* (E), p. 48.
98 Ibid., p. 73; not in (G).
99 Ibid., pp. 79–80.
100 Marx, 'The method of political economy', *Grundrisse* (Harmondsworth, Penguin edn., 1973), pp. 100–9.
101 Korsch, *KM* (E), pp. 79–80.
102 Bukharin, *Historical Materialism*, p. 20.
103 Gramsci, *Selections from the Prison Notebooks*, p. 246.
104 Marx, Preface to *A Contribution to the Critique of Political Economy*, *MESW*, pp. 181–2; *MEW*, vol. 13, p. 8.
105 Korsch, *KM* (E), pp. 195–6; (G), p. 133.
106 Engels, *Socialism: Utopian and Scientific*, *MESW*, p. 416; *MEW*, vol. 19, p. 215.
107 Korsch, *KM* (E), p. 63; see also ibid., p. 54.
108 Ibid., p. 169.
109 Ibid., p. 171.
110 Ibid., pp. 176, 177.
111 Ibid., pp. 158, 174, 175.
112 See pp. 112 ff.
113 Korsch, 'Introduction to Capital', in *Three Essays on Marxism*, p. 46.
114 Korsch, 'Dialektik des Alltags', IISG MS. (1932), p. 2.
115 Korsch, *KM* (E), p. 111.
116 Ibid., pp. 131–2.
117 'Thesen über "Hegel und die Revolution" ', *La Critique Sociale* (1932), pp. 11–12, and in IISG MS.; 'A Lecture Given to the Society for Empirical Philosophy, Berlin' (1931) respectively.
118 Korsch, 'Thesen ...', p. 12.
119 Lukács, *The Young Hegel*, passim.
120 Korsch, *KM* (E), p. 178.
121 Ibid., p. 179.
122 Ibid., p. 179.
123 Ibid., p. 54.
124 Ibid., p. 65.
125 Ibid., pp. 181–2.
126 *KM* (G), p. 204. The corresponding chapter in (E), pp. 232 ff., omits this.
127 Ibid., p. 204; (E), p. 231 is less forceful: 'In a partly philosophical form, it has yet achieved a great number of important scientific results which hold good to this day'.
128 *KM* (E), p. 174.
129 Ibid., p. 62.
130 *KM* (G), p. 78, not in corresponding (E), p. 111.
131 *KM* (E), p. 20.

132 Ibid., p. 20.
133 Lukács, *The Young Hegel*, p. xxvii.
134 Korsch, *KM* (E), p. 230.
135 Ibid., p. 94.
136 Ibid., p. 111.
137 There is a very stimulating exposition of the theory in I. Rubin, *Essays on Marx's Theory of Value*, section 1, pp. 5–60, where it is claimed that

> proponents as well as opponents of Marxism have dealt with the theory of fetishism mainly as an independent and separate entity, internally hardly related to Marx's economic theory. They present it as a digression which accompanies Marx's basic text [p. 5].

138 Korsch, *KM* (E), p. 234.
139 Ibid., p. 18.
140 Ibid., p. 19; instead of 'earlier time' (G), p. 4, says 'revolutionary period of development'.
141 *KM* (E), p. 18.
142 *KM* (G), p. 243; not in (E).
143 See ibid., p. 229, ' "Ökonomie, Politik, gesellschaftliche Bewusstseinsformen (Ideologien)'.
144 Ibid., p. 229; not in (E). Also: 'Review of Sombarts *Verstehende Nationalökonomie*', *Grünberg-Archiv* (1930), pp. 436–48.
145 Korsch, *KM* (E), p. 203.
146 Ibid., p. 204.
147 Bukharin, op. cit., p. xiv.
148 Gramsci, op. cit., p. 426.
149 Korsch, *KM* (G) p. 229.
150 See T. B. Bottomore, *Marxism and Sociology*, pp. 67–74.
151 Korsch, *KM* (E), p. 23.
152 Ibid., p. 235.
153 Korsch, *MP*, p. 85.

8 BEYOND MARXISM?

1 *Interview with HK*, pp. 21, 22.
2 See F. Neumann et al., *The Cultural Migration* (Philadelphia, 1953), p. 18.
3 L. Fermi, *Illustrious Immigrants* (Chicago, 1968), p. 29.
4 H. Pross, *Die deutsche akademische Emigration nach den Vereinigten Staaten 1933–1941*, p. 45: between 1933 and 1939, 7·3 per cent of German émigrés were from the academic professions.
5 P. Lazarsfeld, 'A memoir', in D. Fleming and B. Bailyn (eds), *The Intellectual Migration: Europe and America 1930–1960*, pp. 270–337; here p. 301.
6 Thus he was Lecturer at the State College of Washington, Pullman, Washington for the spring term of 1942; Visiting Assistant Professor at Tulane University of Louisiana, New Orleans, 1943–5. His lectures at Seattle in connection with military training programmes are in the IISG MSS. as:

'Collapse of Germany'; 'Patterns of Collapse'; 'Germany after the Armistice of 1918' (all 1943): 'Germany Today' (1944).
7 Korsch, 'Thesen über Ökonomie und Politik' (1935), Theses 3, 21; in *KM* (G), p. 217.
8 Korsch and Lewin, 'Mathematical Constructs in Psychology and Sociology', *Journal of Unified Science* (1939), pp. 113–21. Lewin's *Die Sozialisierung des Taylorsystems* (Berlin, ?1920) had appeared in Korsch's series 'Praktischer Sozialismus'.
9 See above, p. 137.
10 M. Jay, *The Dialectical Imagination*, p. 305.
11 Interview with *HK*, p. 22.
12 Letter to Paul Partos, 30 July 1939. As 'Über Amerikanische Wissenschaft' *Alternative* (1965), p. 76.
13 Ibid., p. 76.
14 Letter to Gerlach, 16 December 1956, *Politische Texte*, p. 393.
15 Letter to Partos, p. 76.
16 P. Mattick, Introduction to the Greenwood reprint of *New Essays* (Westport, 1970) not paged, fourth page.
17 Ibid., first page.
18 See above, pp. 124 ff.
19 See above, pp. 58 ff., 72 ff.
20 Korsch, 'State and Counter-revolution', *Modern Quarterly* (1939), p. 60.
21 Korsch, 'Collapse of Germany', first of four lectures in Seattle, summer 1943, IISG MS., p. 8.
22 Ibid. p. 11.
23 Korsch, 'Revolution for What?, a Critical Comment on Jan Valtin's *Out of the Night*', *Living Marxism* (1941), p. 27.
24 Korsch, 'Prelude to Hitler', *Living Marxism* (1940), p. 14.
25 Korsch, 'The Fascist Counter-revolution', *Living Marxism* (1940), p. 33.
26 Korsch, 'Prelude to Hitler', p. 14.
27 Korsch, 'The Structure and Practice of Totalitarianism', *New Essays* (1942), pp. 47, 48.
28 Korsch, 'The Fascist Counter-revolution', p. 34.
29 Ibid. pp. 34–5.
30 See Korsch's review, 'The Structure and Practice of Totalitarianism', pp. 43–9.
31 Korsch, 'The Fascist Counter-revolution', p. 31.
32 Ibid., pp. 32–3.
33 Korsch, 'State and Counter-revolution', p. 61.
34 Ibid., p. 61.
35 Ibid., p. 66.
36 Korsch, 'The Fascist Counter-revolution', p. 29.
37 Korsch, 'The Fight for Britain, the Fight for Democracy and the War Aims of the Working Class', *Living Marxism* (1941), p. 2.
38 Ibid., p. 3.
39 Ibid., p. 6.
40 See note 6 above.
41 Brecht letter to Korsch, Santa Monica, end March 1945, in *Alternative* (1965), p. 45. The proposed versification appears in ibid., pp. 46–53; Korsch's reply,

New Orleans, 4 April 1945, sentence quoted in ibid., p. 54.
42 Korsch, 'Human Nature: The Marxian View, by Vernon Venable', *Journal of Philosophy* (1945), pp. 712–18.
43 Ibid., p. 717.
44 Ibid., p. 714.
45 Korsch, 'The World Historians: From Turgot to Toynbee', *Partisan Review* (1942) p. 355.
46 See F. Deppe *et al.*, *Kritik der Mitbestimmung, passim*.
47 I have not been able to find the English original, so here I have used the German text from *Alternative* (April 1965).
48 Ibid., p. 86.
49 Ibid. p. 86.
50 Ibid. p. 88.
51 R. Rosdolsky, *The Making of Marx's 'Capital'* (London, 1977).
52 Note to text of '10 Theses . . .' *Alternative* (April 1965), p. 89.
53 Cf. *Interview with HK*, p. 22.
54 Cf. also 'Restauration oder Totalisierung?', *Politische Texte*, p. 370; 'Marx' Stellung in der Europäischen Revolution von 1848', *Die Schule* (1948), pp. 165–74 *passim*.
55 'Ten Theses . . .', *Telos* (winter 1975/76), p. 40.
56 Ibid. p. 40.
57 Ibid., p. 40.
58 G. E. Rusconi, 'Introduction to *What is Socialisation?*', *New German Critique*, no. 6 (1975), p. 50.
59 L. Trotsky, *The Platform of the Left Opposition* (1927) (London, 1963), p. 87.
60 Korsch, *MG*, p. 81.
61 Korsch, *MP*, p. 115.
62 Korsch, 'Marxism and the Present Task of the Proletarian Class Struggle', *Living Marxism* (1938), p. 118.
63 Korsch, *KM* (G), p. 7.
64 Ibid., p. 230.
65 Korsch, 'A Non-dogmatic Approach to Marxism', retranslated from the German, *Politikon* (1971), p. 10; originally in *Politics* (1946), pp. 151–4.
66 Lenin, 'What Is To Be Done?', *CW*, vol. 5, p. 369.

Bibliography

KORSCH'S WRITINGS

Notes:
1. Other bibliographies of Korsch's writings are: (1) a typescript by Hedda Korsch, summer 1962. This has many omissions and a number of inaccuracies; (2) M. Buckmiller, *Bibliographie der Schriften Karl Korschs*, in C. Pozzoli (ed.), *Über Karl Korsch* (Frankfurt-am-Main, 1973). This is comprehensive and accurate, and my bibliography is virtually identical. A difficulty in compiling bibliographies of Korsch's writings is that Korsch often (e.g., in his articles for *Living Marxism*) signed his articles 'k', 'K. Rops', 'l.h.' or wrote anonymously (e.g. for *Kommunistische Politik*).
2. Korsch's manuscripts are mainly to be found in the International Institute for Social History, Amsterdam (referred to in the text as IISG); a smaller number are still in Hedda Korsch's possession. The interested reader should consult Section C of Michael Buckmiller's bibliography in C. Pozzoli (ed.), op. cit., pp. 100–2.
3. Where the same article appeared in English and other languages, I have usually given a reference to the English version only. Buckmiller's bibliography lists all versions.

Abbreviations:
Inprekorr: *Internationale Presse—Korrespondenz*.
Internationale: *Die Internationale* (Berlin), KPD theoretical journal
JH: *Jenaer Hochschulzeitung*
Kompol: *Kommunistische Politik*
LM: *Living Marxism*
NZ: *Neue Zeitung*
RF: *Rote Fahne*
Tat: *Die Tat*
Zfs: *Zeitschrift für Sozialforschung*

Karl Korsch

A BOOKS AND PAMPHLETS

1 *Die Anwendung der Beweislastregeln im Zivilprozess und das qualifizierte Geständnis* (Bonn, 1911). Enlarged dissertation.
2 *Was ist Sozialisierung?* (Hanover, 1919). Reprinted in *Schriften zur Sozialisierung*, edited and introduced by E. Gerlach (Frankfurt-am-Main, 1969).
3 *Quintessenz des Marxismus: Eine gemeinverständliche Darlegung* (Berlin and Leipzig, 1922).
4 *Arbeitsrecht für Betriebsräte* (Berlin and Leipzig, 1922).
New edition with a foreword by E. Gerlach, introduction by Dieter Schneider (Frankfurt-am-Main, 1968). The second part of the book is abbreviated.
5 *Kernpunkte der materialistischen Geschichtsauffassung: Eine quellenmässige Darstellung* (Berlin, 1922).
6 *Karl Marx: Randglossen zum Programm der Deutschen Arbeiterpartei*, with an introduction by Korsch (Berlin and Leipzig, 1922).
7 *Marxismus und Philosophie* (Leipzig, 1923). 2nd enlarged edition, with *Der gegenwärtige Stand des Problems 'Marxismus und Philosophie': Zugleich eine Antikritik*. Edited and introduced by E. Gerlach (Frankfurt-am-Main, 1966).
English: Translated by F. Halliday (London, 1970).
French: Translated by C. Orsoni, introduction by Kostas Axelos (Paris, 1964).
Italian: Translated by G. Backhaus, introduction by M. Spinella (Milan, 1966).
8 *Der Weg der Komintern: Diskussionsrede des Gen. Korsch auf der Konferenz der politischen Sekretäre und Redakteure der KPD* (16 April 1926), with appendix: 'Die Plattform der Linken'. (Berlin, 1926).
9 *Um die Tariffähigkeit: Eine Untersuchung über die heutigen Entwicklungstendenzen der Gewerkschaftsbewegung* (Berlin, 1928).
10 *Die materialistische Geschichtsauffassung: Eine Auseinandersetzung mit Karl Kautsky* (Leipzig, 1929). New Edition (Frankfurt-am-Main: Europäische Verlagsanstalt, 1971). Italian translation with introduction by G. Rusconi (Milan, 1971).
11 *Karl Marx*. (London and New York, 1938). Edition revised by Korsch, New York, 1947. New edition, New York, 1963.
German edition, following the original German manuscript, edited by G. Langkau (IISG) (Frankfurt-am-Main, 1967).
French edition (Paris, 1946).
Italian: Translated by A. Illuminati, introduction by G. Bedeschi (Bari, 1969).
12 *Das Kapital*. 1872 edition, with an introduction by Korsch (Berlin, 1932).

B COLLECTIONS

1 *Karl Korsch: Schriften zur Sozialisierung.*, edited and introduced by Erich Gerlach (Frankfurt-am-Main, 1969).
2 *Consigli di fabbrica e socializazzione* (Bari, 1970). Contains (1) above, and *Arbeitsrecht fur Betriebsräte* (1968 abbreviated version).

3 *Kommentare zur deutschen 'Revolution' und ihrer Niederlage* (s'Gravenhage, The Netherlands, 1972).
4 *Die materialistische Geschichtsauffassung und andere Schriften*, edited by E. Gerlach (Frankfurt-am-Main, 1971).
5 *Revolutionärer Klassenkampf* (Berlin, 1972).
6 *Politische Texte*, edited and introduced by E. Gerlach and J. Seifert (Frankfurt-am-Main, 1974).
7 *Three Essays on Marxism* (London, 1970; New York, 1972).
8 *Karl Korsch o el Nacimiento de una Nueva Epoca* (Barcelona, 1973).
9 *Karl Korsch: Revolutionary Theory*, edited by D. Kellner (Austin, Texas, 1977).

C ARTICLES AND REVIEWS
1908
1 'Die Stellung der Arbeiterinnen im Erwerbsleben', *JH* (15 February).

1909
2 'Wider den Aesthetizismus in Wissenschaft und Leben in und ausserhalb der Hochschule', *JH* (20 January).
3 'Japanische Arbeitsverhältnisse', ibid.
4 'Einführung in die Lehren der deutschen Bodenreform', *JH* (2 February).
5 'Unnütze Ideale', *JH* (16 February).
6 'Was fordert unsere Zeit von der studierenden Frau?', *JH* (26 February).
7 'Monismus, Reinkevortrag, Toleranz und freie Studentenschaft', *JH* (7 May).
8 'Das "Verhältnis" ', ibid.
9 'Soziale Studentenblätter', *JH* (26 May).
10 'Duellanhänger und freistudentische Ehrengerichte', *JH* (11 June).
11 'Allgemeine Volksschule und Mädchenschulreform', ibid.
12 'National, ein negativer und ein positiver Begriff', *JH* (10 July).
13 'Die "hochverräterische" Freie Studentenschaft', ibid.

1910
14 'Die Forderung eines Universitätsgesetzes im preussischen Abgeordnetenhaus', *JH* (24 June).

1911
15 'Die Reform des juristischen Studiums', *Akademische Rundschau*, pp. 63–9.

1912
16 'Rechtsformen für die Verwirklichung freistudentischer Ideen', *Akademische Rundschau*, pp. 4–10.
17 'Kleists Examinatorium in Frage und Antwort', ibid., pp. 19–20 (review).
18 'Recht und Wirtschaft', nos. 1 and 2, ibid., pp. 20–1 (review).
19 M. Rintelen, 'Schuldhaft und Einlager im Vollstreckungsverfahren des altniederländischen und sächischen Rechtes', *Kritische Vierteljahresschrift für Gesetzgebung und Rechtswissenschaft*', pp. 128–42 (review).
20 'Würzburger Abhandlungen zum deutschen und ausländischen Prozessrecht',

220 Karl Korsch

21 'Die Fabian Society', *Tat*, pp. 422–7.
22 'Die sozialistische Formel für die Organisation der Volkswirtschaft', ibid., pp. 507–9.

1913
23 ' "Eugenics" in England', *Tat*, pp. 581–3.
24 'Das Problem "Aufsteigen geistig Begabter" ', ibid., pp. 611–13.
25 'Londoner Kinderwohlfahrtsausstellung 1913', ibid, pp. 644–6.
26 'Die Technik der öffentlichen Debatte in England', ibid., pp. 714–17.
27 'Das 100,000 M Preisausschreiben der "Zeit im Bild" ', ibid., pp. 321–3.
28 'Die erste Märtyrerin fur das Frauenstimmrecht', ibid., pp. 426–7.
29 'Vom englischen Zeitungswesen', ibid., pp. 461–6.
30 'Die Sommerschule der Fabian Society', ibid., pp. 501–4.
31 'Die Freiheit in England', ibid., pp. 661–74.
32 'Rassenhygiene und Volksgesundheit', ibid., pp. 758–60.
33 'Das Examen als politisches Problem', ibid., pp. 770–82.
34 'John Galsworthy', ibid., pp. 961–4.

1914
35 'Beiträge zur Kenntnis und zum Verständnis des englischen Rechts', *Zeitschrift für Internationales Recht*, pp. 273–301.
36 'Soziale Agrarpolitik im modernen England', *Tat*, pp. 1030–40.
37 'Soziale Caritas', ibid., pp. 1063–7.
38 'Die Rassenhygiene in der wissenschaftlichen gemeinverständlichen Literatur des englischen Sprachgebiets', *Tat*, pp. 1159–64.
39 'Ablehnung von Mandaten in England', *Juristische Wochenschrift*, pp. 396–9.
40 'Probleme und Aussichten englischer Universitätsentwicklung', *Tat*, pp. 154–64.
41 'Freirechtsbewegung und Kodifikationsidee', ibid., pp. 429–33.

1917
42 'Gedanken über Menschlichkeit', ibid. pp. 461–3.

1918
43 ' "Akademisch-Soziale Monatsschrift" ', ibid., pp. 973–6.
44 'Jugendbewegung und Jugendpolitik', ibid., pp. 1052–4.
45 'Zum problem des preussischen Wahlrechts II', ibid., pp. 131–3.
46 'Beruf und Jugend', ibid., pp. 314–18.

1919
47 'Die Kultur des modernen England', ibid., pp. 863–71.
48 'Die Politik im neuen Deutschland', in *Geist der neuen Volksgemeinschaft*, ed. Zentrale für Heimatdienst, Berlin, pp. 63–71.
49 'Sozialisierung und Arbeiterbewegung', *Freies Deutschland*, pp. 40–3.
50 'Vorbemerkung des Herausgebers', in K. Korsch (ed.), B. Shaw, *Der Sozialismus und die Geistig Begabten: Eine Erwiderung an Herrn Mallock*, (Praktischer Sozialismus: Eine sozialpolitische Schriftenreihe) (Hanover, 1919), pp. 5–8.
51 'Realpolitiker des Sozialismus', *Tat*, pp. 55–7.

52 'Über die Möglichkeiten einer sozialistischen Aufklärungsarbeit', ibid., pp. 67–9.
53 'Die Sozialisierungsfrage vor und nach der Revolution', *Der Arbeiterrat*, p. 14.
54 'Die Arbeitsteilung zwischen körperlicher und geistiger Arbeit und der Sozialismus', ibid., pp. 11–14.
55 'Das sozialistische und syndikalistische Sozialisierungsprogramm', *Der Sozialist*, pp. 402–5.

1920
56 'Gutachten zur Frage der Arbeiterräte bei der Firma Carl Zeiss, Jena', *NZ* (1 January).
57 'Praktischer Sozialismus', *Tat*, pp. 735–41.
58 'Robert Wilbrandts *Sozialismus*', ibid., pp. 782–7.
59 'Sozialismus und soziale Reform', *Der Arbeiterrat*, pp. 7–9.
60 'Die sofortige Sozialisierung unseres Export- und Importhandels', *Der Sozialist*, pp. 65–7.
61 'Die Verwaltung der Produktion durch die Arbeiter in Sowjetrussland', *NZ* (29 January and 1 February).
62 'Grundsätzliches über Sozialisierung', *Der Arbeiterrat*, pp. 7–9; *Tat*, pp. 900–11.
63 'Was kann jeder Mann und jede Frau für die Befreiung des Proletariats tun?', *NZ* (1 May).
64 'Räteschule der Jenaer Arbeiterschaft (Entwurf)', *NZ* (13 August).
65 'Die Sabotage der "W.B." an der Jenaer Rateschule', (26 August).

1921
66 'Wandlungen des Problems der politischen Arbeiterräte in Deutschland', *NZ* (7–9 March).
67 'Karl Marx' Promotion zum Dr Phil. In Jena am 15 April 1841', *NZ* (1 September).
68 'Die Umwälzung der Naturwissenschaft durch Albert Einstein', *NZ* (September).
69 'Zur Debatte des Parteitages über Steuern und Staatsfinanzen', *NZ* (1 September).
70 'Allerhand Nachdenkliches über Wahl und Krisenzeiten', *NZ* (10 September)
71 'Stinnes Kostgänger Staat. Eine kritische Würdigung der Goldkreditvorschläge der Industrie', *NZ* (19 September).
72 'Zur Geschichte der sozialistischen Parteiprogramme. Das Kommunistische Manifest und der Weg nach Görlitz', *NZ* (10 October).

1922
73 'Der 18 Brumaire des Hugo Stinnes', *NZ* (17 March); *RF* (18 March).
74 'Marxistisches zur Frage der kommunalen Selbstverwaltung, I and II', *NZ* (20–21 March).
75 'Die SPD. Die Entwicklung zur Stinnespartei', *RF* (26 March); *NZ* (28 March).
76 'Kommunistische Literatur (Selbstanzeige)' *NZ* (26 April).
77 'Die neueste Phase in der Entwicklung des wirtschaftlichen "Rätesystems" nach Art. 165 der Reichsverfassung, I and II', *NZ* (14–15 June).

78 'Eine Antikritik', *Internationale*, pp. 586–8.
79 'Allerhand Marxkritiker, I-III', ibid., pp. 165–70 198–203, 225–8.
80 'Die im Wandel der Zeiten unveränderliche bürgerliche Marxkritik', *Kommunistische Internationale*, pp. 129–31; *Rotes Echo* (22 July).
81 'Ein kurzes letztes Wort', *NZ* (3 August).
82 'Die tote USPD und der lebendige Stinnes', (7 September).
83 'Rosa Luxemburg über Koalitionspolitik oder Klassenkampf?', *NZ* (16 September); *Der Kämpfer* (21 September).
84 'Die wirtschaftliche Lage und die Aufgaben der Gewerkschaften', *NZ* (20 September).
85 'Tischgespräch', *Freiheit* (supplement to *NZ*) (21 September).
86 'Die Betriebsrätewegung im Reich', *NZ* (21 September).
87 'Der Umfall der Führer', *NZ* (6 October).
88 'N. Auerbach, *Marx und die Gewerkschaften*', *Inprekorr*, pp. 1163–4; *Der Kommunistische Gewerkschafter*, pp. 330–3 (review).
89 'Der Kampf um den Staat', *Inprekorr*, pp. 1295–6, as 'König Kapital und seine Hofnarren', *NZ* (7 October).
90 'Der tote Sinzheimer und der lebende Marx', *Inprekorr*, pp. 1843–4 (review).
91 'Das Wesen der Arbeitsverfassung nach bürgerlichem und sozialem Recht', *Arbeitsrecht*, pp. 614 ff.

1923

92 'Die Inauguraladresse der Internationalen Arbeiterassoziation und die Geschichtsfälschungen des Herrn Kautsky', *Inprekorr*, p. 82 (review).
93 'Um die Arbeiterregierung', Diskussionsrede des Gen. Korsch auf dem Leipziger Parteitage, *NZ* (10 February).
94 'Die Marxsche Dialektik'. *Inprekorr*, pp. 330–1.
95 'Karl Marx', *Gothaer Volksblatt: Sonderausgabe* (14 March); *NZ* (17 March), as 'Die Internationale und der Marxismus'.
96 'Die wichtigsten neueren Schriften auf dem Gebiet des Arbeitsrechts', *NZ* (3 July).
97 'Aus der Kinderstube des Herrn Dietzgen', *Inprekorr*, pp. 539–40.
98 'Cunow-Kautskys Kampf um den Staat', ibid., p. 960.

1924

99 'Kommunistische Abrechnung mit der kapitalistischen Diktatur und ihren Helfershelfern', Rede des Genossen Korsch im Thüringer Landtag am 28 February, *NZ* (3 March).
100 'England' (report), *Internationale*, pp. 26–7.
101 'France' (report), ibid., pp. 44–5.
102 'Brief an das Thüringische Ministerium für Volksbildung vom 22 Marz 1924', *NZ* (1 April).
103 'Kritisches und Positives zur Frage der Taktik der Kommunistischen Partei', I-III, *NZ* (2–4 April).
104 'Die Gottgesandten', *NZ* (3 May); *Internationale*, pp. 253–5.
105 'Über materialistische Dialektik', *Internationale*, pp. 376–9.
106 'Georg Lukács, *Lenin, Studie über den Zusammenhang seiner Gedanken*', ibid., pp. 413–14 (review).
107 'Proletarische Niederlagen, proletarischer Sieg', *NZ* (21 July).

Bibliography

108 'Paul Levi—und was dann?', *NZ* (6 August).
109 'Der Wortlaut des Dawes—und McKenna—Berichts', *Internationale*, pp. 283–4.
110 'Lenin und die Komintern', ibid., pp. 320–7.
111 'Des Pudels Kern', *NZ* (26 August).
112 'Die Konferenz der Arbeitsminister in Bern über den Achtstundentag', *NZ* (11 September); *RF* (12 September).
113 'Die Hochzeit', *NZ* (29 August).
114 'Die Durchführung des Dawes-Gutachtens und der Kampf um den Achtstundentag', *Internationale*, pp. 547–60.
115 'Kämpft für die revolutionäre Produktionskontrolle', *NZ* (29 September).
116 'Der Marxismus der Ersten Internationale', *Internationale*, pp. 573–5; *NZ* (29 September); *RF* (26 September).
117 'Stalin, *Lenin und der Leninismus*', *Internationale*, pp. 668–70 (review).
118 'Internationale Parteipolitik', *NZ* (1 November).
119 'Der Faszismus ist tot—nieder mit dem Faszismus', *NZ* (5–6 November).
120 'Die Rolle der SPD zum gegenwärtigen Wahlkampf: I-II', *NZ* (3–4 December).
121 'Das Problem der Goldinflation in den Vereinigten Staaten', *Internationale*, pp. 708–16.
122 'Trotzki als Geschichtsschreiber: I-II', *NZ* (4–5 December).
123 'Der junge Marx als aktivistischer Philosoph', *Geistige Politik*, pp. 41–5.

1925
124 'Die Theorie der Grundrente bei Varga und bei Marx', *Internationale*, pp. 42–7.
125 'E. Vargas Beiträge zur Agrarfrage', ibid., p. 41.
126 'Der Massenschrei nach Amnestie', *NZ* (4 January).
127 'Leninismus und Trotzkismus', *NZ* (28 February).
128 'Vom Imperialismus zum proletarischen Staatskapitalismus', *NZ* (7 March).
129 'Über die Zeitschrift *Die Internationale*', *NZ* (21 March) and *Inprekorr*, pp. 518–19.
130 'Monarchie oder Republik—und was für eine?', *NZ* (28 March).
131 'Wer Marx liebt, wählt Hindenburg', *NZ* (24 April).
132 'Karl Marx über Republik und Monarchie', *NZ* (27 April).
133 'Republik Hindenburg', *NZ* (22 May); *Die Rote Studentenfahne*, no. 4, pp. 3–4.
134 'Die klassische deutsche Philosophie und der Marxismus', *Die Rote Studentenfahne*, pp. 1–3.
135 'Wie helfen die Kommunisten den Inflationsopfern?', *NZ* (4 June).
136 'Militäristische Restauration im Reichsausschuss', *NZ* (19 June).
137 'Die Tragödie der Inflationsopfer', *NZ* (23 July).
138 'Was wird aus der Amnestie?', *NZ* (10 August).
139 'Eine Berichtigung des Gen. Korsch', *NZ* (18 September).
140 'Nieder mit dem kleinbürgerlichen anti-Bolschewistischen Geist', Beilage, *Rote Fahne* (22 September).
141 'Eine Erklärung des Gen. Korsch', *NZ* (24 September).
142 'Konkrete Erklärung über meine angeblichen antibolschewistischen Ausführungen in Frankfurt a.M', *NZ* (6 October).

143 'Feststellung', *NZ* (8 October).
144 'Die Bekenntnisse der schönen Seele eines modernen deutschen Staatsanwaltes', *NZ* (7 November).
145 'Revolution', *Thüringischer Volkskalender*, pp. 9–12.
146 'Der geschichtliche Charakter der marxistischen Wissenschaft', *Der Ring*, pp. 71–81.
147 'Die Verfassung der Vereinigten Sozialistischen Sowjet-Republiken', *Das Neue Russland*, pp. 28–34.

1926
148 'Der Bericht des Agenten über das erste Jahr des Dawesplans', *Internationale*, pp. 27–31.
149 'Die gesellschaftliche Wirklichkeit des Werts', *Der Ring*, pp. 139–46.
150 'Der neue Kompromissentwurf der Regierungsparteien gegen Volksbegehren und Volksentscheid über die Fürstenenteignung', *RF* (12 March).
151 'Rede des Genossen Korsch', *NZ* (31 March).
152 'Zum Ausschluss der Gen. Korsch und Schwarz', *Kompol*, no. 4.
153 'England, Polen und die Komintern', *Kompol*, nos. 7–8.
154 ' "Völkerbundsergänzung" oder internationale Klassensolidarität', ibid.
155 'Kleinen Briefkasten. Genosse Karl Korsch "Entschiedene Linke" ', *Die Aktion*, pp. 197–200.
156 'Unter falscher Flagge', ibid, pp. 226–7, *Kommunistische Arbeiterzeitung* (September).
157 Letter to the *Kommunistische Arbeiterzeitung*, 28 September 1926.

1927
158 'Über den Terror in Sowjetrussland und über die Aufgaben des Proletariats angesichts des näher rückenden Krieges', *Kompol*, nos. 11–12.
159 'Amsterdam und Moskau', *Kompol*, no. 14.
160 'Zehn Jahre Klassenkämpfe in Sowjetrussland', *Kompol*, nos. 17–18.
161 'Die zweite Partei', *Kompol*, nos 19–20.

1928
162 'Die Amsterdamer Gewerkschaftsinternationale (IGB) sucht einen Kopf!', *Kampf-Front* (23 January).
163 'La gauche marxiste Allemagne et les tâches des révolutionnaires marxistes dans l'Internationale', *Le Réveil Communiste* (February-March).
164 'Um die Tariffähigkeit', *Kampf-Front* (26 March).
165 'Argumente gegen die Tariffähigkeit der revolutionären Gewerkschaften', *Kampf-Front* (April).
166 'Weitere Argumente gegen die Tariffähigkeit der revolutionären Verbände', *Kampf-Front* (23 April).
167 'Auf dem Wege zur Wirtschaftsdemokratie?', ibid.
168 'Das letzte Argument gegen die Tariffähigkeit der revolutionären Gewerkschaften', *Kampf-Front* (7 May).
169 'Wohin gehen die freien Gewerkschaften', *Kampf-Front* (21 May).
170 'Avant les élections de 1928', *Contre le Courant: Organe de l'opposition communiste*, pp. 13–15.

Bibliography

171 'Karl Marx und die Moral', *Fanal*, p. 237.
172 'Der Weg der Henriette Roland Holst', *Die Aktion*, pp. 234–8.

1929
173 'Die materialistische Geschichtsauffassung', *Grünberg-Archiv*, pp. 179–279.
174 'Aufruf für Mjasnikow: Genosse Mjasnikow aus Russland geflüchtet', *Die Aktion*, p. 85.
175 'Blutiger Mai in Berlin', ibid., pp. 91–4.
176 'De taak van het proletariaat in de huidige periode', *De Arbeid*, pp. 2–4.
177 'Revolutionäre Kommune I', *Die Aktion*, pp. 176–81.
178 'Die Stellung des revolutionären Proletariats zur Wehrfrage', ibid., pp. 181–4.

1930
179 'Von der bürgerlichen Arbeiterpolitik zum proletarischen Klassenkampf, *Kampf-Front* (11 January).
180 'Das Problem Staatseinheit—Föderalismus in der französischen Revolution', *Grünberg-Archiv*, pp. 126–46.
181 'Sombarts *Verstehende Nationalökonomie*', ibid., pp. 436–48 (review).
182 E. Paschukanis, *Allgemeine Rechtslehre und Marxismus*; K. Renner, *Die Rechstinstitute des Privatrechts und ihre soziale Funktion*, ibid., pp. 301–10 (review).

1931
183 'Die spanische Revolution', *Die neue Rundschau*, pp. 289–302; *De Nieuwe Weg*, pp. 63–70.
184 'Revolutionäre Kommune, II', *Die Aktion*, pp. 60–4.

1932
185 'Zur Geschichte der marxistischen Ideologie in Russland', *Gegner*, pp. 9–12; *LM* (1938), pp. 44–50 (enlarged).
186 'Thesen über "Hegel und die Revolution" ', *La Critique Sociale* (1932).
187 'Thesen zur Kritik des faschistischen Staatsbegriffs', *Gegner*, p. 20.
188 'Ausgang der Marx-Orthodoxie', ibid., pp. 7–9; *International Council Correspondence* (December 1937), pp. 7–11.
189 'Die dialektische Methode im "Kapital" ', *Aufbau*, pp. 144–50; slightly altered, as 'Die alte Hegelsche Dialektik und die neue materialistische Wissenschaft', *Gegner*, pp. 20–2; *International Council Correspondence*, pp. 16–21.
190 'Kommunistischer Klassenkampf gegen Marx' Kapital', *Die Aktion*, pp. 36–42.
191 '15 jaren October revolutie. Legenden en werkelijkheid van het socialisme in Sowet-Russland', *De Nieuwe Weg*, pp. 327–30.
192 'Ernest Posse, *Der Marxismus in Frankreich 1871–1905*', *Zfs*, pp. 186–7; *La Critique Sociale* (January), p. 37 (review).
193 'Carl Schmitt, *Der Hüter der Verfassung*', *Zfs*, pp. 204–5 (review).
194 'Philipp Frank, *Das Kausalgesetz und seine Grenzen*', ibid., pp. 404–5 (review).
195 'Julius Schaxel, *Das Weltbild der Gegenwart und seine gesellschaftliche Grundlagen*', ibid., pp. 405–6 (review).

196 'V. I. Lenin, Über den historischen Materialismus', ibid., pp. 423–4; La Critique Sociale, p. 34 (review).

1933
197 'Das Kausalgesetz und seine Grenzen', Die linke Front, pp. 48–53 (review).
198 'Über einige grundsätzliche Voraussetzungen für eine materialistische Diskussion der Krisentheorie', Proletärier, pp. 20–5.
198 'Karl Marx', Encyclopaedia of the Social Sciences (London and New York), vol. 10, pp. 172–5; La Critique Sociale, pp. 94–6; De Nieuwe Weg, pp. 38–41.
200 'Michael Freund, Georges Sorel. Der revolutionäre Konservatismus', Zfs, pp. 116–17 (review).

1934
201 'Ernst Wilhelm Eschmann, Vom Sinn der Revolution', ibid., pp. 142–3 (review).
202 'Donosco Cortes, Der Staat Gottes: Eine katholische Geschichtsphilosophie', ibid., p. 266 (review).
203 'F. O. H. Schulz, Untergang des Marxismus', ibid., p. 274 (review).
204 'Wilhelm Tempel, Aufbau der Staatsgewalt im faschistischen Italien', ibid., pp. 302–3 (review).
205 'T. J. Murphy, Preparing for Power', ibid., pp. 450–1 (review).
206 'W. Milne-Bailey, Trade Unions and the State', ibid., pp. 452–3.
207 'Zur Neuordnung der deutschen Arbeitsverfassung', Räte-Korrespondenz, pp. 1–20.

1935
208 'On the New Programme of the "American Workers Party" ', International Council Correspondence (January), pp. 15–25.
209 'Why I am a Marxist', Modern Monthly (April) pp. 88–95.
210 'Remarks on the Theses Regarding the Next World Crisis, Second World War and the World Revolution', International Council Correspondence (May), pp. 13–22.
211 'Marxism as a Religion', International Council Correspondence (June-July), pp. 17–24 (review).

1937
212 'Origin and Impact of Marxian Materialism', Marxist Quarterly (April-June). Pre-publication excerpt from Karl Marx.
213 'Leading Principles of Marxism: A restatement', Marxist Quarterly (October-December), pp. 356–78. Pre-publication excerpt from Karl Marx.
214 'The passing of Marxian Orthodoxy', International Council Correspondence, p. 11.

1938
215 'Planning New Depressions', LM, pp. 15–20.
216 'Collectivisations: L'oeuvre constructive de la révolution espagnole', Zfs, pp. 469–74.
217 'Economics and Politics in Revolutionary Spain', LM, pp. 76–82.

218 'Marxism and the Present Task of the Proletarian Class Struggle', ibid., pp. 115–19.
219 'Lenin's Philosophy: Some Additional Remarks to J. Harper's Recent Criticism of Lenin's Book *Materialism and Empiriocriticism*', ibid., pp. 138–44.
220 'The Marxist Ideology in Russia', *Living Marxism*, pp. 44–50.

1939
221 'Collectivisation in Spain', ibid., pp. 178–82.
222 'Ignazio Silone, *The School for Dictators*', ibid., pp. 188–90 (review).
223 'Mathematical Constructs in Psychology and Sociology', *Journal of Unified Science*, pp. 113–21.
224 'State and Counter-revolution', *Modern Quarterly*, pp. 60–7.

1940
225 '*The Marxist Philosophy and the Sciences*, by J. B. Haldane', *LM*, pp. 59–61 (review).
226 'Prelude to Hitler: The Internal Politics of Germany, 1918–1933', ibid., pp. 7–14.
227 'The Fascist Counter-revolution', ibid., pp. 29–37.

1941
228 '"The New German Empire", by F. Borkenau', ibid., pp. 61–3 (review).
229 'Revolution for What? A Critical Comment on Jan Valtin's *Out of the Night*', ibid., pp. 21–9.
230 'The Workers' Fight against Fascism', ibid., pp. 36–49.
231 'The Fight for Britain, the Fight for Democracy and the War aims of the Working Class', ibid., pp. 78–80.
232 'Towards Full Use of Resources', ibid., pp. 60–3.
233 'War and Revolution', ibid., pp. 1–14.
234 'Nickerson Hoffmann, *The Armed Horde: 1793–1939*', *Zfs*, pp. 358–61 (review).

1942
235 'The Dynamics of War and Revolution', ibid., pp. 244–7 (review).
236 'The World Historians: From Turgot to Toynbee', *Partisan Review* (May-June), pp. 354–71.
237 'Notes on History', *New Essay* (Fall), pp. 1–9.
238 'The Structure and Practice of Totalitarianism'. *New Essays* (Fall), pp. 43–9 (review).
239 '*The Nature of Modern Warfare*, by Cyril Falls', ibid., p. 79 (review).
240 'H. A. de Weerd, *Great Soldiers of the Two World Wars*', *Partisan Review* (January-February), p. 89 (review).

1943
241 'A Historical View of Geopolitics', *New Essays* (Spring), pp. 8–17 (review).
242 'And Keep Your Powder Dry! An Anthropologist Looks at America, by Margaret Mead', ibid., pp. 70–4 (review).

1945
243 '*Human Nature: The Marxian View* by Vernon Venable', *Journal of Philosophy*, pp. 712–18; *La Critique Sociale*, no. 19 (1947) (review).

1946
244 'A Non-dogmatic Approach to Marxism', *Politics*, pp. 151–4.
245 'W. S. Halperin, *Germany Tried Democracy*' *Commentary*, pp. 196–98 (review).
246 'Restoration or Totalization? Some Notes on Trotsky's Biography of Stalin and on the Revolutionary Problem of Our Time', *International Correspondence*, pp. 10–13 (review).
247 'Independence Comes to the Philippines', *Asia* (original reference not traceable); *Alternative* (in German) (1965), pp. 85–8.

1948
248 'Marx' Stellung in der Europäischen Revolution von 1848', *Die Schule* (Hanover), pp. 165–74.
249 'A Letter from Karl Korsch', *Southern Advocate for Workers' Council* (Melbourne, Australia), pp. 9–10.

1954
250 'A Bakunin Sampler', *Dissent*, p. 110.

1959
251 'Zehn Thesen über Marxismus heute', *Arguments* (Paris 1959) (written in 1950).

SECONDARY SOURCES

BOOKS AND ARTICLES CONSULTED

No further reference is thought necessary to the standard works of Marx, Engels and Lenin (see p. 188).

ADGB, Jahrbuch (1922).
Adler, M., *Demokratie und Rätesystem* (Vienna, 1919).
Adler, M., *Marxistische Probleme* (Stuttgart, 1913).
Althusser, L., *For Marx* (London, 1969).
Althusser, L. *Lenin and Philosophy, and Other Essays* (London, 1971).
Anderson, Perry, *Considerations on Western Marxism* (London, 1976).
Andreas, B., and Haupt, G., 'Bibliographie der Arbeiterbewegung, heute und morgen', *International Review of Social History* (1967), pp. 1–30.
Angress, W. T., *The Communist Bid for Power in Germany* (Princeton, 1963).
Ayer, A. J., *Language, Truth and Logic* (London, 1946).
Bahne, S., 'Zwischen "Luxemburgismus" und "Stalinismus", die Ultralinke Opposition in der KPD', *Vierteljahreshefte für Zeitgeschichte* (1961), pp. 359–83.
Bahne, S., 'Sozialfaschismus in Deutschland', *International Review of Social History* (1965), pp. 211–45.
Bauer, O., 'Marxismus und Ethik', *Neue Zeit* (1906), pp. 485–99.
Bauer, O., *Der Weg zum Sozialismus* (Vienna, 1919).
Bechtel, H., *Wirtschaftsgeschichte Deutschlands im 19 und 20 Jahrhundert* (München, 1956).
Bendix, R., *Max Weber: An Intellectual Portrait* (London, 1966).

Bericht des Gen. Zinoviev über die Tätigkeit des Exekutivkomittees der Kommunistischen Internationale, Der V Weltkongress der KI, 1924, Protokoll (Berlin, 1924).
Bericht über die Verhandlungen des Vereinigungsparteitages der USPD (Linke) und der KPD (Spartakusbund) (Berlin, 1920).
Bernstein, E., *Evolutionary Socialism: A Criticism and an Affirmation* (London, 1909).
Borkenau, F., 'Review of Karl Marx', *Sociological Review* (1939), pp. 117–19.
Born, K. E., *Moderne Deutsche Wirtschaftsgeschichte* (Cologne, 1966).
Bottomore, T. B., *Marxism and Sociology* (London, 1975).
Braunthal, J., *History of the International*, vol. 2 (London, 1967).
Brinkmann, C., 'Review of Lukács' *History and Class Consciousness*, *Archiv für Sozialwissenschaft* (1924), pp. 717–19.
Broué, P., *La révolution en Allemagne, 1917–1923* (Paris, 1971).
C. B. Burdick and R. H. Lutz, *The Political Institutions of the German Revolution, 1918–1919* (New York 1966).
Bukharin, N., *Theory of Historical Materialism* (New York, 1925).
Carr, E. H., *A History of Soviet Russia*, vols 1–7 (London, 1950–64).
Carr, E. H., *Karl Marx* (London, 1934).
Carsten, F. L., *Revolution in Central Europe, 1918–1919* (London, 1972).
Caute, D., *The Fellow-Travellers: A Postscript to the Enlightenment* (London, 1972).
Cole, G. D. H., *Guild Socialism Re-stated* (London, 1920).
Cole, G. D. H., *A History of Socialist Thought* (London, 1956).
Cole, G. D. H., *Self-government in Industry* (London, 1917).
Cole, G. D. H., *Syndicalism* (London, 1921).
Cole, G. D. H., *Workers' Control in Industry* (London, 1919).
Collotti, E., *Le Parti communiste allemand de 1918 à 1933: Une contribution bibliographique* (Milan, 1961).
Communist International, World Congress, *Bulletin 1–32*, Fourth Conference (Moscow, 1922); Fifth Conference, *Report*.
Communist International Executive Committee, *Bericht Über die Tätigkeit der Exekutive . . . vom 4 bis 5 Weltkongresses* (Hamburg, 1924).
Die Lehre der deutschen Ereignisse. Das präsidium des EKKI zur deutschen Frage, January 1924 (Hamburg, 1924).
Cornu, A., *Karl Marx, l'homme et l'oeuvre; de l'Hégélianisme au matérialisme historique, 1818–1845* (Paris, 1934).
Deak, I., *Weimar Germany's Left-wing Intellectuals* (Berkeley, 1968).
Deborin, A., 'Lukács und seine Kritik des Marxismus, *Arbeiterliteratur* (1924), pp. 615–40.
Degras, J., *The Communist International, 1919–1943*, 3 vols (London, 1956–65).
Deppe, F., et al., *Kritik der Mitbestimmung* (Frankfurt-am-Main, 1970).
Dersch, H., 'Neue Schriften zum sozialen Recht', *Archiv für Sozialwissenschaft und Sozialpolitik* (1924), pp. 505–16.
Deutscher, I., *The Prophet Unarmed, 1921–1929* (London, 1970).
Deutscher, I., *The Prophet Outcast, 1929–1940* (London, 1970).
Diederichs, E., *Aus meinem Leben* (Leipzig, 1942).
Diederichs, E., *Leben und Werk. Ausgewählte Briefe und Aufzeichnungen*, ed. Lulu von Strauss and T. Diederichs (Jena, 1936).
Diederichs, E., *Selbstzeugnisse und Briefe von Zeitgenossen* (Düsseldorf, 1967).
Drabkin, J. S., *Die Novemberrevolution in Deutschland* (East Berlin, 1968).
Eberlein, A., *Die Presse der Arbeiterklasse und der sozialen Bewegung*, 4 vols (Berlin,

1968–9).
Ertl, F., *Alle Macht den Räten?* (Frankfurt-am-Main, 1968).
Fabian, W., *Klassenkampf um Sachsen, 1918–1930* (Löbau, 1930).
Fabian Society, *Committee of Inquiry on the Control of Industry* (Letchworth, C. 1910).
Fabian Society, *Lecture Lists* (London, 1886–1914).
Fabian Tract no. 51, S. Webb, *Socialism: True and False* (London, 1899).
Fabian Tract no. 70, *Report on Fabian Policy and Resolutions Presented by the Fabian Society to the International Socialist Workers and Trade Union Congress* (London, 1896).
Fabian Tract no. 150, E. Davies, *State Purchase of Railways* (London, 1910).
Fabian Tract no. 169, W. Stephen Sanders, *The Socialist Movement in Germany* (London, 1913).
Fabian Tract no. 171, H. Schloesser, *The Nationalisation of the Mines and Minerals Bill* (London, 1913).
Fabian Tract no. 192, G. D. H. Cole, *Guild Socialism* (London, 1920).
Feldman, G. D., *Army, Industry and Labour in Germany, 1914–1918*, Princeton, N.J., 1966).
Fetscher, I., *Marx and Marxism* (New York, 1971).
Fischer, R., *Stalin and German Communism* (Cambridge, Massachusetts, 1948).
Flechtheim, O. K., *Die KPD in der Weimarer Republik* (Offenbach, 1948).
Fleming, D., and Bailyn, B. (eds.), *The Intellectual Migration: Europe and America, 1930–1960* (Cambridge, Massachusetts, 1969).
Gabel, J., 'Korsch, Lukács et les problèmes de la conscience de classe', *Annales: Economie, société, civilisation* (1966), pp. 668–80.
Gay, P., *The dilemma of democratic Socialism: Eduard Bernstein's Challenge to Marx* (New York, 1952).
Gay, P., *Weimar Culture: The Outsider as Insider* (London, 1969).
Geschichte der deutschen Arbeiterbewegung: Biographisches Lexikon, 8 vols. (East Berlin, 1966–).
Goldmann, L., *Human Science and Philosophy* (London, 1969).
Goode, P., 'The Law of Value and Marxist Method', *Conference of Socialist Economists Bulletin*, Autumn 1973, pp. 64–70.
Gramsci, A., *Selections from the Prison Notebooks* (London, 1971).
Grebing, A., *Geschichte der deutschen Arbeiterbewegung* (Munich, 1973).
Greiling, W., *Marxismus und Sozialisierungstheorie: eine Untersuchung des Ergebnisses der deutschen Sozialisierungsliteratur* (Berlin, 1923).
Guillebaud, C. W., *The Works Council [Betriebsrat]* (Cambridge, 1928).
Gustaffson, Bo., *Marxismus und Revisionismus: Eduard Bernsteins Kritik des Marxismus und ihren ideengeschichtlichen Voraussetzungen* (Frankfurt-am-Main, 1972).
Halperin, S. W., *Germany Tried Democracy* (New York, 1946).
Hausenstein, W., and Kranold, A., *Der deutsche Student einst und jetzt* (Munich, 1920).
Hegel, G. W. F., *Logic*, translated from the *Encyclopaedia of the Philosophical Sciences* by W. Wallace (Oxford, 1892).
Hilferding, R., *Das Finanzkapital* (Vienna, 1909).
Hilger, G., *The Incompatible Allies: A Memoir-history of German-Soviet Relations, 1908–1941* (New York, 1953).
Hobsbawm, E. J., *Revolutionaries* (London, 1973).

Bibliography 231

Hyppolite, J., *Études sur Marx et Hegel* (Paris, 1955).
Jakubowski, F., *Ideology and Superstructure in Historical Materialism* (London, 1976).
Jay, M., *The Dialectical Imagination: A History of the Frankfurt School and the Institute of Social Research 1923–1950* (New York, 1973).
Joravsky, D., *Soviet Marxism and Natural Science* (London, 1961).
Kant, I., *Critique of Pure Reason*, translated by N. Kemp Smith (London, 1929).
Kautsky, K., 'Review of Marxism and Philosophy', *Die Gesellschaft* (1924), pp. 306–14.
Kautsky, K., *Bernstein und das sozialdemokratische Programm: Eine Antikritik* (Stuttgart, 1899).
Kautsky, K., *Ethik und materialistische Geschichtsauffassung* (Stuttgart, 1906).
Kautsky, K., *Die materialistische Geschichtsauffassung*, 2 vols (Berlin, 1927).
Kautsky, K., *Richtlinien für ein sozialistisches Aktionsprogramm* (Berlin, 1919).
Kolakowski, L., *The Alienation of Reason: A History of Positive Thought* (New York, 1968).
Kolb, E., *Die Arbeiterräte in der deutschen Revolution* (Düsseldorf, 1962).
Kommunistische Partei Deutschlands, *Bericht über den 4 Parteitag der KPD* (Berlin, 14–15 April 1920).
Bericht über die Verhandlungen . . . 2 Parteitag der KPD., August 1921 (Berlin 1921).
1926 Konferenz aller Polleiter und Chefredakteure aus den Bezirken, 16–17 April 1926 (Berlin, 1926).
Kongress der Gewerkschaften Deutschlands, *Zur Sozialisierungsfrage . . . Sonderabdruck aus dem Protokoll der Verhandlungen* (Berlin, 1919).
Kranold, H., *Die freie Studentenschaft in Vergangenheit und Zukunft*, Schriften der Münchner Freien Studentenschaft no. 3 (Munich, 1914).
Kranold, H., Reichenbach, H., and Landauer, K., *Freistudentum. Versuch einer Synthese der freistudentischen Ideen* (Munich, 1913).
Kreuzer, L., *W. A. Döblin* (Stuttgart, 1970).
Kun, B., 'Die Propaganda des Leninismus', *Die Kommunistische Internationale* (1924), pp. 16–21.
Laqueur, W. Z., *Young Germany: A History of the German Youth Movement* (New York, 1962).
Lefebvre, H., *Dialectical Materialism* (London, 1968).
Lichtheim, G., *Marxism* (London, 1961).
Lösche, P., *Der Bolschewismus im Urteil der deutschen Sozialdemokratie 1903 bis 1920* (Berlin, 1967).
Lukács, G., *History and Class Consciousness*, translated by R. Livingstone (London, 1971).
Lukács, G., *Lenin* (London, 1972).
Lukács, G., *Political Writings, 1919–1929* (London, 1972).
Lukács, G., *The Young Hegel* (London, 1975).
Marck, S., 'Neukritische und neuhegelsche Auffassung der Marxsche Dialektik', *Die Gesellschaft* (1924), pp. 573–8.
Marcuse, H., 'Das Problem der geschichtlichen Wirklichkeit', *Die Gesellschaft* (1931), pp. 350–67.
Marcuse, H., 'Review of Biographies of Karl Marx', *Zeitschrift für Sozialforschung* (1935) pp. 103–5.
Marcuse, H., *Soviet Marxism* (New York, 1958).
Marcuse, H., *Studies in Critical Philosophy* (London, 1972).

Marcuse, H., *Reason and Revolution* (London, 1955).
Marx, K., *Capital*, ed. Dona Torr (London: Allen & Unwin, 1957).
Mayer, G., *Friedrich Engels* (Berlin, 1934).
Mayer, J. P., *Max Weber and German Politics* (London, 1944).
McBriar, A. M., *Fabian Socialism and English Politics, 1884–1918* (Cambridge, 1962).
Merleau-Ponty, M., *Les aventures de la dialectique* (Paris, 1955).
Meszaros, I., *Lukács's Concept of Dialectic* (London, 1972).
Neuberg, A., *Armed Insurrection* (London, 1970).
Neumann, S., *Die Parteien der Weimarer Republik* (Stuttgart, 1932).
von Oertzen, P., *Betriebsräte in der Novemberrevolution* (Düsseldorf, 1963).
Pannekoek, A., *Lenin als Philosoph* (Frankfurt-am-Main, 1969).
Parkinson, G. H. R. (ed.), *Georg Lukács* (London, 1970).
Pease, E. R., *The History of the Fabian Society* (London, 1963).
Praeger, E., *Geschichte der USPD* (Berlin, 1922).
Preobrazhensky, E., *The New Economics* (Oxford, 1965).
Protokoll über die Verhandlungen des Ausserördentlichen Parteitags in Halle, 12–17 October 1920 (Berlin, 1920).
Pross, H., *Die deutsche akademische Emigration nach den Vereinigten Staaten. 1933–1941* (Berlin, 1955).
Radvanyi, L., 'Review of *Marxism and Philosophy*', *Archiv für Sozialwissenschaft* (1925), pp. 528–35, reprinted and translated in *Telos* (1971), pp. 133–7.
Reichel, E., *Der Sozialismus der Fabier. Ein Beitrag zur Ideengeschichte des modernen Sozialismus in England* (Heidelberg, 1947).
Reichenbach, H., Schwab, A., Birnbaum, I., Kaiser, J., *Studentenschaft und Jugendbewegung* (Munich, 1914).
Riazanov, N., *Marx and Engels* (Moscow, n.d., ? 1927).
Ritter, G. A. and Miller, S., *Die deutsche Revolution—Dokumente* (Frankfurt-am-Main, 1968).
Rosdolsky, R., *The Making of Marx's 'Capital'* (London, 1977).
Rosenberg. A., *A History of the German Republic* (London, 1936).
Rubin, I. I., *Essays on Marx's Theory of Value* (Detroit, 1972); first published Moscow, 1928.
Rudas, L., 'Orthodoxer Marxismus?', 'Die Klassenbewusstseinstheorie von Lukács', *Arbeiterliteratur* (1924), pp. 493–517, 669–97, 1064–89.
Rusconi, G. E., *La teoria critica della società* (Bologna, 1968).
Ryder, A. J., *The German Revolution* (Cambridge and London, 1967).
A. S., 'Die bürgerliche Konterrevolution und der Renegat Korsch', *Die Internationale* (1926), pp. 562–7.
Sandkühler, H. J. and de la Vega, R. (eds.), *Austromarxismus* (Frankfurt-am-Main, 1970).
Schmidt, A., *The Concept of Nature in Marx* (London, 1971).
Schorske, C. E., *German Social-democracy, 1905–1914* (New York, 1955).
Schuster, Sir Ernest, *Die bürgerliche Rechtspflege in England* (Berlin, 1887).
Seidel, R., *The Trade Union Movement of Germany* (Amsterdam, 1928).
Slater, Phil, *The Origins and Significance of the Frankfurt School* (London, 1977).
Sontheimer, K., 'Der Tatkreis', *Vierteljahreshefte für Zeitgeschichte* (July 1959), pp. 229–60.
Sozialisierungskommission, *Berichte* (Berlin, 1921, 1922).

Bibliography

Stalin, J., *Dialectical and Historical Materialism* (London, 1941).
Stammler, R., *Wirtschaft und Recht nach der materialistischen Geschichtsauffassung* (Leipzig, 1896).
Sten, Jan, 'Die Grundaufgaben der propagandistischen Arbeit', *Inprekorr* (1925) pp. 499–502.
Stolper, G. E., *The Germany Economy 1870–1940* (New York, 1940).
Thèses, manifestes et résolutions adoptés par les premiers quatre congrès de l'Internationale Communiste, 1919–1923 (Paris, 1934).
Trotsky, L., *Écrits*, vol. 1 (Paris, 1955).
Trotsky, L., *Lessons of October* (New York, 1937).
Trotsky, L., *The First Five Years of the Comintern*, 2 vols (New York, 1945).
Trotsky, L., *The Third International after Lenin* (New York, 1970).
USPD Unity Conference (with KPD), 3 December 1920, *Bericht* (Berlin, 1921).
USPD *Protokoll über die Verhandlungen des ausserördentlichen Parteitags in Halle, 12–17 October 1920* (Berlin, 1920).
Vacca, G., *Lukács o Korsch?* (Bari, 1969).
Valtin, Jan (pseudonym of R. Krebs), *Out of the Night* (New York, 1941).
Verhandlungen des deutschen Reichstags. (Berlin, 1921–).
Verhandlungen der Sozialisierungskommission über den Kohlenbergbau im Winter 1918–19 (Berlin, 1921).
Vorlander, K., *Kant und Marx* (Tübingen, 1911).
Wagner, V. F., and Marbach, F., *Wirtschaftstheorie und Wirtschaftspolitik* (Berlin, 1953).
Webb, S. and B., *Industrial Democracy* (London, 1920).
Weber, H. (ed.), *Der deutsche Kommunismus: Dokumente* (Cologne and Berlin, 1963).
Weber, H., *Die Wandlung des deutschen Kommunismus*, 2 vols. (Frankfurt-am-Main, 1969).
Wilbrandt, R., *Sozialismus* (Jena, 1919).
Wittfogel, K. A., *Geschichte der bürgerlichen Gesellschaft* (Vienna, 1924).
Witzmann, G., *Thüringen von 1918–1933: Erinnerungen eines Politikers* (Meisenheim am Glan, 1958).
Zeman, Z. A. B. and Scharlau, W. B., *The Merchant of Revolution: The Life of Alexander Helphand (Parvus)* (Oxford, 1965).

SOME RECENT WORKS ON KORSCH

(Contemporary reviews of Korsch's books are to be found in 'Books and Articles Consulted'. See above pp. 228–33.

1 E. Gerlach, 'Karl Korsch gestorben', *Sozialistische Politik* (1962), pp. 7–12.
2 P. Mattick, 'Karl Korsch: His Contribution to Revolutionary Marxism', *Controversy* (1962), pp. 11–22.
3 W. Rasch, 'Der marxistische Lehrer von Brecht', *Merkur* (1963), pp. 988–1003. 998–1003.
4 P. Mattick, 'The Marxism of Karl Korsch', *Survey* (1964), pp. 86–97.
5 E. J. Salter, 'Bertolt Brecht und Karl Korsch', *Forum*, no. 132 (1964).
6 E. Gerlach, 'Karl Korsch's Undogmatic Marxism', *International Socialism*, no. 19 (1964), pp. 20–8; *Neue Kritik*, no. 18 (1963).
7 E. Volker, 'Der Stückeschreiber und sein Lehrer', *Die Zeit* (3 December 1965)

(on Brecht and Korsch).
8 *Alternative*, no. 41 (April 1965); special number on Korsch.
9 R. Paris, 'Review of *Marxism and Philosophy*', *Giovane critica* (1965), pp. 45–52.
10 L. Colletti, 'Review of *Marxism and Philosophy*', *Problemi del socialismo* (1966), pp. 777–8.
11 Anon. (E. J. Hobsbawm), 'Marxism Re-opened', *Times Literary Supplement* (1968), pp. 305–7 (on *Marxism and Philosophy*).
12 P. Manganaro, 'La teoria dei consigli operai nel pensiero di Korsch', *Giovane critica* (1969), pp. 74–7.
13 L. Ceppa, 'Lo sviluppo del pensiero di Karl Korsch', *Rivista di filosofia* (1969), pp. 328–55.
14 G. E. Rusconi, 'Korsch e la strategia consiliare sindacale', *Problemi del socialismo* (1969), pp. 762–77.
15 T. Pasquinelli, 'Né Lukács né Korsch', *Critica Marxista* (1970), pp. 178–96.
16 F. Cerutti, 'Hegel, Lukács, Korsch: Zum dialektischen Selbstverständnis des kritischen Marxismus'. pp. 195–210 of O. Negt (ed.), *Aktualität und Folgen der Philosophie Hegels* (Frankfurt-am-Main, 1970).
17 T. Perlini, 'A proposito di Korsch', *La critica sociologica*, no. 15 (1970), pp. 33–69; part 2, no. 16 (1971) pp. 8–34.
18 *Politikon*, no. 38 (1971); special number on Korsch, with essays by Seifert, Rusconi, Vacca.
19 P. Breines, 'Praxis and its Theorists: The Impact of Lukács and Korsch in the 1920s', *Telos*, no. 14 (Spring 1972), pp. 67–104.
20 J. Seifert, 'Anmerkungen zu Korschs Rechtstheorie', *Kritische Justiz* (1972), pp. 149–53.
21 C. Pozzoli (ed.), *Über Karl Korsch* (Frankfurt-am-Main, 1973); includes essays by Buckmiller, Marramao, Rusconi, Wolff, Negt, Brüggermann, Riechers.
22 *Telos*, no. 26 (Winter 1975/76); Largely devoted to Korsch, including essays by Ceppa, Kellner, Negt, Marramao, Cerutti, Breines.

Index
(Individual works are listed under the author's name)

ADGB, 41
Adler, M., 32, 95, 120
Althusser, L., 3, 77
anarchism, 77
anarcho-syndicalism, 33
Austro-Marxists, 32, 33
Avenarius, R., 124

Bakunin, M., 132
Ballod, 18
Bammel, 105
Base and superstructure, 43, 44, 58, 59, 61, 145
Bauer, Bruno, 140
Bauer, Otto, 32, 33, 57, 109, 120
    Der Weg zum Sozialismus, 32, 57
Berkeley, G., 126
Bernstein, E., 9, 13, 66, 109, 128
Blanqui, L. A., 132
Bochum, E., 18
Bolsheviks, 31, 72
Bolshevisation, 38, 105ff
Bolshevism, 182
Bordiga, A., 110
Brandler, H., 99, 100
Brecht, B., 136, 140, 178, 179
Breslau/Schlesien, 41
Brüggemann, H., 136
Bukharin, N., 79–81, 104, 121, 127, 156, 167
    Theory of Historical Materialism, 79, 89, 167

capital, 150, 154
capitalism
    consumers', 22
    state, 131
Catalonia, 133
causality, 148
Ceppa, L., 134
co-determination, 24, 52, 180
Cole, G. D. H., 34
Colletti, L., 3
Comintern, 1, 38, 72, 107, 108, 111, 118, 122, 173, 174
    Executive Committee (EKKI), 101, 105, 106
    Stalin and, 1
    Third Congress, 41, 93, 102
    Fourth Congress, 41, 93, 98, 102
    Fifth Congress, 1, 93, 94, 102, 103
Commission on the Socialisation of Industry (Berlin 1918–19), 18, 19, 40, 133, 191
Committee of Inquiry on the Control of Industry (Fabian Society), 13, 14
commodity fetishism, 149, 164, 165
Commune, Paris, 132
communes, Spanish, 133
Comte, A., 137, 166

235

Index

constitution of labour, 48, 59
contract of labour, 59
Cornu, A., 138
Council Communists, 172
Councils (*Räte*), 26, 28, 59
  dictatorship, 111
  factory (*Betriebsräte*), 37, 40, 41, 46, 47, 180
  Factory Council Law (1920), 40
  movement (*Rätebewegung*), 18
  Workers' and Soldiers', 17, 18, 31, 32

Dawes plan, 106, 107
Deborin, A., 105
democracy
  bourgeois, 54
  industrial, 35, 54, 56, 57
  parliamentary, 18
  and political rights, 42
  workers', 31
dialectic
  Hegelian, 67, 71, 153, 158
  Marxist, 67, 91
dialectical materialism, 67, 72, 86, 116, 126, 127, 145, 159
dialectics, 128, 161, 162
  of nature, 80, 85, 146
dictatorship
  of the party, 110
  of the proletariat, 30, 59, 111
Diederichs, E., 8
Döblin, A., 136, 137
Dühring, E., 21

Ebert, F., 31, 100
Elm, 29
Engels, F., 75, 80, 85, 87, 126, 127, 140, 144–7, 157, 159, 179
  Anti-Dühring, 126
  Dialectics of Nature, 85
  Ludwig Feuerbach and the End of Classical German Philisophy, 95, 126, 127
  Socialism: Utopian and Scientific, 75
Entschiedene Linke, 107, 109, 110
eugenics, 9
Eurocommunism, 3

Fabianism, 11–14, 19, 26, 34, 35
Fabian Nursery, 9–11
Fabian Society, 9–16, 34
Farquharson, A., 137
Fascism, 2, 130, 174–6
Feudalism, 151, 152
Feuerbach, L., 140, 144, 159
Fichte, J. G., 140
First International, 77
First World War, 17, 177
Fischer, R., 2, 99, 101, 106
Fogarasi, A., 94
Fourth International, 173
Francke, A. H., 18
Frankfurt Institut, 71, 171
Frankfurt School, 137
Free Student Movement, 6–8

Galileo, 148
Gans, E., 140
Gerlach, E., 30, 102
Ginsberg, Morris, 137
Goebbels, P. J., 175
Gramsci, A., 72, 156, 167
Graziadei, A., 103, 104
Grünberg-Archiv, 91
Guild Socialism, 19, 33, 34, 35

Hegel, G. W. F., 63, 64, 69, 70, 86, 88, 90, 91, 95, 143–6, 152, 153, 160–3, 179
  Logic, 70, 71
  Philosophy of Fine Art, 163
  Philosophy of History, 162
  Philisophy of Right, 43, 162, 163
Hilferding, R., 18, 66, 95
  Das Finanzkapital, 95, 128
Hilfsdienstgesetz (1916), 40
historical specification, principle of, 151, 155, 156–8
Hitler, A., 136–8, 174, 177, 181
Hobson, S. G., 34
Holbach, P. H. D., 124

Ideology, 67–9, 71–8, 84, 86, 123–32
Imperialism, 180
Imperialist epoch, 52, 53
International Communists of Holland, 137

Jacobinism, 177
Jacobins, 131, 140
Jena, University of, 8, 43
Jenaer Hochschulzeitung, 7, 8
Junkers, 6, 31
Jurisprudence, 5, 6, 43

Kant, I., 63, 86, 91, 95, 116, 120, 121, 140, 158
Critique of Pure Reason, 92
Kautsky, K., 13, 18, 77, 83, 104, 115–22, 127, 134, 185
Bernstein und das sozialdemokratische Programm: Eine Antikritik, 128
Ethik und materialistische Geschichtsauffassung, 120
The Materialist Conception of History, 115–23, 125, 134, 185
Kleine, A., 99
Kommunistische Politik, 97, 109, 110, 114
Korsch, Hedda, 8, 136
Korsch, Karl
and Brecht, 136
early life, 5
Fabian Society, 9–15
Frankfurt School, 137
and Free Student Movement, 6–8
and Kautsky, 76, 77, 82, 114–35 *passim*
and Lenin, 3, 58, 68–70, 107–9, 118–35 *passim*, 183–7 *passim*
and Lukács, 3, 49, 72–4, 80–4
and *Sozialpolitik*, 8, 20
and *Die Tat*, 8
WORKS
Anti-Critique, 81, 89, 97, 123–35
'Das Problem Staatseinheit-Föderalismus in der französischen Revolution', 131
'Die sozialistische Formel für die Organisierung der Volkswirtschaft', 14–16
Karl Marx, 1, 28, 60, 81, 136–69 *passim*, 171, 176, 179, 181
Kernpunkte der materialistischen Geschichtsauffassung, 42, 178
Labour Law for Factory Councils, 3, 37–61 *passim*, 79, 112, 113,

129, 183, 184
Marxism and Philosophy, 1–3, 27, 36, 48, 59, 62–96 *passim*, 142, 145, 146, 153, 155, 158, 161, 162, 169, 185
'The Marxist Ideology in Russia', 130
The Materialist Conception of History, 97, 115–35 *passim*, 159
Quintessenz des Marxismus, 42, 43, 62
'Ten Theses on Marxism Today', 181–3
Um die Tariffähigkeit, 112, 130
What is Socialisation?, 19–36 *passim*, 170
K.P.D., 1, 28, 57, 60, 81, 97–113 *passim*, 173, 174
Kun, Bela, 105

Labriola, A., 114
Lassalle, F., 81, 125
Law, reform of, 8, 9
Lazarsfeld, P., 171
Lenin, V. I., 1, 3, 41, 66, 70–2, 82, 96, 102, 105, 110, 118–25, 127, 183, 187
Imperialism: The Highest Stage of Capitalism, 49, 50, 59, 128
Materialism and Empirio-Criticism, 125–8, 135, 146
'One Step Forward, Two Steps Back', 127
Philosophical Notebooks, 126, 128, 135
The Proletarian Revolution and the Renegade Kautsky, 118–19
State and Revolution, 70
What Is To Be Done?, 124, 128
Leninism, 3, 102, 110, 113, 118, 121, 124–9, 145, 182, 183, 185
Levi, P., 41
Lewin, K., 148, 171, 179
Lichtheim, G., 134
Liebknecht, K., 174
Living Marxism, 178
Lukács, G., 1, 3, 4, 43, 49, 66, 70–2, 82, 96, 102, 105, 110, 118–25, 127, 183, 187

Index

History and Class Consciousness, 62, 71, 80, 92, 93, 163
  'Reification and the Consciousness of the Proletariat', 92
  'Towards a Methodology of the Problem of Organisation', 93
  'What is Orthodox Marxism?', 84
The Young Hegel, 160, 163
Luxemburg, R., 38, 103, 132, 174

Mach, E., 108, 158
Machism, 105, 124
Mannheim, 166, 167
'March Action', 41, 196
Marck, S., 85, 104
Marcuse, H., 138
Marx, K., 25-7, 30, 44-6, 63-7, 73-8, 115-17, 121, 144-6, 147-87 *passim*
  Capital, 76, 77, 141, 143, 159
  Communist Manifesto, 76, 151, 178
  Contribution to a Critique of Political Economy, 75, 156, 157, 162
  Critique of The Gotha Programme, 30, 86
  Critique of Hegel's Philosophy of Right, 67
  Economic and Philosophical Manuscripts, 138-41, 160
  Eighteenth Brumaire, 90
  The Poverty of Philosophy, 78
  Theses on Feuerbach, 117, 169
Marxism
  German, 10
  Leninism, 129
  Russian, 129, 130
  Soviet, 130, 146
Marxist political economy, 163-5, 168
Maslow, A., 99, 101, 106
Mattick, P., 137, 172
Mecklenburg-Strelitz, 99
Meiningen, 17
Merleau-Ponty, M., 94
Mjasnikov, 110
monarchy
  absolute, 54, 57
  constitutional, 58

Moses Hess, 140
Müller, General, 100
Mussolini, B., 130, 181

Nazism, 101, 174, 175
Neo-Kantianism, 121
Neubauer, A., 100
Neue Zeitung, 39, 41, 42
Neumann, F., 175
New Economic Policy (NEP), 131
New Essays, 178

Pannekoek, A., 137
Pareto, V., 137, 165
Partos, P., 172
Parvus, 128
Plekhanov, G. V., 114, 128
Positivism, 79, 91, 146-9, 158, 161, 168
Proudhon, P. J., 132

Rathenau, W., 21
Reichstag, 109-11, 136
Renner, K., 43
Revolution
  bourgeois, 51, 56, 131, 133, 152
  French (1789), 18
  German (1923), 184
  proletarian, 51, 56, 152, 161
  Russian (1905), 129
  Russian (1917), 31, 111
Riazanov, N., 138
Ricardo, D., 144, 152, 153, 163
Rosdolsky, R., 181
Rumney, J., 139
Rusconi, G. E., 129, 142, 183
Russian Communist Party, 108, 109

Sapronow-Smirnow democratic centralist group, 110
Saxony, 100, 101
Scheler, M., 166
Schelling, F. W. J., 140
Schlagewerth, H., 110
Schleiermacher, F., 140
Schmoller, G., 7
Scholem, W., 106
Schumpeter, J. A., 18
Schuster, A., 9, 17
Schwarz, B., 108, 110

Schwarz-Lossau group, 109
science
  natural, 121, 140, 145–9, 153, 155, 156
  social, 73, 78, 83, 91, 94, 145–8, 150, 153, 163, 186
Second International, 29, 63, 71, 73, 88, 94, 118, 125, 130, 134, 142, 154
Smith, Adam, 163
socialisation (of industry), 11, 19–26
socialism, 14, 15, 21, 23, 28–31, 50, 53
sociology, 89, 145, 157, 165, 166–8
Sombart, W., 166
Sorel, G., 133
Soviet Union, 107, 110, 130, 138, 176
Sozialpolitik, 7, 9, 20, 47, 52
Spartakus League, 38–40
S.P.D., 6, 8, 14–16, 22, 23, 38, 39, 45, 48, 63, 64, 76, 99, 106, 131, 135, 172
Spencer, H., 166
Spinoza, B., 124, 158
Stalin, J. V., 1, 103, 109, 138, 147
Stalinism, 2, 173
Steffin, 136
Sternberg, F., 136
Stinnes, M., 50
Stirner, M., 140
Strauss, D. F., 140
Studentenkorps, 6
syndicalism, 15, 22, 23, 182

Die Tat, 8
Tenner, A., 100
Thüringia, 38, 39, 41, 98, 100

Tönnies, F., 166
Tretyakov, 136
Troeltsch, E., 166
Trotsky, L., 105, 107, 110, 128, 184
Trotskyism, 102, 173
Tylor, E., 137

Umbreit, P., 18
United Front policy, 41, 102
Unter dem Banner des Marxismus, 120
USPD, 19, 29, 32, 38, 174

Vacca, G., 85
Veblen, T., 137
Verein für Sozialpolitik, 7
Vernon Venable, 179
Vogelstein, 18

Wagner, A., 7
Walras, L., 165
Webb, S., 57, 58
Webb, Mrs, 14
Weber, H., 105
Weber, Max, 7
Weil, F., 71
Weil, H., 171
Wilbrandt, R., 18, 191
Wissell-Mollendorff plan, 21
Wittfogel, K. A., 71, 79–81
Workers' control, 31
Workers' government, 98

Zeigner, E., 100
Zeitschrift für Sozialforschung, 137, 138, 171
Zinoviev, G., 1, 39, 93, 94, 100, 103, 104, 110

GPSR Compliance
The European Union's (EU) General Product Safety Regulation (GPSR) is a set of rules that requires consumer products to be safe and our obligations to ensure this.

If you have any concerns about our products, you can contact us on

ProductSafety@springernature.com

In case Publisher is established outside the EU, the EU authorized representative is:

Springer Nature Customer Service Center GmbH
Europaplatz 3
69115 Heidelberg, Germany

www.ingramcontent.com/pod-product-compliance
Lightning Source LLC
LaVergne TN
LVHW040735250326
834688LV00031B/306